The Sociology of Military Science

The Sociology of Military Science

Prospects for Postinstitutional Military Design

Chris Paparone

B L O O M S B U R Y
NEW DELHI • LONDON • OXFORD • NEW YORK • SYDNEY

BLOOMSBURY INDIA
Bloomsbury Publishing India Pvt. Ltd
Second Floor, LSC Building No. 4, DDA Complex, Pocket C–6&7,
Vasant Kunj, New Delhi 110070

BLOOMSBURY, Bloomsbury Academic India and the Diana logo are trademarks of Bloomsbury Publishing Plc

First published in India 2021
First published 2013

This edition published with permission from Bloomsbury Publishing Plc,
50 Bedford Square, London, WC1B3DP, UK

British Library Cataloguing-in-Publication Data
A catalogue record for this book is available from the British Library.

Library of Congress Cataloging-in-Publication Data
A catalog record for this book is available from the Library of Congress

ISBN: 978-93-54352-18-8

For sale in the Indian subcontinent only

Typeset by Deanta Global Publishing Services, Chennai, India
Digitally printed and bound in India by Replika Press Pvt. Ltd.

Bloomsbury Publishing Plc makes every effort to ensure that the papers used in the manufacture of our books are natural, recyclable products made from wood grown in well-managed forests. Our manufacturing processes conform to the environmental regulations of the country of origin.

To find out more about our authors and books
visit www.bloomsbury.com and sign up for our newsletters

CONTENTS

Acknowledgments vi
About the Author vii
Preface viii

1 The Institutionalization of Modern Military Science 1
2 Frame Awareness 27
3 A Critique of "The Usual Suspects" for Military Design 71
4 Relationalism 105
5 The Reconstruction of Military PROFESSION 147
6 *Un Petit Récit* from the Field 175
Coda: Designing Meanings In- and On-Action 201

References 205
Index 223

ACKNOWLEDGMENTS

I would like to lovingly thank my wife Carrie, and our children, Kimberly, Scotty, and Carl, for their loving support and patience while I took time and attention away from them as I prepared this book. I would also like to extend that lovingness to my Mom, Lois, may she rest in God's hands, and Dad, Lieutenant Colonel (Retired) C. R. Paparone, a career veteran who served in four theaters (World War II, Korea, Cold-War Germany, and Vietnam), who inspired and mentored me through my own career in the US Army. I would like to recognize my contributing authors, Major Grant Martin and Major Ben Zweibelson, for writing Chapter 6, "*Un Petit Récit* from the Field" in their own time while being very busy with their families, and serving on active duty, and writing—even while deployed to combat zones. What more could an army ask for in terms of intellectual dedication and officership? I appreciate the encouragement and many reviews of my friend and colleague from National Defense University, George Topic. Also, I would be remiss if I did not recognize my teaching team at the US Army Command and General Staff College (CGSC), Fort Lee, Virginia Campus, for their support and friendship over the years: Bryan Berg, Lieutenant Colonel Dave Biacan, Bill Davis, Jim Donivan, Rebecca Freeze, Lieutenant Colonel Todd Huderle, Bob Kennedy, Penny Koerner, Major Dan McKeegan, Peter Menk, Mark Solseth, and Chris Stowe. Finally, what makes my job so much fun and interesting are the midgrade officers in the CGSC seminar room who never cease to amaze me with their intelligence and "war stories."

ABOUT THE AUTHOR

Chris Paparone is a retired US Army Colonel who is serving as an associate professor of strategy and military operations at the Fort Lee, Virginia, USA campus of the US Army Command and General Staff College. While on active duty, he served in various command and staff positions in the continental United States, Panama, Saudi Arabia, Germany, and Bosnia. He is a proud graduate of the US Naval War College (Command and Staff) and received his PhD in public administration from The Pennsylvania State University, Harrisburg. He and his family reside in the picturesque county-city of Chesterfield, Virginia.

About the contributing authors

Major Grant Martin is a US Army Special Forces officer who has served two tours in Afghanistan and multiple deployments in support of United States Special Operations Command, South. Major Ben Zweibelson is a US Army Infantry officer from Connecticut who has over 18 years of combined enlisted and commissioned service, served two tours in Iraq, and is presently serving in Afghanistan.

PREFACE

Of facts . . . they lie unquestioned, uncombined.
Wisdom enough to leech us of our ill
Is daily spun; but there exists no loom...

EDNA ST. VINCENT MILLAY[1]

This book is about the discovery of refreshing meanings for Military Design. One of the most important aspects of finding exciting sources of meaning comes from a critical examination of the institution's existing science.[2] My purpose (and passion) for writing this book is to assist others in the community who may be intrigued by a seemingly radical proposition: sociologically, there must be, and always will be, a disunity of military knowledge.[3] Henceforth, I attempt to inquire: *Can there be a variety of ontological, epistemological, and methodological frames of reference for the design of militaries and their interventions?*[4] I believe the answer is "yes," and the principal theme that will guide my answer is captured in the word *postinstitutional* (i.e. rejecting the premise of *foundationalism*—the *science of everything*).[5] Indeed, this book represents a call for *institutional reflexivity*[6]— the process of exposing and exploring hypostasized frames of reference (i.e. as soon as "we"—the collective mind—settle on a frame, we become both victims and beneficiaries of institutionalized knowledge).[7] Reflexivity is an ethic that demands that institutional members continuously dismantle, attack, disrupt, deconstruct, and so forth, otherwise habituated frames of the collective mind. The ideal of the *military profession* demands one to remain critical about institutionalized science and exercise epistemic reflexivity. *Reflective practice* should always have relevance and arguably define the profession, no matter what the theory-for-military-action *du jour*. My hope is to give the reader fresh sociological avenues to become more institutionally reflexive—to offer a refreshing variety of frames of reference well beyond those used in conventional designs.[8]

What peeves my emotional sense of humanity is when military organizations and their intervention activities are designed too narrowly—as "science projects" (the way of the modernist). I feel compelled to preface this book with a series of examples and critical portrayals of how modernist military institutions have gone too far to legitimate their knowledge constructions as would natural (physical) scientists. I turn to my youngest son's 11th grade chemistry textbook to make the point. *Science*, according to the authors (Wilbraham et al. 2005), is about

- Matter—the object is "anything that has mass and occupies space" (p. 7); (Ontological orientation: objectivism);
- The science of measurement "directed toward a practical goal or application" (p. 9) (Epistemological orientation: quantitative); and
- A specific form of problem-solving: "making observations, testing hypotheses, developing theories" which explain laws (i.e. how matter behaves) (pp. 22–3). (Methodological orientation: "scientific").

This ontological realism, the epistemology of pragmatism (common sense), and the methodological steps to problem-solving are very enticing to those inculcated into the modernist worldview. Indeed, this pattern of sensemaking is quite seductive to the modernist institutions; hence, it is no surprise that assumptions of contemporary military science look something like

- A military has mass and occupies space;
- We apply the military toward a practical goal (also called "objectives," and the foreknowledge we seek is determined from measures of performance and effect); and
- The first "law" of military intervention, before committing forces, is to define the problem[9] and then use the tools of military science to solve it.

In short, the military is designed as an independent variable (the solution) manipulated to affect the dependent variable(s) (the problem). Modern military knowledge is assumed by the institution as part of a larger, monistic body of positivist science—in its ideal state, it is destined neither to be ontologically disparate, epistemologically separable, nor methodologically unique. In short, the modernist institution links its structures to the promise of Cartesian-scientific foundationalism. That is, modern military science is legitimated only when it is unified through the natural science values of nominalism (e.g. taxonomic naming conventions), nomotheticism (e.g. seeking law-like principles of war), and progressivism (e.g. knowledge gets better and better). Hence, the worthiness of modern military science is based on how it contributes to the eventual science of everything—where ontology, epistemology, and methods merge into an isomorphic, *utopian* sameness (Mannheim 1936). I find this homogenized worldview of military science both constraining and unnerving. My intent is to critique these modernist assumptions toward knowledge unification.

Indeed, I write this book principally to dispute the unification assumptions of modern military science and expose them as constituting a taken-for-granted, rather narrow-minded ideology. My overall purpose is to assist members of the modern military institution's philosophical emancipation with institutional reflexivity—assisting in the transcendence of traditional approaches to Military Design beyond the otherwise sedimentary objectivist ontology, Cartesian epistemology, and the accompanying "scientific" method.

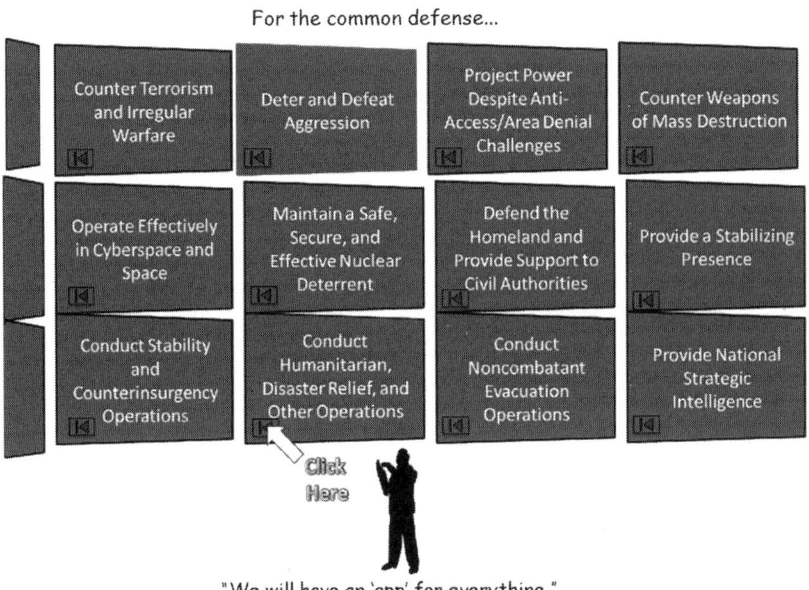

Graphic by author.

There is an abundance of evidence that both the administrative and operational arms of the US Department of Defense (DOD) are set on assuring the unity of knowledge in its military contributions to the science of everything. Today's military science, replete with tangible consequences, is based on the logic that MILITARY DESIGN = A SCIENCE PROJECT.[10] For example, the following is an extract from a report that is sadly humorous, expensive and, from a humanistic point of view, quite scary:

> When you think of the latest and most powerful military technology you might imagine smart bullets that can bend around corners or advanced stealth technology that can render a soldier virtually invisible, but underwear? Probably not, but that is exactly what the U.S. military is adding to its seemingly endless arsenal. As reported by Fox News, researchers at the U.S. Army Medical Research and Material Command office . . . and Telemedicine & Advanced Technology Research Center . . . have developed some digital-drawers capable of monitoring a soldier's

> vital statistics such as heart rate, skin temperature, respiration, and heart rate. Utilizing gel-free sensors, the high-tech underoos gather the collected vitals from a soldier and relay it to a central system allowing for an unprecedented level of monitoring and training soldiers on and off the battlefield. In theory, soldiers that maintained more balanced vital levels during stressful training situations could then be picked for missions with a greater degree of difficulty (Iliaifar 2012).

Another case in point. While in the process of writing this book, my employer, the US Army Training and Doctrine Command (TRADOC)—an administrative arm of the Department of the Army—is spending millions of taxpayer dollars for advanced technology in education (a funding program called "Classroom XXI"). The justification is officially reported as follows:

> TRADOC Regulation 350-70 (dated March 9, 2009) *Systems Approach to Training Management, Processes, and Products*: Classroom XXI is defined as the training environment in which the military and civilian personnel of the 21st Century will train. This environment is built by leveraging the technology of the information age to gain training efficiencies while maximizing training effectiveness . . . . Classroom XXI . . . requires technological modernization of the training institution. Technology will transform current classrooms from an instructor-centered environment to a student-centered multimedia environment with worldwide access to approved training material. To create the Classroom XXI environment, considerable investments must be made in networks, hardware, facilities, and software to create an open, compatible environment of classrooms and depositories of approved training material connected via cyberspace (Department of the Army 2009b).

Each of our "upgraded" classrooms at the US Army Command and Staff College on my campus at Fort Lee, Virginia, now contains the latest "advanced learning technologies" in everything, from video-teleconferencing to very expensive 70-inch plasma, touch screen televisions—two in each classroom. There are also two other, very expensive, computer projectors, drop-down screens, and an extra 50-inch flat screen monitor in the same classroom as well. I thought it appropriate to mention this program to illustrate just how far the US Army has embraced the progressiveness promised by modern science to the point of equating the quality of its officer education with the expensive and expanded use of advanced technology and audiovisual engineering. TRADOC seems to have spared no expense, justified by the institutionalized structures of "modern science," even in the midst of an ongoing and devastating recession and a government debt crisis. In the tongue-in-cheek mode, perhaps military officer education should be measured by TRADOC as a correlation of available PowerPoint projection screen square inches to student ratios; therefore, the faculty can educate officers in a geometrically more effective way. I cannot help but cringe at the institutional belief that advanced electronic technology (a derivative conviction of the eventual utopian science of everything) will somehow result in more creative, better-thinking, better-acting graduates.

About the time of this writing, my teaching team received results from a Research and Development Corporation (RAND) study commissioned by my college to assess the standardization of grading practices of the faculty. Here is one interpretation from a staff member who attended the presentation of the results and sent an email to the faculty of my teaching department:

> Our department had 50 instructors selected to each grade 4 . . . exams. One exam was an A exam, 2 were B exams and one was a C. We had 11 instructors complete the task. The average score for the A paper was 72.6 for the B papers 77.8 and for the C paper 74.2. . . . Due to sample size it could not be confirmed, but it appears there is a problem with what makes and [sic] A, B or C. It should be noted that the standard deviation for most instructors did show a range of answers, but they did not match the pre-grading assumption of what a grade should be. I mean the instructors as individuals had a grade spread, but it did not match each other nor did it make what was the assumed grade of the paper to start with (electronic mail from an unnamed staff member in a teaching department at Fort Leavenworth, Kansas 2011).

I had to smile as I read this. The college had just directed a new policy of identifying the top 20 per cent of graduates of our program. To validate the policy and ensure equity, the institution had to find a way so that the grading of essay exams was "standardized" across the faculty. My guess is that the faculty who were compelled to participate in the study not only objected to the premise of the exercise, but (ironic to the intent of the study) also displayed some active-aggressiveness in how they approached this illusive "scientific" experiment. I admit that I would be happier if they did.

Other examples of the DOD pursuing the science of everything are news stories I obtained from various official press releases (I found these rather startling):

> Fort Leavenworth, Kansas (August 4, 2011) *Fort Leavenworth Lamp*: Volunteers are being sought to participate in a study to see if electrical activity in the human brain is linked to behaviors, beliefs and values that distinguish effective from less effective leaders. Col. Sean Hannah, from the Center for the Army Profession and Ethic, Combined Arms Center, is working with David Waldman and Pierre Balthazar, from the W. P. Carey School of Business

> at Arizona State University, to see if this information could help identify appropriate people for particular leadership positions. It could even be used to develop leadership potential and optimize the brain activity of existing leaders. Hannah's team has demonstrated that behaviors associated with effective leaders can be neurologically mapped and predicted by comparing traditional psychological assessments, such as leadership behaviors and values, to a set of "brain maps" produced through electroencephalogram technology (Fort Leavenworth Lamp 2011).

Even more disturbing is the DOD's serious attempt to treat issues of human existentialism (in the above case, leadership as a variable) as one would scientifically manipulate independent variables associated with suicide. According to an official press release, the Task Force on the Prevention of Suicide by Members of the Armed Forces has spent time and money framing the increase in suicides among its service members in the design of a science project:

> WASHINGTON, Aug. 23, 2010/PRNewswire-USNewswire .... Since its formation in August, 2009, the Task Force mandate has been to look at the issue of suicide across all branches of the military at all levels, to "make recommendations regarding a comprehensive policy designed to prevent suicide by members of the Armed Forces." Specific deliverables as outlined in the Congressional memorandum directed the Task Force to:
>
> - Assess the Services' suicide prevention and education programs
> - Assess if any military career fields have higher risk
> - Assess trends and causal factors of military suicides
> - Assess the processes and procedures for military suicide investigations.... (PR Newswire 2010).

One essay that claimed to "reframe" suicide in the military, selected for publication in the prestigious US Army War College journal, *Parameters*, ended with a call for more science: "Efforts at prevention of suicide in the military will be most effective when they are rooted in as complete and accurate an understanding of the factors leading to suicide as possible" (Mastroianni and Scott 2011, p. 19). This conclusion goes unchallenged, as the handling of the issue evidently was another science project based on a belief that one can scientifically, through factorial analyses, predict suicide in the military. Such modernist quests seek to find independent variables (find the causal factors) to predict suicide (the dependent variable). The underlying monistic view of epistemology in these studies seems to be that the study of suicide is reducible with a scientific methodology.

Through manipulation of the independent variables (i.e. the proper "policies" and "process and procedures"), the DOD will ultimately change the dependent variable (premature death) of those who are considering or who commit suicide. Not surprisingly, I have heard that the identified independent variable in the studies tends to orient on leadership (what lately has become the multipurpose, independent variable of the modernist military institution).[11] I also found a related story that the US Army is trying to use "spirituality" as an independent (predictor) variable, operationalized by a

> . . . computerized survey that is mandatory for all Army members. Those surveyed are asked to rate their responses to statements such as, "I am a spiritual person. I believe that in some way my life is closely connected to all of humanity. I often find comfort in my religion and spiritual beliefs," or, "In difficult times, I pray or meditate." The test then ranks their emotional, social, family and spiritual "fitness." According to the Army, the test was developed to help spot soldiers who might be depressed or suicidal, two issues that have impacted servicemen returning from Iraq and Afghanistan. It says the results are provided to help point troops to services that can help them. Brig. Gen. Rhonda Cornum, the director of Comprehensive Soldier Fitness, said, "Researchers have found that spiritual people have decreased odds of attempting suicide, and that spiritual fitness has a positive impact on quality of life, on coping and on mental health" (Pasadena Sun 2012).

We also see how this "science" is useful in justifying large military budgets and correspondent searches for high-technologies that objectify otherwise subjective foreign policy narratives that make it difficult for the US Congress to say no. As such, DOD acquisition science is closely linked to the utopian science of everything. The DOD (that is now spending about three to four trillion dollars every decade on high-technology procurements) has developed its modern science of acquisition. In its *2010 Annual Report*, the Defense Acquisition University (DAU) celebrates its scientific management knowledge construction much like NASA would celebrate its rocket science that led to its Apollo-moon program (DAU 2010). Even the social aspects of DAU scientific acquisition is vested in deterministic forms of educating "acquisition professionals," an even more pronounced scientism than the Army's:

> The Intact Team Trainer is a micro-world based in an office setting. With rooms and tools corresponding to office, conference room, and break room environments, players interact with each other to perform real-world tasks. Computer capture of interactions allows the facilitator to have a wealth of information to discuss with the team and draw out lessons learned (p. 7).

The US government's Office of Personnel Management (OPM), whose largest single customer agency is the DOD, apparently seeks to harness civilian "human resources" as part of the quest for a value-free, nonpartisan, dehumanization of people, reducing them to a form of capital:

> We constantly seek new ways to accomplish our work and to generate extraordinary results. We are dedicated to delivering creative and forward-looking solutions and advancing the modernization of human resources management. . . . OPM will design and implement Federal personnel management practices consistent with our merit system principles. These principles . . . guide our efforts to treat all Federal job applicants equitably when making hiring decisions, retain employees based on their performance, support employees with effective education and training, and protect them from partisan influence.... Equal pay should be provided for work of equal value. . . . The strategic goals are presented in an order that follows the *lifecycle* of a Federal employee. The "Hire the Best" strategic goal concentrates on improving the Federal hiring process. OPM's "Respect the Workforce" strategic goal focuses on employee retention through training and work-life initiatives. The "Expect the Best" strategic goal aims to provide the necessary tools and resources for employees to engage and perform at the highest levels while holding them *accountable* (emphasis added, OPM 2010, pp. 5–6 and p. 9).[12]

The OPM narrative implies viewing the human worker as a well-controlled independent variable that will, by quantitative measures, assure efficient and effective performance (the dependent variable). Thus, the human science of performance is "scientifically" designed in the DOD in the pursuit of measurable efficiencies. The echoes of Frederick Taylor's (1913) treatise on scientific management are rather astonishing (e.g. Thayer 1972; Merkle 1980).

Written artifacts about designing military interventions reveal the same belief patterns. In the 2011 introduction to the US military's capstone doctrine entitled *Joint Operations*, note this imbedded sense of scientific ontology, epistemology, and methodology:

> The fundamental purpose of military power is to deter or wage war in support of national policy. In these capacities, military power is a coercive instrument, designed to achieve by force or the threat of force what other means have not. While leaders may employ this power in more benign ways for a variety of important purposes across a wide range of situations, they must understand that these other uses can imperil this Nation's fundamental ability to wage war (Department of Defense 2011b, p. I-1).

The logic of a unified, modern science is at least implicitly at work in this narrative. Here, the military itself is seen as an independent variable (or, in the DOD's functionalist jargon, *instrument of power*), scientifically designed for a specified function (i.e. to deter or wage war) with respect to dependent variables (the object-achievement of national policy), through power or force (words that are akin to the science of physics). The implications are that (1) if the "leaders" (the elected officials or political appointees who govern the military) (2) do not use the science appropriately (according to the causal relationships established in science), then (3) the United States may be at perilous risk (i.e. warning of amateurish misunderstanding and misuse of modern military science).

Extending this logic (some have called this the *Vietnam Syndrome*; perhaps appropriately updated as the *Afghanistan-Iraq Syndrome*), military interventions are analogous to the science of physiology—prescribing the right medicine, hence, one has to correctly diagnose the kind of ailment at hand before one applies the scientifically determined remedy (the application of armies, air forces, etc.). Here's a *USA Today* extract with a recent example of quantitative measures of effectiveness that mimics the hard sciences:

> Since 2005, more than 50 [NATO] troops had been killed and 48 wounded by Afghan troops, according to data released before the policy changed and USA Today research. In 2011, Afghan troops killed at least 13 ISAF [NATO's International Security Assistance Force] troops. Anthony Cordesman, a military analyst at the Center for Strategic and International Studies, said information about the killing of U.S. troops by Afghan troops or police is important because it shows whether the U.S. withdrawal plan is realistic (Brook 2012).

This propensity of the modernist institution to seek officers with a quantitative science education has been around in the military community at least as long as there has been the US Military Academy at West Point. My teaching-team and nineteenth-century historian friend and office colleague, Professor Christopher S. Stowe (2005), writes:

> . . . West Point of the 1830s provided a number of critical services for America and its citizenry. Its scientific, mathematical curriculum, emphasizing training in military and civil engineering, produced young officers possessing the kind of specialized expertise held in universal demand as the republic embarked upon a period of unmatched geographic and qualitative expansion. To these well-schooled subalterns fell the preparatory tasks of nation building, which besides the army's traditional frontier constabulary and warmaking duties included surveying and cartography, geographic and hydrographic exploration, and the construction of roads, lighthouses, railways, and canals (p. 71).

Likewise, one of the later passionate calls for increasing the Western science of war was by British military theorist Colonel J. F. C. Fuller. In his treatise, *The Foundations of the Science of War*, reflecting on World War I, after his nation faced over 1 million casualties, he writes:

The Lack of the Scientific Study of War

> What was the difficulty? It was that soldiers possessed no means of analyzing facts; they saw things as cows see them, and they were unable to work scientifically. Had they been able to discover the true meaning-the truth-of facts, the rest of the problem would have all but solved itself (Fuller 1925, p. 29).
>
> . . .
>
> Method creates doctrine, and a common doctrine is the cement which holds an army together. Though mud is better than no cement, we want the best cement, and we shall never get it unless we can analyze war scientifically and discover its values. This, then, is the object of my method-to create a workable piece of mental machinery which will enable the student of war to sort out military values. Once these values are known, then can they be used like bricks to build whatever military operation is contemplated. My system, I believe, will enable the student to study the history of war scientifically, and to work out a plan of war scientifically, and create, not only a scientific method of discovery, but also a scientific method of instruction. Normal man will not think; thinking is purgatory to him; he will only imitate and repeat. Let us turn, therefore, these defects to our advantage; let us, through clear thinking and logical thinking, obtain so firm a mental grip on war that we can place before this unthinking creature a system which, when he imitates it, will reflect our intention and attain our goal. Let us look upon normal man as a piece of human machinery, a machine tool controlled by our brain. Let us devise so accurate a system, and let us present it to him in so simple a form, that without thinking, without perhaps knowing what we intend, he with his hands will accomplish what our brains have devised (p. 35).
>
> . . .
>
> What is science? Science is coordinated knowledge, facts arranged according to their values, or, to put this definition still more briefly and to quote Thomas Huxley, science is "organized common sense," common sense being, in the opinion of this great thinker, "the rarest of all the senses" (p. 36).
>
> . . .
>
> If we can establish a scientific method of examining war, then frequently shall we be able to predict events-future events-from past events, and so

> extract the nature and requirements of the next war possibly years before it is fought (p. 38).

Fuller's quote from Huxley particularly epitomizes the military institution's well-documented ("organized common sense") artifacts of modern science: doctrinal publications. Fuller's assertion of the value of determining the future of warfare reflects foundationalism that persists in today's modern military institutions in the scientific quest for a more logical-positivist doctrine.

Today, military "think tanks," such as the RAND, prosper on the basis of this ideal of a predictive knowledge about war in the footsteps of West Point's origins and J. F. C. Fuller's scientism. RAND's Cartesian mantra includes the following:

> Through our dedication to high-quality and *objective research and analysis and with sophisticated analytical tools* developed over many years, RAND engages clients to create knowledge, insight, information, options, and solutions that will be both effective and enduring (emphasis added, RAND 2011).

What follows is an extract from a more recent RAND study confirming that strategy and operations in military interventions may be designed as scientific experiments. The study was funded by the DOD and titled, *Dilemmas of Intervention Social Science for Stabilization and Reconstruction*:

> **Operations as Experiments**
>
> Because of the uncertainties and complications discussed above, those developing strategy for S&R [stability and reconstruction] will be well advised to think of the chosen *strategy as an experiment*, one that will probably have to be adapted to reinforce what is working and to find substitutes for what does not. This requires monitoring developments, which requires signposts of success or failure. Metrics can either help or hurt in this regard, depending on how well they are constructed and how well they reflect the idiosyncratic nature of the particular intervention. We believe that *improved metrics can be constructed* using the results of our survey and its system depictions . . . (emphasis added, Davis 2011, pp. xlv–xlvi).

Here is a similar script from the DOD's attempt to forecast the future (the future projections are claimed to be into the 2016–28 range) and its correspondent soothsaying of how the force will have to fight:

> The Joint Operations Concepts—consisting of the Capstone Concept for Joint Operations (CCJO), and the various Joint Operating Concepts

> (JOCs), the Joint Functional Concepts, and the [Joint Integrating Concepts] JICs—provide a *common vision* of how the Department of Defense would like to *operate in the future*, along with the desired attributes of the force. . . . These documents provide . . . an assessment of how well the current or programmed force performs that mission; and the functional solutions analysis (FSA), an analysis of *possible solutions* to shortcomings in mission performance. . . . The results of *experimentation* may be used as input to . . . or, the results of the . . . may direct *new experimentation efforts* or identify areas where additional technology development is required to deliver the required capability (emphasis added, Department of Defense 2010, p. A-1).

Also in the JFC Fuller tradition, what this narrative describes is the publication of official documents that foretell how the joint force will operate, compare this desired capability to how capable the force is now, and then expend resources, through programs and budgets, to fill the gaps. This is a classic modernist exemplar in creating Military Design justifications with the illusion of science.[13]

If you do not find issues with the assumptive structures in the sampling of these modern military science narratives, you may not want to read this remainder of this book. What follows in six chapters is a *nonfoundationalist* view of military science.[14] The principal argument is that military science is (and must be) a messy, eclectic, socially interactive, multidisciplinary, inventively isomorphic, politically discursive, technically unstructurable, countercultural, artful, existential, often institutionally deviant, risky, adaptive, meta-philosophical, and mindful process. There will be no monistic military science. There will be no science of everything. Any claim to the contrary is an epistemic illusion.

The six chapters that follow include

Chapter 1, "The Institutionalization of Modern Military Science," forays into a philosophical critique of the modernist approach to military science while suggesting a multiple-frames approach to critical inquiry. The first chapter will also introduce a theory of institutionalization and present some speculation about how modernism flourished around the ideal of a modern general staff, the rise of operations research and systems analysis (ORSA), and a short discussion of US involvement in Vietnam (I tend to use the Vietnam War for fruitful heuristics concerning military sociology throughout the book). In light of these experiences, the chapter then offers to unmask the objectification military science through a postinstitutional form of reflexivity—the *Affirmative Postmodern Approach*.

Chapter 2, "Frame Awareness," addresses the fact that modernist military institutions reify jargon and communicate theories for action with dead metaphors. We must admit that our linguistic capacity is very limited and human speech, "the first social institution" (Rousseau 1966, p. 5), is insufficient to describe phenomena.[15] All logic is relational, all grammar symbolic, and all rhetoric analogously incomplete; hence, we should find ways to question meanings, remain mindful that meanings are creatively derived from analogical reasoning, and be playful in redesigning them. The conceptualizations intertwined in modern defense institutions are largely dominated by the pretense of knowledge that natural science metaphors provide.[16] This chapter offers a Multi-Framing, *Typology of Metaphors* that will aid the military designer in exposing institutionalized frames of reference and offer him creative sources for reframing.

It seems existential searches for meaning occur when militaries are "in the presence of extremity that they can best talk about meaning of life" (Morris 1966, p. 4). Military institutions fall back on the "usual suspects" in explaining failures or ambiguities of success.

Chapter 3, "A Critique of 'The Usual Suspects' for Military Design," comprises my speculations about the etymology of meanings of what I consider are *iconic meaning containers* that have become hypostasized (or should I say, downright worshipped) in modernist militaries. I divide this chapter into three parts—Part 1. Frame Reflection on Strategy, Part 2. Frame Reflection on Leadership, and Part 3. Frame Reflection on Planning. I offer alternative ways to reframe them or discard them entirely (at least temporarily). My hope is to introduce some element of doubt about these human-invented attributions and perhaps convince doctrinaires not to promote these wares so authoritatively and positively.

Chapter 4, "Relationalism," explores the paradoxes revealed in postinstitutional Military Design. I attempt to employ ideas garnered from the important treatise of Gibson Burrell and Gareth Morgan (1979), which permits *interparadigmatic journeys*. I propose, again in the interest of institutional reflexivity, that we can view military structures and military interventions through the quadigenous (four-way) views from *functionalism*, *radical humanism*, *radical structuralism*, and *interpretive* paradigms and speculate how these perspectives may present Military Design as paradox.

Chapter 5 is entitled, "The Reconstruction of Military Profession," where I identify sociological issues with dominant modernist constructions of *military profession*, as they may prevent broader interpretations of Military Design and blind us to the alternative prospects for critical inquiry. I propose a postinstitutional (reconstructionist) view of military profession that may help overcome the otherwise unchallenged, bureaucratic values and rules that restrict critical inquiry into modernist conventions of Military Design.

Chapter 6, "*Un Petit Récit* from the Field," is the conversation between two majors who have served as planners and designers on wartime staffs: Grant Martin, US Army Special Forces, and Ben Zweibelson, US Army Infantry. They come together to dialogue about their institutional experiences in Military Design. I asked these officers to take sociophilosophical positions and describe important interpersonal aspects as they (quite courageously) attempted to work within the institution, as what I would characterize, in postinstitutional, artful ways.

Coda. At the end of the book, I provide some closing remarks.

Notes

1 This excerpt is from the poem "Upon this age, that never speaks its mind" © 1939, 1967 by Edna St. Vincent Millay; reprinted here by the gracious permission of Holly Peppe, Literary Executor, The Millay Society (www.millay.org). I selected this epigraph to illustrate the idea that there is not one way (a single "loom") to make sense of the world; no matter how many "facts" are available. Karl Mannheim (1936) said it this way: ". . . seemingly isolated and discrete facts must be comprehended in ever-present but constantly changing configurations of experience in which they are actually lived. Only in such a context do they acquire meaning" (p. 110).

2 In my research, I found that scant attention is paid to *epistemic reflexivity* in the military sociology literature. The one exception is an article by Zeev Lerer and Sarit Amram-Katz (2011), which concludes that the turbulence associated with concepts about warfare "is deeply rooted in the minds, knowledge, organization structures, and institutionalized practices of the military. Its cultural dominance makes it a default scheme – a prototype – against which circumstances and contexts are conceived, compared, and understood. . . . [recent experience] shows how models of 'textbook war' and 'textbook companies' still frame the reactions and interpretations of soldiers and commanders alike in operational situations that do not conform to these models" (pp. 67–8).

3 I use the terms *science* and *knowledge* interchangeably throughout the text. My personal bias is to portray *knowledge* in terms of the liberal arts' Trivium: the *logic*, *grammar*, and *rhetoric* of social meanings associated with our linguistics system (Joseph 2002/1937, p. 9). My key assumption in this book is that any system of meaning is man-made; therefore, all knowledge that language represents is subject to criticism—all science, after all, is interactively expressed symbolically (Blumer 1969).

4 Critical examination of *ontology* would question the assumptions of "human being" and "being human," along a subjective::objective continuum, and is associated with the question of *what* is real or appears to be real. Critiques of *epistemology* would then question truth-of-knowledge coherency (e.g. simplified::complexified) associated with *grounds* for communicating it to be real or appear to be real. Critical aspects of *methodology* include deconstruction of research traditions and associated processes of investigation and assimilation that are assumed to legitimize knowledge as real or appearing to be real.

5 Another way to describe postinstitutionalism is a "rejection of rational-actor models . . ." with the critical view that "institutionalization is both a 'phenomenological process by which certain social relationships and actions come to be taken for granted' and a state of affairs in which shared cognition

defines 'what has meaning and what actions are possible'" (Powell and DiMaggio 1991, p. 9). Postinstitutionalism implies that the institution is a state of being unreflexive; so, it is critical to studying it from an etic (outsider) position, and, when emic ("inside it" as I am in writing this book), striving to be as reflexive as humanly possible.

6 See Karl Maton (2003) for his rendition of "epistemic reflexivity" which is similar to the idea I am offering here.

7 I use the terms *hypostasized*, *reified*, *objectified, routinized, habitualized*, and *institutionally sedimented* as synonyms—conveying the socialization of making conceptual meanings into concrete, *a priori* meanings. Making concepts concrete also contributes to the idea of *ideology*. And *ideology* is closely related to the idea of making sense from the perspective of a *worldview* or from inside a Kuhnian *paradigm*. For examples, later, in Chapter 3, I explore how *strategy*, *leadership*, and *planning* have come to have hypostasized military frames of reference (i.e. these are believed foundational "meaning containers" within the modernist ideology of military science). I heuristically call these (in addition to *military profession,* which I attempt to reconstruct in Chapter 5), the "usual suspects" when it comes to institutional searches for meaning. I propose that these become "rally points" for searches-for-meaning occur when institutionalized knowledge becomes problematic for finding meaning in intervention situations (such as after the United States' involvements in the Vietnam War and her recent wars in Iraq and Afghanistan-Pakistan).

8 For example, a recent booklet published by United States Army Research Institute (2012) renders "design" as a methodology (inconsiderate of a broader philosophical view that would include addressing ontological and epistemic issues) and subordinates that methodology into an unquestioned (institutionalized) planning paradigm. "The Army Design Methodology (ADM) offers Commanders and planning staff a tool for the conceptual component of an integrated planning process" (p. 4). There seemed to be no room in this "insider" (self-referential) research report to question the idea of planning itself.

9 *Operationalism* (defining phenomena, like war, in terms of measurable independent and dependent variables) is an example of treating existential issues as rigid, unemotional science projects. Modern military science demands such operationalism, giving the illusion of methodological rigor in pursuit of reliable causation (Sjoberg 1959, p. 623). Operationalism may be the single biggest fallacy of modern military science; yet, it explains why we call the execution of military interventions "operations."

10 The history of French military science in the wake of the Enlightenment also portends of its later questionable efficacy. See, for example, Azar Gat's (1992) treatise that discusses French military modernism (the likes of Jomini contrasted with German-Clausewitzian romanticism) through the nineteenth century in the first chapter. Coincidently, Gat also thoroughly links the dialectical philosophy of Clausewitz to Marxian theory in Chapter 5 of his book. I will also address the Marxian-related sociological paradigms of *radical humanism* and *radical structuralism* (I will cover these in Chapter 4) as

alternatives to the *functionalist* view that dominates modern military thought today.

11 In its expressed design policies, the US military has a predetermined set of independent variables. At the time of this writing, they are: *doctrine*, *organization*, *training*, *materiel*, *leadership*, *personnel*, and *facilities* (DOTMLPF). Design of the military is based on manipulations of these operationalized variables. In many ways, these are the institutional *solutions that look for problems* (Cohen et al. 1972).

12 I have to point out the use of the words “lifecycle management” that are the same as that the Defense acquisition community uses to describe its scheme for procurement management of materiel systems. The not-so-hidden text is that human resources should be managed similarly to materiel systems—a machine-like approach to capability inventories, the engineering of military work, and the retirement of the obsolete.

13 While the future-telling approach is hardly more than a Shaman rain dance, when reading this 149-page manual that prescribes, in excruciating detail, the methods to find these gaps, one can easily lose track that all of these procedures are based on nothing more than unimaginative and poorly written science fiction.

14 This nonfoundationalist view of knowledge construction may be referred to as “postpositive epistemology.” For example, what D.C. Phillips and Nicholas Burbules (2000) describe as “believing that human knowledge is not based on unchallengeable rock-solid foundations—it is *conjectural*. . . . there are all kinds of sources of our knowledge, but *none has authority*” (p. 26, emphasis in original). I use the term *postinstitutional* to signify the same idea of “nonfoundational.”

15 Jean-Jacques Rousseau’s (1966) specific quote is: “Speech distinguishes man among the animals; language distinguishes nations from each other; one does not know where a man comes from until he has spoken. Out of usage and necessity, each learns the language of his own country. But what determines that language is that of his country and not of another? In order to tell, it is necessary to go back to some principle that belongs to the locality itself and antedates its customs, for *speech, being the first social institution*, owes its form to natural causes alone” (emphasis added, p. 5).

16 I refer to this *pretense of knowledge* also as an *artless rhetoric*, meaning the “scientificized” language that conveys an assumed absence of emotion and *genericization* (Simons 2010)—sterilization of situations, away from contextual uniqueness.

1

The Institutionalization of Modern Military Science

Philosophy is an attitude of mind towards doctrine ignorantly entertained. . . . The philosophical attitude is a resolute attempt to enlarge understanding of the scope of application of every notion which enters our current thought.

ALFRED NORTH WHITEHEAD,
Modes of Thought

. . . mathematics and physics . . . This type of thinking is applicable only under quite special circumstances, and what can be learned by analyzing it is not directly transferable to other spheres of life. Even when it is applicable, it refers to a specific dimension of existence which does not suffice for living human beings who are seeking to comprehend and to mold their world.

KARL MANNHEIM,
Ideology and Utopia

The order of ideas must follow the order of institutions.

GIAMBATTISTA VICO,
The New Science

In this book, I treat military organizations and interventions as complex sociological phenomena; therefore, I use sociology as the principal basis of inquiry.[1] My intent, in the footsteps of Karl Mannheim (1936), is to examine the social construction of military knowledge and whether such an inquiry will lead to greater insights about designing (not to be confused with planning) militaries and military interventions.[2] The central argument is that modernism—as an institutionalized episteme—has served to limit frames of reference for Military Design.[3] My quest here is both to disprivilege modern military science and to emancipate the designer or design team from its confines (Woolgar 1988, p. 8). As a secondary reason for inquiry, my hope is that the book will help demystify "artistry" with the hope of shaping a more flexible praxis for Military Design.

Critique of the modernist approach to military design

I argue that modern military science has been inadequate for practitioners who must deal *sui generis* with military organization and interventions. Modernism asserts that there is only one kind of knowledge—that which is legitimated only through an objectivist worldview and associated with the socialization of "normal science" (Kuhn 1996), where assumptions include

- *Progressivism* (the belief that all "problems" can be solved and that aprioristic knowledge accumulates and undesirable events and problems recur; one only acts rationally, with a substantially proven theory in mind—that planning for the future (the construction of foreknowledge) is more and more possible as theories become more valid and reliable predictors of future events and ready-made solutions are more and more viable);
- *Logical positivism* (a conviction that all causal relations are knowable and become more and more context-free in application—conveying the expectation of "the science of everything");
- *Reductionism* (variables can undoubtedly be separated and structured in functionalized relationships with others and assessed through the "scientific" method); and
- *Empiricism* (an undaunted realist's quest for physical sensory data as proof of truth, particularly tied to measurements which may serve tentatively as in-lieu-of proofs until scientific testing is complete).

In studying social phenomena, modernism would add derivative assumptions associated with the theory of evolution and microeconomic theory with correspondent derivative theories of structural functionalism and behaviorism. At its highpoint in the context of twentieth-century industrialization, modernism can be construed as a rather colorless, sterile, and drab "culture marked by both the benefits of mass production and the burden of alienation, depersonalization, excessive specialization, and bureaucratization" (Merkle 1980, p. 1). I assert that these underlying ontological beliefs continue to dominate the epistemology of modern military institutions and serve to limit Military Design as would

- ideologies in partisan politics that limit design of *public policy* (Schneider and Ingram 1997)
- science of *engineering* that would aesthetically deprive the architect who is focused exclusively on the functional design of a building (Lawson 2006)
- scientific management of efficient *automobile production* that deprives attention to the artful design of what is being produced (Lutz 2011) and
- *computer-based instruction* that focuses on knowledge comprehension and technical application while devaluing the emotional aspects of critical collaborative inquiry, limiting heuristic value, and restricting the possibility of improvisational and tacit knowledge.[4]

In contrast, postinstitutional interpretations recognize a contextual shift in shaping Military Designs governed by these "postmodern" characteristics (I compiled these from Moskos et al. 2000; Boëne 2003; Sookermany 2011)[5]:

- ambiguity over "civil-military" governance when warring with supranational militants (a.k.a. "irregular forces" who fight "irregular wars")
- confusion that ensues when militaries attempt to operate outside the traditional modernist sociological frame of "organized violence" and reframed more broadly into "organized anarchy"[6]
- erosion of the "sovereignty" (to include citizenship identity) of the modern nation state and the inept theories of *realpolitik* (perhaps paradoxical to *idealpolitik* expressed by Boëne 2003)
- moving away from quantity toward quality and technical specialization of forces
- purposeful manipulation by modern militaries through public relations and leaning more toward institutional survival
- insufficiency of titular doctrinal concepts applied to military interventions that are too complex for a stable, positivist science to work
- epistemological displacement from expertness in knowing-in-military-practice to the skeptical awareness of the certain ambiguity of learning-in-military-practice and
- supranational warring parties that make the efficient, modern, behavioral-engineering of organizational design (e.g. mass production of materiel and replication of tasks, conditions, and standards of

training and specialized military education) of military mobilization inadequate (perhaps making improvisation-in-action a more important value)

This interpretive shift demands alternative sociological paradigms for framing Military Design. Other sensemaking options, antithetical to institutionalized modernist frames, may include interpreting military interventions as

- complex social phenomena that may be alleviated or managed but never, in the mathematical sense, "solved"
- researched through exploration of *social constructions of reality* (e.g. Berger and Luckmann 1967; Blumer 1969; Searle 1995)
- context-specific with historic resemblances[7]
- emotionally charged and spiritually motivated
- artfully crafted and aesthetically pleasing
- fraught with competing values, ethical dilemmas and paradox
- addressed through ongoing, pluralistic judgments and
- requiring endless, existential-like, searches for meaning by those who participated and by the historians who make sense of them in context.

These become the revised conditions for *thinking*[8] about military action—constructed with both meaning and behavior. While modernist epistemology would focus on the latter, henceforth, I will especially emphasize linguistic structures and the deeper meanings associated with military action.[9]

A postinstitutional approach to Military Design, then, admits that experience is *sui generis* and that each situation requires a continuous, pluralist search for extra-institutional frames that can provide alternative meanings. The following guidelines reflect postinstitutional (more pluralistic) ethics that would support the demands of this shift toward this more eclectic, transdisciplinary practice of Military Design:

- Treat military interventions as context-dependent (not necessarily tied to a modernist view of the history of warfare which aims to progressively turn historic knowledge into positive, context-free knowledge, often labeled "lessons learned," "best practices," or "doctrine" and reorient on situational uniqueness);
- Remain ontologically and epistemologically flexible (doubtful of claims to "expert" knowledge, doctrinal entertainments, "operationalized" variables, and pre-engineered tasks while appreciating continua that serve interpretations oscillating between objective to subjective ontology and between atomistic and "chaoplexic"[10] epistemology) (Mannheim 1936, p. 13);

- Value *institutional reflexivity* (always faced with novelty, refrain from turning to rational-analytic models of choice and strive to remain humble, open to "radical" methods of inquiry, pragmatic skepticism, and deviance-in-practice);
- Promote critical discourse among a multiplicity of participants in as democratic ways as possible (recognize that appeals to oligarchic and "expert" authorities are doubtful when dealing with sociological phenomena; remain vigilant that military science is sociologically relational rather than objectively conclusive); and
- Accept that Military Design may require a considerably long period of time to reflect on the merits or disappointments in- or of- militaries and their interventions that were intended to alleviate social situations and that the "side-effects" of complex interventions depend on meanings and interpretations that people attach to them (there is no objective "truth" in reflection on merits or disappointments; rather, various "truths" emerge, sociologically, over time; hence, "truth" involves retrospective judgment and never as prospective as, say, proponents of operations research and systems analysis—ORSA—would claim).

My intent, with the help of my colleagues who wrote Chapter 6, is to weave these ideas into the fabric of the book with the hope that the reader can return to explore deeper meanings that may unfold around them.

Multiple-Frame approach to military design

The first thing any ethical scholar of warfare should do is to admit his or her philosophical bases (and biases) of argument (often hinted by epigraphs such as the ones at the start of this chapter). I feel that I have already waited too long in this introduction to express them. To set this stage, my favorite description of philosophy comes from Lewis Feuer (1975), who sees the philosopher's lofty goal as a "genuine, un-counterfeit, un-imitative expression of the person's experience in relation to the universe. . . ." He continues:

> . . . a philosophy is the fullest self-discovery of an individual and what [s/he] stands for. A philosophy is one's own to the extent that the individual rids himself of the effects of clichés and catchwords, placards, parades, slogans, and watchwords; disengaging [her/himself] from the social counterpressures of ideological clubs, circles, peer and populist groups, professional orthodoxies and associations, thereby surmounting the laws of fashion, the individual can define for [her-/him- self, her/his] individual standpoint (p. 187).

Compare this with his description of ideology:

> . . . the outcome of social circumpressures; it takes philosophy, and reduces it to the lowest common social denominator. . . . the emphasis is on the being 'one of us,' and the free, uncontrolled, venturing idea is suspect. An ideology is an 'ism,' that is, a philosophical tenet which has been affirmed as the axiom for a political group. . . . But above all, the ideology closes the door to search and doubt . . .; the ideology claims answers that are certainties . . .; it closes questions; it records terminal collective decisions; it is not a franchise for the individual questioner (p. 188).

From Feuer's descriptions, one can sense that philosophy inherently calls for both a passion for wisdom and challenging social taboos—the desire to look outside the potential psychic prison of our institutionalized ideologies, struggle to suspend disbelief in alternate framings, and peer through window frames that offer relational points of view.[11] This ideal of wisdom, intertwined with a sense of humbleness, is so eloquently described by John A. Meacham (1990):

> The essence of wisdom . . . lies not in what is known but rather in the manner in which that knowledge is held and in how that knowledge is put to use. To be wise is not to know particular facts but to know without excessive confidence or excessive cautiousness . . . [to] both accumulate knowledge while remaining suspicious of it, and recognizing that much remains unknown, is to be wise. . . . [Thus] the essence of wisdom is in *knowing that one does not know*, in the appreciation that knowledge is fallible, in the balance between knowing and doubting (emphasis added, p. 187 and p. 210).

Equally compelling, and more concise, is Karl E. Weick's version, "Wisdom is the quality of thought that is animated by a dialectic in which the more one knows, the more one realizes the extent of what one does not know" (2009, p. 19). Note in these expressions how doubt becomes a near synonym with wisdom. This view of philosophy, imbedded in my mindfulness while writing this book, is: if one appreciates the limits of explaining complex, ever-changing phenomena, one's best hope is to find as many articulations as possible, never accepting just one. Nevertheless, one can still act while at the same time exercising disciplined speculation about one's meanings about the action. Sociologist Peter L. Berger (1963) put it this way: "the liar knows he is lying, but, by definition, the ideologist does not" (p. 112). In the critical mode of postinstitutional sensemaking, designers seek to expose those institutional representatives who appear sincere, not as liars, but who are stuck on hypostatized meanings—that is the designer has the potentially socially dangerous obligation to reveal those who find meaning for action in their own propaganda (p. 109).[12]

Lastly, there is the humbling long view of man's limitation that exceeds all generations of "knowledge," expressed by Carl G. Jung (1956):

> It would be a ridiculous and unwarranted presumption on our part if we imagined that we were more energetic or more intelligent than the men of the past – our material knowledge has increased, but not our intelligence. This means that we are just as bigoted in regard to new ideas, and just as impervious to them, as people were in the darkest days of antiquity. We have become rich in knowledge, but poor wisdom (p. 20).

Jung forces us to accept that no matter how much of what he calls "material knowledge" we have accumulated (and now abundantly available on the internet), the presence of "wisdom" has regressed of late.

In regard to the idea of exercising disciplined speculation, I admit to have been deeply influenced by the proponents of the multi-frame approach for the inquiry into, and interpretation of, social phenomena, particularly employing the ideas put forth by Karl Mannheim's (1936) treatise on the sociological philosophy of knowledge.[13] The following authors and their books, to include Mannheim's classic work, were mind-expanding in that regard (and it would be a fair wager that a multidisciplinary master's degree program could be designed around them).[14] I selected a quote from each book (listed in order of publication year) that seems to best reinforce the multi-framing idea:

- Karl Mannheim (1936), *Ideology and Utopia*: ". . . it is precisely the multiplicity of the conceptions of reality which produces the multiplicity of our modes of thought, and that every ontological judgment that we make leads inevitably to far-reaching consequences. . . . [W]e begin to suspect that each group seems to move in a separate and distinct world of ideas and that these different systems of thought, which are often in conflict with one another, may in the last analysis be reduced to different modes of experiencing the 'same' reality" (p. 99). Frames include: Bureaucratic Conservatism, Conservative Historicism, Liberal-Democratic Bourgeois Thought, Social-Communist Conception, and Fascism.
- Stephen C. Pepper (1966), *World Hypotheses*: "Having done all that we can do rationally to organize the evidence on the topic in question in terms of structural corroboration, and finding as a rule that therefore four equally justifiable hypotheses explaining the nature of the subject, we shall have the wisdom not to conclude that we know nothing about the topic, but, on the contrary, that we have four alternative theories about it, which supply us with a great deal more information on the subject than any one of them alone could have done." Pepper calls his multi-frame approach reasonable postrational eclecticism (p. 331). Frames include: formism, mechanism, contextualism, and organicism.

- Henry Mintzberg (1973) *The Nature of Managerial Work*: "The task I set for myself in this book is to extract the useful findings from the literature and blend them with the findings of my own study to present a comprehensive description of managerial work. As a beginning, this chapter describes eight major schools of thought on the manager's job" (p. 8). "Schools" of thought include: Classical, Great Man, Entrepreneurship, Decision Theory, Leader Effectiveness, Leader Power, Leader Behavior, and Work Activity. [Mintzberg has subsequently published other important works that present multiple frames, to include *Mintzberg on Management* (1989) and *The Rise and Fall of Strategic Planning* (1994).]
- Hayden White (1978), *Tropics of Discourse*: The "fourfold schema of tropes [serves] as a model of modes of mental association characteristic of human consciousness. . . . [L]anguage provides us models of the direction that thought itself might take in its effort to provide meaning to areas of experience not already regarded as being cognitively secured by either common sense, tradition, or science" (p. 13 and p. 73, emphasis in original). Frames (he calls "master tropes") include: metaphor, metonymy, synecdoche, and irony.
- Kim Cameron and Robert Quinn (1988), *Paradox and Transformation*: ". . . one must have the cognitive capacity to use multiple frames, and the behavioral capacity to use skills that match the frames" (p. 306). Frames include: Human Relations, Open Systems, Rational Goal, and Internal Process.
- Keith Grint (1997), *Leadership*: ". . . this model [of leadership] encompasses epistemologically and methodologically different perspectives on leadership that should facilitate a greater understanding . . ." (p. 4). Frames include: Situational Leadership, Constitutive Leadership, Trait Leadership, and Contingent Leadership.
- Mary Jo Hatch (1997), *Organization Theory*: "Organizational complexity can be colorfully illustrated by the Hindu parable of the blind man and the elephant. . . . Only when viewing these numerous perspectives all at once do you get any sense of the magnitude of the problem you face. . ." (p. 7). Frames include: Modern, Symbolic, and Postmodern.
- Deborah Stone (1997), *Policy Paradox*: "Reasoned analysis is necessarily political. It always involves choices to include some things and exclude others and to view the world in a particular way when other visions are possible. Policy analysis is political argument, and vice versa. . . . What people care about and fight about are interpretations of fetuses, shootings, wars, and economies. What communities decide about when they make policy is meaning, not matter [of fact]. And science cannot settle questions of meaning" (pp. 575–6). Frames include: Equity, Efficiency, Security, and Liberty.

- Graham T. Allison and Philip Zelikow (1999), *Essence of Decision*: "Multiple, overlapping, competing conceptual models are the best that the current understanding of foreign policy provides" (p. 401). Frames include: Rational Actor, Organizational Behavior, and Governmental Politics.
- Paul A. Sabatier (1999), *Theories of the Policy Process*: "Knowledge of several different perspectives forces the analyst to clarify differences in assumptions across frameworks, rather than implicitly assuming a given set" (p. 6). Frames include: Rational, Multiple Streams, Long Wave, and Comparative Systems.
- Nicholas Rescher (2001a), *Philosophical Reasoning*: ". . . it is unlikely in the extreme that there will soon be a restoration of the ambitious single-author systemizations that have characterized philosophical productivity in the past. . . it has become multilateral and diffuse—no longer the product of single minds" (p. 273). Frames [interesting that he calls these a "network of contexts"] include: cognitive, scientific, social, technical, and political.
- Gareth Morgan (2006), *Images of Organization*: "When we recognize that competing theories are competing metaphors, we can. . . . set grounds for a much more reflective approach. . . where people rather than theories are in the driving seat" (p. 364). Frames include: Machines, Organisms, Brains, Cultures, Politics, Psychic Prison, Flux and Transformation, and Instruments of Domination.
- Antoine Bousquet (2009), *The Scientific Way of Warfare*: ". . . the endurance of the general phenomenon of war, its myriad manifestations have been shaped by the diversity in the material and ideational characteristics of the societies and cultures that have waged it" (p. 243). Frames include: Mechanism, Thermodynamics, Cybernetics, and Chaoplexity.[15]

What these multi-framers have in common is that they seek not only to doubt, but also to criticize institutionalized frames of reference. They advocate the insights that come from employing a plurality of frames. My intent in this book is to convince the reader that what these pioneers have accomplished in other fields or study can be done in military science as well.

The multi-framing approach proposes that: (1) all meanings are interpreted and adopted through a sociopolitical process; (2) institutions tend to adopt singular or settled meanings to frame events; and, (3) the designer, through critical discourse, can seek a plurality of alternative meanings to frame the same events. The underlying assertion of the present book is built upon Mannheim's and many that followed his lead—that *all* forms of knowledge are socially constructed. Those meanings and explanations are subject to critical reflection and creative generation of multiple frames or angles for interpretation. The process may seem regressive to the more conservative members of the institution as it represents a call for returning (at least temporarily) to a pre-institutionalization stage of situational framing and a recognition of the sociality of problematization.[16] The postinstitutional outcome of the multi-frame approach is ideally an intellectual, emotional, and emancipatory experience.

The institutionalization of modern general staff

One remedy to sedimentation of knowledge is in finding reason to admit there is sedimentation.[17] Military institutions may be defined as the formal and informal structures and actions through which a larger social system legitimates military intervention. Liberally paraphrasing James G. March and Johan P. Olsen (1989), institutionalized structures consist of degrees of habituated rules (routines, policies, classifications, conventions, organization charts, roles, strategies, organizational forms, and technologies) and inculcated values (beliefs, scripts, paradigms, codes, norms, mores, and assimilative knowledge) that, through social interactive processes, *frame* individual and collective action (p. 22). From these ideas, Pamela S. Tolbert and Lynne G. Zucker (1996) have synthesized the process of institutionalization into a descriptive model that can be adapted to inquire and speculate about military institutions.

Tolbert and Zucker theorize that the stages of the process are: pre-institutionalization, semi-institutionalization, and full institutionalization (p. 176). Innovation is prominent in the pre-institutional stage, influenced by idea-generative forces such as experiences in human conflict, technological changes, laws, and economics. Innovation is characterized by artful imitation and adaptation which can happen in an interorganizational context, making change more attractive. Habitualization is the continued mimetic process of pre-institutionalization that adapts the stories of others' innovations into the organization in order to provide approaches to solving problems in reaction to perceived similar stimuli (in this book, another military intervention). The innovations of the Franco-Prussian War served to set exemplars for evaluating performance during the Spanish-American War. A short history follows.

Secretary of War Elihu Root's push to reform the US War Department (1899–1904) was arguably a creative adaptation of Prussian general staff structures employed in the Franco-Prussian War (1870–71) (Hewes 1975). Nations were aghast at the speed with which the believed-to-be inferior forces of Prussia penetrated deep into France threatening Paris and the toppling of the French regime. David Kahn (2007) writes that other militaries attributed a sort of dark, mystical power to the Prussian general staff system—believed to be the most decisive aspect of the War (pp. 499–500). What was seductive to other military observers at the time was the apparent ability of the Prussian staff to see into the future—the soothsaying quality of comprehensive military staffs and their detailed planning technologies began to form an occult-like belief system that still exists today. Kahn writes: "The desire to know the unknowable and to control it tinges that desire with mysticism, because the black arts promise to reveal the future. That gives the general staff the image of . . . a 'dark force'; it explains why. . . the Prussian general staff [was called] 'the mythical monster'" (p. 500). Kahn goes on to speculate about the imitative process as other militaries adapted the Prussian military staff and planning models:

> Of course as knowledge objectifies and mathematizes, it bleaches out the occult. But the desire to predict the future makes it unlikely that humans will ever extirpate mysticism from their activities. . . . So studies of the general staff may benefit from examining the hermeticism and magic . . . as a wellspring of modern science (p. 500, emphasis added).

Root was also heavily influenced by this belief system and he found a window of opportunity for institutional reforms in response to US political reflections on mobilization for the Spanish American War (1898), where the US War Department was found to be administratively ill-equipped.[18] The US military bureaucracies were redesigned to meet the needs of future American interventionism based on the uncanny success of the Prussian general staff a quarter of a century before.

By 1910, the US War Department had transformed itself to the semi-institutional stage employing many organizational structures which were innovated by the Prussians. This stage was also influenced by the concurrent US "scientific management" movement in mass-production manufacturing led by Frederick Taylor (Hewes 1975, p. 18; Merkle 1980).[19] Objectification is an inherent quality of the semi-institutional stage—a "movement toward a more permanent and widespread status" and seen in the permanency of structures as partial hypostatization sets in—where borrowed, extended, and displaced articulations are becoming a shared reality (Tolbert and Zucker 1996, p. 176). The process occurs when members of an organization "develop general, shared social meanings attached" to the behaviors shared in the pre-institutionalization stage—"a development that is necessary for the transplantation of actions to contexts beyond their point of origination" (p. 175). Rationalization, characterized by the diffusion of new structures, is motivated by virtue that institutional decision-makers perceive that more organizations have adopted the innovation; therefore, the costs and benefits of new structures are apparently favorable (p. 177).

Continuing with post-Spanish American War reforms, the US National Security Act of 1947 legalized the existence of a "unified" Department of Defense and legitimized the "joint staff"—the original ideas by now so extended and displaced from the Prussian staff approaches as to become a fading or dead metaphor. The structures associated with planning rules and associated staff values are no longer meaningfully attached to originating innovations. These are all but forgotten by the institution, and the central purpose of the ideas go unquestioned as "progress" continues through smaller increments of adaptive change.

According to Tolbert and Zucker, *sedimentation* is the condition that results from the eventual full-institutionalization of structures. The process rests "on the historical continuity" of rules and values—especially on their "survival across generations of organizational members" (p. 178). The chief quality of sedimentation is the social process of reification, defined as the "degree to which typifications are 'experienced as possessing a reality of their own reality that confronts the individual as an external and coercive fact'" (p. 175, citing Berger and Luckmann 1967). The authors explain this unreflective state more fully:

> Sedimentation is characterized both by virtually complete spread of structures across the group of actors theorized as appropriate adopters, and by the virtually complete spread of structures over a lengthy period of time (p. 178).

Continuing with the Prussian general staff case study, the US Goldwater-Nichols Act of 1986 signified the sedimentation of a more integrated US national military staff. The roles, functions, and elaborately regulated procedures, joint knowledge repositories, etc. of the Chairman of the Joint Chiefs of Staff in the US Department of Defense, extended and displaced from the Prussian model (now vaguely reminiscent), are today quite sedimentary ("the way we do things in the DOD"). In summary, the mysticism of the Prussian general staff system has become modern military science—the institution's reification that frames "the complexity of the world onto the institutional structure that exists" (March and Olsen 1989, p. 28).

Other histories of modernist military sedimentations are endless. One more exemplar is the institutionalization of ORSA in the US Defense Department presented briefly here:

- *Pre-institutionalization.* Military applications of operations research began with the British military staff during World War I, becoming a full-fledged discipline in 1937 with innovative developments for the integration of radar and Hurricane fighter-interceptor squadrons (Shrader 2006, p. 5). The British conveyed these analytic-optimization modeling methods to the Americans in 1940. Throughout World War II, the usefulness of ORSA was witnessed particularly in structuring the optimal use of limited antisubmarine and bombing capabilities. Over the course of World War II, these quantitative research and analytical methods began to be applied to wartime policy-level decision-making (Miser 1980, pp. 139–46). In the 1950s and early 1960s, this field grew more and more popular even when faced with objections from senior military folks (usually World War II veteran officers) who stipulated that simulations, RAND studies, and so forth be subordinated to a more intuitive approach to decision-making (see Ghamari-Tabrizi 2000, for an excellent history of the rise of ORSA during this time period).

- *Semi-institutionalization.* The emergent military "science" became linked to the social meanings of Victory in Europe and Victory in Japan (hence the process of reification was already under way). One of the US War Department's military staff (Office of Statistical Control) who learned and embraced ORSA was Army Captain Robert S. McNamara, who later made use of this "science" as an executive at Ford Motor Company (more and broader social habituation) before being appointed Secretary of Defense in the Kennedy Administration. McNamara and his "whiz kids" use the mathematical modeling decision science of ORSA to develop the Department's PPBS (planning, programming, and budgeting system) (Schlesinger 1963) and to manage the impending escalation of the Vietnam War under President Johnson. Despite the US debacle in Vietnam, in which the quantitative mentality of the Whiz Kids (with the ORSA artifacts of enemy body counts, and "stop light" charts representing probabilities of Viet Cong village strongholds) was mainly in display, DOD leaders emerged with an even greater penchant for ORSA-style decision-making (Shrader 2006).
- *Full-institutionalization.* By 1963, James R. Schlesinger (a disciple of McNamara) reduced the Pentagon problem of managing the military "... into two parts: (a) How much resource to divert to defense and (b) How to use such resources" (Schlesinger, p. 295). Schlesinger (later appointed US Secretary of Defense 1973–75) painted a world of predictability through a detailed analysis, thereby confirming the institutionalized qualities of ORSA. Today, ORSA-produced models dominate decision-making in the Pentagon to the point where other decision theories and practices are not viable. The four major decision systems in the Department, based soundly on ORSA decision science, include: the Planning Program, Budgeting, and Execution process, Materiel Acquisition System, the Joint Capabilities Integration and Development System, and the Joint Strategic Planning System. ORSA has become the hypostatized "modern science" officiating over US national defense knowledge structures and

policy decisions. ORSA is so sedimentary to the management of the US defense institution that it has remained essentially unchallenged for the better part of a century. The steps for solving problems in virtually any context (weapons procurement, operations planning, etc.) according to ORSA science, include

- The *definition of the problem* and the determination of the means of measuring its critical elements
- The *collection of data* (either by direct observation, the use of historical data, or the use of computer-generated data)
- The *analysis of the collected data* (using both mathematical and nonmathematical methods)
- The *determination of conclusions* based on the analysis of the collected data and
- The *recommendation* to the military decision-maker of a course of action designed to correct or improve weapons and equipment, organization, doctrine, strategy, or policy (Shrader 2006, p. v).

Note how the values and rules of ORSA complement the parallel institutionalization of general staff structures and decision processes—underpinned by the "science project" ideology. Vaunting to solve any type of problem at any level of organization or analysis, the general staff system, coupled with ORSA-styled processes, today constitutes nothing less than the essence of modern military science for the US Defense institution.

Modernist military science has seemed quite efficient to societies in that the institutionalization process makes it possible to *rationalize* the design and finance large-scale, diversified military forces before interventions. Such rationalizations have to appear conceptually consistent (the hallmark of modernism) if resources are to be reliably produced and obtained. When the products of these rationalizations are presented to political decision-makers, the ideology seems spirally reinforcing. Modernism manifests in the creation and sustainment of military structures that, over time, become sedimentary; that is, they may be described as solutions looking for problems (March and Olsen 1989, p. 17).[20]

There are instances when complex problem settings are so dynamic that they do not "respond" well to the use of sedimentary solutions, particularly those of the modern military staff and their decision sciences. Modernist attempts to update meaning structures (commonly called lessons learned and best practices) from the field through the "scientific method," provide only fleeting theories of action and serve as a reason why militaries tend to fight the last war and pay less attention to other histories of military intervention.[21]

The American intervention in Vietnam

No military intervention better illustrates the institutional myopia of modernism than the American involvement in Vietnam. Frances FitzGerald's 1972 Pulitzer Prize winning book, *Fire in the Lake*, is essentially a treatise on this explanation of institutional (a.k.a. ethnocentric) failure:

> . . . in the third year of the war, after the US mission had set up a weak military dictatorship and dismantled the economy, after the American troops had killed countless thousands of Vietnamese, had burned their villages and destroyed their crops, all the talk of "social revolution" and nation-building evidenced an extreme removal from reality. In many respects this [problem] was institutional. The high officials of the mission had created a system by which they could receive no bad news . . . for instance, all civilian province officials filled out a single report every month describing not what the situation was but what the "Free World Forces" had done in their province for the past month. The aim of this report was patent, as its title was "Progress Report." And it did indeed show progress up to the point of perfect tautology. . . . The equivalent accounting system in the military was the description of all US actions undertaken, followed by an enumeration of enemy deaths and enemy "structures" destroyed. . . . [The report] suggested that death and destruction had some absolute value in terms of winning the war. . . . To admit that the war was excessively destructive or that it was not being won was to admit to personal as well as institutional failure – an admission difficult for anyone to make (pp. 363–5).

Witness the premature American claims of all but defeating the Viet Cong in 1967 prior to the Tet Offensive of 1968—ironically objectified from McNamarian ORSA models—represented by the sincerity of US Commander, General William Westmoreland (Westmoreland 1976, p. 410). Modernist framing continued for the rest of the war and dominates institutional rationalizations of that War even today.

Indeed, novelty in intervention settings continues to challenge modernist military institutions.[22] Modernism relies on sedimentary frames of reference (finding the one best way) so as to consistently obtain resources and deal technically with an expected range of enemies and physical circumstances. Military history demonstrates that potential foes are very creative at finding new advantages against such established structures. The dynamic that ensues between rationalized institutions and "irrational" opponents makes such progressive, "applied science" approach to war problematic. The problem of the institutionalization of modernism is that it ignores the fact that each second, minute, and day of an intervention is different in some way from the previous one. There is no *intervention in general*, only intervention in particular; uniquely and historically situated. Hence, postinstitutional designers should treat referent (indoctrinated) frames as a very narrow set of heuristics, not the promised context-free knowledge claimed by the modernists.

After all, military historians are continuously reframing past interventions.[23] Why should modernist-oriented strategists and commanders think they can preunderstand (an apriority requirement of commanders in modern military doctrine[24]) the interventions they are about to undertake if historians, armed with more data, cannot settle these understandings for decades, centuries, and millennia later?[25] The illusion of understanding is how the sedimentation of modern militaries sets conditions for surprise when standard meanings do not seem adequate to explain what is going on and guide a person how to act. The more lengthy and complex the intervention, the more likely that members of the institution will be in a continual state of astonishment – perhaps enough to "punctuate" a paradigm shift.[26]

This is why I advocate a multiple-frame approach to Military Design, signaling eclectic searches for alternative sensemakings in light of inevitable institutional "failures-to-frame" action well. Members realize that their failure to invoke continuous reframing will, at some point, involve perpetual frustration. Designers using only modern military science face intractable situations, even as they and their fellow practitioners are institutionally trapped from employing other frames. They have difficulty in effectively articulating the fact that modernism has become a contributing factor to failure. Hence, Karl Mannheim's central point about the sociology of knowledge is that knowledge is nonfoundationalist—that is, what we know is tentative and not wedded to any assumptions of modernism based on progressive knowledge and which includes the disputing of all claims to positive knowledge (Phillips and Barbules 2000, p. 24). A postinstitutional military design effort that subscribes to this nonfoundationalist assumption would strive to embrace surprise as "normal," employing disciplined speculation while creatively seeking to uncover and critically challenge new, seemingly radical frames that would guide action.

The affirmative postmodern approach

One approach to such a critical exposé is the affirmative postmodern approach, adapted from the work of Martin Kilduff and Ajay Mehra (1997). By "affirmative," I mean not to argue that better Military Design should always result from some sort of solipsistic, radical postmodernism philosophy and corresponding nihilistic deconstruction methodologies. Rather, the positive approach is an attitude that seeks to identify and criticize sedimentary beliefs and assumptions, in other words, help expose what knowledge structures modern military institutions take for granted.

My hope is to equip military designers with a critical method that may help them escape from sedimentary ways of framing situations. For example, with such a critique, we may better include nontraditional framings exemplified by more equivocal terms, such as "irregular warfare," while not rejecting the modernist frames, but including them as part of the multi-framing approach. Military Design becomes more "macroscopic" by embracing *multiple* frames, requiring *all* the instruments of traditional proof and more (in this case, subjection to the postmodern critique).

There are no required or sequential steps to the affirmative postmodern critique as there would be with rationalistic realism or its ontological offspring, modern military science. The idea is to pursue, critically and creatively, challenges to conventional wisdom with a purpose to help reveal and examine institutionalized monistic forms of framing, characteristic of modernism. The critique entails mixing and matching styles of inquiry to achieve an aesthetic and multidisciplinary approach to antithetical arguments. The intent of this unconventional approach is to increase an important creative tension that can lead to transcendence of old ways of thinking beyond hypostatized knowledge. For example, while the inquiry for postinstitutional Military Design may be informed by modern military doctrine and claims to historic justifications, it remains ambivalent toward them. The affirmative postmodern critique both celebrates and denies tradition and the myth of progress, emphasizes the polysemic quality of language,[27] values the presence of paradox, accepts irony in the situation, promotes multidisciplinary eclecticism, and embraces ontological pluralism.

Employing this critique, the skeptical designer can now view modernist doctrines as potential examples of dogmatic frame consensus. Perhaps better described as propaganda, military doctrine seeks to govern the legitimacy of its reified frames of reference and enforce them through oligarchic power structures. Rather than calling upon military doctrinaires to try and synthesize them or find epistemological closure, the postinstitutional designer embraces a diversity of positions that may remain open indefinitely (as the social constructionist's view of knowledge demands). With this flexible critique, designers should believe that certain aspects of the historic and contemporary military thinking should be reevaluated. Especially under complex, ambiguous conditions of military intervention, the postinstitutionalist can also claim that marginal and softer voices may have as much meaning as those in the formally empowered, hierarchical positions. Vested in more pluralistic forums, military designers may transgress oligarchic claims of authoritative knowledge, challenge conventional wisdom, and amplify voices previously silenced. Postinstitutional designers, then, see military interventions as messy affairs that can and should be investigated through peer-disciplined speculation and out-of-the-box sensemaking. There is a difference between puzzle-solving—using sedimentary framings to explain phenomena—and innovation—using bold conjecture, controlled by values associated with criticism (Schön 1963, pp. 53–4). These permit the design effort to drive back into the time and context to reinterpret and question the frames that seemed so appealing in the pre-institutional stage.[28] The objectified world created by modernist military writers is only then revealed to be no more than an intersubjective interpretation comprised of "official" schemata (that modern militaries call "doctrine") that are "legitimated" only through another human's power to make them so.

I think it is appropriate here to address a short linguistic case study with critical intent, employing the underpinnings of the affirmative postmodern approach. At the time of this writing, US joint service doctrine (arguably, the principal artifact of modern military science) is officially defined as

> *Fundamental principles that guide the employment of US military forces in coordinated action toward a common objective. . . . It is authoritative but requires judgment in application* (Department of Defense 2011a).[29]

With a sense of the history of modern warfare, this definition may seem clear, accurate, precise, and relevant (i.e. rational); however, the assumptions encased in this definition can be exposed and criticized. First, how shall one argue that these doctrinal *principles* are indeed *fundamental*? The word *fundamental* indicates a kind of unquestioned or self-evident underpinning and unjustified progressive view of knowledge upon which all other modern military science is to be built (i.e. reflects foundationalism). What is *fundamental* seems to have little substance other than a flag officer (in this case, the Director of the Joint Staff, a vice admiral) having approved the text to "make it so." Absent in this definition is an auditable trail of discourse that demonstrates how this assertion of *fundamentality* comes to be and whether the claim is logically challengeable. Arguably, the logic of *fundamental principles* in that US military doctrine is analogous to the *fundamentalism* inherent to stereotyping by social groups—should these *fundamental principles* be better described as "military proverbs" rather than giving the impression that they are objective, aprioristic, and scientific?

Indeed, in the context of modern military science, the use of the word *principles* is often abused, appealing to a family resemblance with the logic, grammar, and rhetoric of Sir Isaac *Newton's Principia Matemática*, advocating a view of the world through a machine-like precision of algebra. As one speculates on the institutionalization of modern military science, one detects mathematical goals of precision that facilitate staff work distribution, categories of resource allocation, and other attractive social architectures that provide the comforting illusion of predictability, control, synchronicity, and other values of scientism. Placed in the grammatology of algebraic formulae, US military science seems structured around a mathematical superset metaphor (symbolized below by ⊇). The following are constructs illustrated with indentations and font sizes that portray a hierarchy of knowledge structure found in modern military doctrinal texts and related artifacts:

Strategy ⊇ Ends + Ways + Means
Strategic Ways ⊇ Diplomacy + Information + Military + Economic
Military Means ⊇ Doctrine + Organization + Training + Material + Leadership + Personnel + Facilities

. . .

War Plans ⊇ Strategic Tasks
Strategic Plans ⊇ Operational Tasks
Operational Plans ⊇ Tactical Tasks
Tactical Plans ⊇ Individual Tasks

. . .

Operational Design ⊇ Command and Control + Intelligence + Fires + Movement and Maneuver + Protection + Sustainment
Command and Control ⊇ Communicating and maintaining the status of information + Assessing the situation in the operational environment + Preparing plans and orders + Commanding subordinate forces + Establishing, organizing, and operating a joint force headquarters + Coordinating and controlling the employment of joint lethal and nonlethal capabilities + coordinating and integrating joint, multinational, other governmental agencies, international governmental organizations, and nongovernmental organization support + Providing public affairs in the operational area . . .
Public Affairs ⊇ puts operational actions in context + facilitates the development of informed perceptions about military operations + helps undermine adversarial propaganda efforts + contributes to the achievement of national strategic, and operational objectives. . .
. . . [And so forth].

Note that the hierarchical knowledge structures (such as *Public Affairs*) listed to the right of the larger sets are all interdependent on the design of the superset, *Strategy*, on the left, indicating the primacy of strategy over everything else. From this functionalist frame, there is an obvious seductive quality of the certainty that only the engineering sciences (knowledge of interconnected parts) could afford. This architecture-like superstructuration of military episteme has arguably become a constricted frame, constituting an ideology for Military Design (Mannheim 1936, pp. 58–9).

When events or situations appear ill-structured, military doctrinaires seek to add or modify their noologic supersets, sets, and subsets of terms and concepts to accommodate such situations and make them appear structured (even if they are not). So, doctrinaires "rearrange the deck chairs" of institutionalized knowledge structures—recycle, rename, repackage the same concepts, separate and combine "functions," and so forth without challenging the efficacy of the functional structuration to begin with—in the modernist attempt to replicate the engineering sciences into a consistent, context-free science of military intervention.[30] Instead of accepting that events and situations in military operations convey their own, unique meanings, modern military science seeks to standardize meanings on events and situations so that it can devise organizational techniques for interventions. That is, modern military science is an attempt to functionally structuralize these complex interventions without making any critical reflection on whether this technically rationalistic epistemology is appropriate. Modern military science can be described as the illusive quest for making terms and concepts look like those of the physical sciences. Some of these concepts may work well for some aspects of Military Design (such as military logistics, weapon systems design, and combat engineering to some degree), but not if one seeks to design the whole of complex social interventions.

The problem with the modernist approach to Military Design is the absence of appreciating the science of muddling through[31] (Lindblom 1959) in practice in the unfolding messiness and uniqueness of the situation. Interdependencies of the elaborated meanings built into the modern military science become difficult to criticize from inside the institution because the hierarchical structuring of strategy, operations, and tactics and the taxonomies of knowledge on which they are built would fall apart into a perceived chaotic nightmare if this criticism were acknowledged by the believers. Mannheim (1936) describes this critical (and alternative) view of modernist knowledge more eloquently than I:

> The general interdependence of all the elements of meaning and their historic relativity has . . . become so clearly recognized that it has almost become a common-sense truth generally taken for granted. . . . Just as the true beauty of a sound literary style consists in expressing precisely that which is intended—in communicating neither too little or too much—so the valid element in our knowledge is determined by adhering to rather than departing from the actual situation to be comprehended (pp. 91–8).

As will be discussed later in the book, the concept of reflection-in-action would then apply to a more artful, postinstitutional Military Design process, and the epistemological challenge is rephrased by Schön (1983) as having ongoing "conversations with the situation" uniquely at hand (p. 95).

Coordinated action in the official definition of doctrine indicates a theory of sociotechnically controlled synchronization where planned activities (categorized across the algebraic breakdown of superset taxonomies shown above) can be orchestrated ahead of time, as would sheets of music that guide those who play instruments (of power?) together. Does this construct imply that there will be intolerance for deviant improvisation? By the way, what kind of knowledge constitutes *coordinated action* for something that has not happened yet? Does planning-for-integration of action (in the doctrinal vernacular, "unified action") imply that causality in war demands a sort of prescience (synonym, foreknowledge)? Paradoxically, one can hardly realize modernist values of empiricism and its companion, objectivity, in planning, so is planning revealed to be anything more than an elaborated fictional story of things to come? Such "operations plans" are better described as soothing causal stories that, like the prescient hopes of science fiction, have some resemblance to the present.

Common objective in the definition implies that the politics of setting goals for military operations (or broader interorganizational activities) have already been settled (which in the US domestic political arena is seldom, if ever, the case, let alone in supranational situations). Political goals are generally ambiguous, transient, and opportunistic, subject to shifting and competing value patterns, and interpreted through various partisan views as to what "success" in military interventions should look like (a question of evaluative judgment) and what policy will work (fictitious, causal narratives about the future) (Vickers 1965; Lyotard 1984; Stone 1997). Asserting that stable goals are possible in an emotionally charged political setting involving military intervention is, therefore, nonsense. If the emotionally charged political discourses over goals for military interventions are inconsistent over time, how can the military science of intervening remain stable as this modernist definition demands?

The affirmative postmodern critique also works to expose the paradox (or perhaps hypocrisy) of the meaning of *authoritative* (linked to an affinity for closure) in juxtaposition with the meaning of *judgment in application* (linked to situatedness). The first tells us that official doctrine contains a demand for institutionalized rule-following (a hierarchic or bureaucratic ethic); the second demands that one should know when to not follow them (arguably, a professional ethic of having the wisdom to deviate). While the affirmative postmodern critique may embrace this sort of paradox and irony as essential to the complexities of life and military interventions, the modern military text seems to ignore this juxtaposition as requiring no further explanation (ignorance is bliss?) rather than explore the deeper (and necessary) paradoxes of demanding simultaneous, yet incommensurate, values from military practitioners.

If the institutional espoused definition of doctrine is assailable through these critical deconstructions, then what is the efficacy of the subordinated texts (in algebraic terms, subsets) that flow from there? These deeply sedimentary, superset ways of framing for the design of military meanings and behaviors in interventions are akin to Lewis Feuer's definition of ideology (mentioned earlier). A postinstitutional philosophy of Military Design would seek to expose how institutionalized frames, such as those formalized in written doctrine, are dominating thoughts about what should be done and would suggest a need to find alternative framings.

Some final introductory thoughts

The essence of the argument in this chapter, and in the remainder of this book, revolves primarily around criticizing the epistemology of modern military institutions. In lieu of strictly modernist approaches to military interventions, I struggle to take on a postinstitutional view of knowledge creation—where modern military science is presented as something socially reified. I concur with Mannheim that there is a sociological explanation for knowledge; hence, all human "reality" is socially constructed into often unquestioned structures of rules and values—that is, *institutions*.

Modern military institutions reflect a belief system that claims aprioristic knowledge, progressivism, and a constrained ontological and methodological bases for epistemology—objectivism and scientificization. Henceforth, my writing partners and I make the case that modern military science is *not* objective knowledge; rather, it is largely *objectified* knowledge. The more we move along the continuum of military knowledge, from natural science (such as computing the probability of a tank round penetration fired into another tank) into social science (such as dealing with the sociopolitical milieu), the less "stable" and more discontinuous the knowledge should be. "Should" indicates this involves a revised ethics of knowledge and investigates how military institutions can so value context-free knowledge application that such an epistemology becomes hypostatized—believed to be foundational.

Modern military science represents sedimentary language (such as the term "doctrine" represents) and processes (such as operations research). Such sedimentations are vulnerable to "attack." Some might venture that this is the postmodernists' nihilistic tack and, while I do not singly embrace that approach, I freely exercise postmodern methods (as with the affirmative postmodern critique) as legitimately as I would with the traditional "scientific method." The morphologist's job (in the spirit of Mannheim) is to expose sedimentary knowledge systems and to try and help students of Military Design decompose the sedimentary modernist epistemology (an act of critical reasoning) and generate new or extended ways to frame (the essence of creativity). I hope this introductory chapter helps refine my thesis and set expectations for what is ahead—what I call postinstitutional approaches to Military Design.

Notes

1 By military intervention, I mean a socially significant imposition that includes militant organizations that can happen anywhere: physically—from inside a foreign nation, a domestic disaster area; and metaphysically—a social-psychological domain, through electronic media such as cyberspace, that considers interpretations of charismatic narratives, and enculturation.

2 Peter Senge (1990) uses a compelling metaphor to speak to the relationships between the ship captain (who designs the journey ahead) and the ship's designer (how the boat is designed) (pp. 341–5). Little credit (or blame) goes to the ship's designer as the ship's captain is solely responsible for everything that happens or doesn't happen. This metaphor speaks to why "design" in the military context should be much broader than just the design of an intervention. Senge speaks to designing *vision*, *values*, *purpose* and two ingredients to framing: *systems thinking* and *mental models* (p. 343). In this book, I strive to extend it to a more inclusive gestalt (e.g. exploring the institutional knowledge structures and finding ways to continuously criticize them—"being postinstitutional" and orienting on the *design of meaning*).

3 I use "frame(s)" and "perspective(s)" interchangeably in the book, using Karl Mannheim's description: "the subject's whole mode of conceiving things as determined by his historical and social setting" (p. 266). In other words, *reframing* conveys the artful reconstruction of meaning (as a sort of "generative metaphor" [Schön 1993]). Note that *frame* is itself a metaphor (more on this in Chapters 2 and 3).

4 For example, the US Department of the Army "trains" its soldiers and workforce on existential issues such as whistle-blowing, suicide, and homosexuality using computer-based instruction technology. In that regard, the US Army defines learning in modernist terms: "When preparing for current operations or full spectrum operations, Soldiers and Army civilians must continuously study Army and Joint doctrine, lessons learned, observations, key insights, and best practices." Even the Army's "self-development" is expressed in terms of "planned, goal-oriented learning that reinforces and expands the depth and breadth of an individual's knowledge base, self-awareness, and situational awareness" as if the knowledge is already there and one just needs to set goals and plan to learn it (Department of the Army 2009a, pp. 3–5).

5 By postinstitutional, I am referring to a position of being mindful and critical about institutional reification of interpretive frames (such as those artifacts of military doctrine). Through *postinstitutional reflexivity* (breaking free of the iron cage of institutionalized thinking and acting), one can find new, liberating ways to interpret that may extend and displace those highly institutionalized ways of making sense of the world. Some sociologists have made the analogy that institutionalized meanings for action are as powerful as instincts are to animals and that institutions create the walls of our "psychic prisons" (Morgan 2006, p. 207). Others have tried to find words to describe a shift. For example, Anthony King (2006) called it "the post-Fordism military"; however, I think that term is too restrictive in that it refers to a shift from an industrial era to a next era of some sort. What I propose here is more like a *Kuhnian paradigm shift* (Kuhn 1996, p. 119, p. 150)—a "tradition-shattering" way of inquiry (p. 6).

6 I added the "organized anarchy" shift borrowing from Michael D. Cohen and James G. March (1986) general properties of organized anarchies: *problematic goals*, *unclear technology*, and *fluid participation* (p. 3).

7 Karl Mannheim (1936) makes this point about *context specificity* clear: "The very fact that every event in history is bound to a temporal, spatial, and situational position, and that therefore what happens once cannot happen

always, the fact that events and meanings in history are not reversible, in short the circumstance that we do not find absolute situations in history indicates history is mute and meaningless only to him who expects to learn nothing from it, and that in the case of history more than that of any other discipline, the standpoint which regards history as 'mere history,' as do mystics, is doomed to sterility" (p. 93).

8 Karl Mannheim (1936) describes thinking as "conscious reflection" or "imaginative rehearsal of the situation" (p. xxii).

9 D. C. Phillips and Nicholas C. Burbules (2000) use an algebraic equation as a metaphor to make this existential point: ACTION = BEHAVIOR + MEANING (p. 70). MEANING, which is the focus of the present book, implies existential searching, sensemaking, relationalism, ethics, and so forth—those things that involve symbolism and multiple views of epistemology. I like the provocative quote from actress Jodie Foster, playing Dr. Arroway in the 1997 movie, *Contact*: "Ironically, the thing people are most looking for, MEANING, is what science has been unable to give them." I will discuss this mathematical metaphor more in Chapter 4.

10 *Chaoplexity* is a portmanteau coined by John Horgan (1996, p. 191) indicating the blending of chaos theory and complexity science. The word is used later in the context of military science by Antoine Bousquet (2009, p. 34).

11 I will cover the philosophical view of *relationalism* in more detail in Chapter 4.

12 *Hypostatized* meanings are human abstractions that are believed to be concrete (hard knowledge). The terms *reification, habituation, sedimentation, objectification, concretization,* and *hypostatization*, or forms thereof, are interchangeable. These sociological processes also relate well to the postmodern concept of *psychic prison* (Morgan 2006) and Karl Mannheim's (1936) sociological concept of *ideology*.

13 The "theory of the social or existential determination of actual thinking" coupled with the hypostatization of that thinking (p. 267).

14 Marianne W. Lewis and Andrew J. Grimes (1999) argue that "With metatriangulation scholars strive not to find *the* truth but to discover comprehensiveness stemming from diverse and partial worldviews" (p. 685).

15 I could find no comprehensive work other than Antoine Bousquet's that attempts to employ a multiple frames approach to military affairs; yet, his remarkable work is focused differently than what I propose here. Bousquet focuses on *when* the history of the physical sciences has corresponded, heuristically, with past and present institutionalized sensemakings about warfare. The present book seeks to broaden the scope as to *why* and *how* military institutions have done so.

16 The ancient Greek philosophers called this sort of questioning, *epoché*.

17 This admission is essential to *institutional reflexivity*. Another way to describe institutionalization is limiting the "very criteria by which people discover their preferences" (Powell and DiMaggio 1991, p. 11). One aspect of being institutionally reflexive would be to expose those criteria and recognizing that these are constraining.

18 The second part of Root's term in office was under reappointment by President Teddy Roosevelt, a bigger-than-life hero of the Spanish American

War. Roosevelt's wartime experience, now empowered by the "bully pulpit" was part of Root's window of opportunity for reform.

19 The Napoleonic wars, which shaped institutionalization of *Levee En Mass* in Western militaries, dovetailed nicely with Taylorism and the science of mass production. Wartime mobilization was an extended metaphor of the industrial sciences, particularly modern automobile manufacturing processes.

20 Another name for "solutions-looking-for-problems" was framed by John L. Gaddis (1982) as the *tyranny of means*. He explains, "It is ironic that this should have occurred under the administrations [Kennedy and Johnson] that prided themselves on their ability to match ends in the most appropriate manner; one cannot help but conclude that the very abundance of means which seemed to be available during those years contributed to the problem. The bracing discipline of stringency, after all, provides more powerful incentives than even the most sophisticated management techniques" (p. 273).

21 This is the essential argument of MacGregor Knox and Williamson Murray (2001).

22 Malcolm Gladwell (2005) tells the story of retired US Marine Lieutenant General Paul Van Riper acting as a red team opponent during the US training exercise, Millennium Challenge 2002, illustrates the contemporary issues with modernism. Van Riper's ingenuity in fighting the modern joint force with novel approaches threw the war game planners "off script" and disrupted the flow of the very expensive exercise. Arguably an institutional maverick, Van Riper has seemed to be what I characterize as a strong advocate of postinstitutional critique and a creative explorer of alternative framings (pp. 99–146).

23 Andrew Roberts (2011) reframes the point of view in his book: how the Axis *lost* World War II rather than argue from the traditional frame that the Allies *won* it.

24 In its modernist doctrine, the US Army stresses the removal of ambiguity in complex situations: "As commanders begin to understand the situation to include the problem, they start envisioning potential solutions." This is arguably a backwards logic as I will attempt to argue throughout this book (i.e. modern militaries are institutionalized solutions looking for problems) (Department of the Army 2011a, pp. 1–4).

25 To their credit, the US Naval War College Strategy and Policy Department, for example, continues to employ Thucydides' (1954) classic history of the Peloponnesian Wars (431–404 BC) in their education of officers, apparently for this reason. I attended that program in the early 1990s and still remember the challenge to study Thucydides' work.

26 Historians have often characterized the *Wehrmacht* of the interwar years as successfully doing this. Macgregor Knox and Williamson Murray (2001) similarly "frame" their treatise around *punctuated equilibrium* theory (a radical-structuralist view of institutional evolutions and revolutions, borrowed metaphorically from the biological sciences) (p. 6).

27 Defined, from a behaviorist point of view, *language* is an observable form or manner in which members of a group use vocal sounds and written signs to convey meanings to each other. From a broader philosophical view (as with Karl Manheim's 1936 treatise on the sociology of knowledge), "language" is

tautological with "contextual" and serves two functions: communication and representation, both forming from a dynamic discursive (social) and reflective cognitive (psychological) process called *symbolic interactionism* (Blumer 1969). When I refer to *language* here and in the remainder of the book, I mean it in the broadest sense—to include images, symbols, narratives, artifacts, and other ways and means social groups remember and communicate remembered meanings. I would argue that language is closely related to the term, "science," for that matter.

28 To paraphrase (Schön 1963) reflexivity involves paying attention to the relationship between the old frame and the new or novel situation at hand (i.e. the frame and the situation interact). Having a "cluster" of frames (multiple frames) gives legitimacy to having several meanings for the same term (i.e. extension and displacement of meaning/generative metaphors). I will extend Donald A. Schön's meaning into the idea of *institutional reflexivity* later in the book.

29 I use **italics** to indicate terms from this definition and to reference later in the text where I attempt to deconstruct and criticize specific word- and phrase-meanings.

30 For example, in the 1980s, the US military characterized the "spectrum of conflict" from "low intensity" to "high intensity." After several iterations, today the same idea is restructured as the "range of military operations" from peace through war (Department of Defense 2011b, p. 1-5). This recurrence of knowledge structures is called *cyclicism* in the philosophy of knowledge (or epistemology) (Rescher 1995, p. 95).

31 Charles E. Lindblom (1959) argues that complex social situations demand small, incremental policy interventions as large-scale attempts to change the situation will risk disastrous consequences that cannot be reversed. The *Science of Muddling Through* is the practice of using *successive limited comparisons*—a method of comparing the situation now with the situation before and making an informed judgment as to whether things seem better.

2

Frame Awareness

This process of understanding can only be tropological in nature, for what is involved in the rendering of the unfamiliar into the familiar is a troping that is generally figurative.

HAYDEN WHITE,
Tropics of Discourse

Another theme of the life of metaphor has to do with certain persistent relations between metaphors and theories based on them. It is a truism to say that culture provides us with the informal theories from which our formal theories are displaced.

DONALD A. SCHÖN,
The Displacement of Concepts

Metaphor is one of our most important tools for trying to comprehend partially what cannot be comprehended totally: our feelings, aesthetic experiences, moral practices, and spiritual awareness. These endeavors of the imagination are not devoid of rationality; since they use metaphor, they employ imaginative rationality. . . . metaphor is not just a matter of language . . . it a matter of conceptual construction.

GEORGE LAKOFF AND MARK JOHNSON,
Metaphors We Live By

There are no live metaphors in the dictionary.

PAUL RICŒUR,
The Rule of Metaphor

Unlike the modernist approach, which is finding meaning in the situation at hand (usually expressed as the *definition of the problem*), the postinstitutional approach is finding the situation among a variety of meanings. Our first task in the proposed postinstitutional approach, then, is to recognize that the designing of language is part of the adaptive framing for military institutions and their interventions. Ken Starkey and Sue Tempest (2009) put it this way:

> Language shapes the problem spaces we deal with by naming and framing them, by making them familiar. This familiarity is a two-edged sword, both enabling and constraining, giving us a perspective on what would otherwise look chaotic, but limiting our vision to the extent that we believe that what we see is the way the world is and needs to be (p. 579).

Any claims by the military modernist to expert knowledge should begin to waiver as we note that all language *is* culturally adaptive as social constructions—it is artificial (Cossette 1998, p. 1357). As such, these communications are polysemic and relatively ephemeral.[1] Studying the morphology (or *mutatis mutandis*) of military language is particularly interesting and as such is subject to the tools of interpretive sociology and critical inquiry—the purpose of this chapter. Key to our inquiry is the study of *communications as metaphor*, and military science is no exception.

The term metaphor is itself a metaphor—derived from the Greek words *meta*, which means "beyond," and *pherein,* which means "to bear." Hence, metaphor takes us beyond the normal content of language and serves as a "container" for the unrealizable literal or objective definitions of phenomena that humans are interested. In short, I argue here that postinstitutional Military Design calls for the *management of metaphors*—that is, designers should mindfully draw from a diversity of meanings that serve as (Brown 1977; Ortony et al. 1993) [my comments in brackets]:

- category errors with a purpose [note the irony]
- linguistic madness with a method [indeed, creativity walks on the edge of madness]
- Giambattista Vico's "credible impossibilities" [note the inherent paradox]
- sensibility-on-loan [i.e. from other knowledge forms]
- exemplars for the otherwise unfamiliar constituency [analogy is better than total ignorance]
- "bridges," from what they tacitly know and cannot say [mysteries], to others' quasicomprehension
- implicit substitutes for inexplicit reality [symbols of reality]

- purposeful ambiguities (equivocations) to gain support from otherwise conflicting interpretations [why often used in political rhetoric]
- something short of ridiculousness and more than an euphemism or hyperbole [yet are defectively absurd if taken literally]
- imaginable idioms or a source for neologisms [insightful ways of looking at things]
- imaginative frames of reference [poetic] and
- metaphysical explanations [permitting pseudo awareness].

With this intention, we shall apply Schön's (1963) displacement of concepts theory and construct a typology of metaphors in the remainder of this chapter. The goal is to spur the intellectual and emotional emancipation of military designers from the unchallenged, "monochromatic," (modernist's categorical) language of military interventions (Black 1993, p. 25).

Schön's displacement of concepts

Faced with the continuous reframing of military intervention and an array of emergent "irregular" adversaries, military designers (as aspiring morphologists) should be seeking less theories of action drawn from the physical sciences and pay more attention to the value drawn from other sources for creative framing. Yet, what should military designers know about creative language design? Where does creativity come from in the construction of military concepts? Is creativity strictly an unexplainable, mysterious process? Can we critically examine how linguistic imagination works toward new theories of action? Can there be a utilitarian logic associated with the language arts when it comes to military interventions?

In his book *The Logic of Scientific Discovery*, Karl Popper (2002/1935), one of the most cited philosophers of the twentieth century, said: ". . . there is no such thing as a logical method of having new ideas," claiming that some mysterious form of "irrationality" is at work (p. 8). However, some who have studied how language is conceptually constructed—largely through the morphology of metaphors and analogies—have disagreed. One such pioneering philosopher is Donald A. Schön (1963). In his rather obscure book *Displacement of Concepts*, Schön develops a remarkable theory of concepts—how humans dislocate new meanings from old. Ironically, Schön employs *metaphoric reasoning* ("giving a thing a name that belongs to something else") to explain how metaphor works—he employs meaning associated with the biological theory of evolution, substituting the human adaptive language process for natural selection (p. 40). Schön's theory is encapsulated in his own concise description of human adaptation of language:

> Theories are selected for displacement on a number of bases: the gifts of the various overlapping cultures involved, the metaphors underlying the ready-made theories in terms of which the new situations are already partly structured, and the demands of those situations—that is, the aptness of the old theory, taken as a projective model, to provide new solutions for the problematic aspects of those situations (p. xi).

To illustrate, here is an excerpt where Schön imaginatively uses a learning-to-swim metaphor to describe the creative process in the evolution of meaning:

> A child who has learned to swim in a pool learns for the first time to swim in the ocean. He has material to work with, patterns of expectation and response. But as he first encounters waves and the buoyancy of salt water, everything he has learned to do must shift. He must learn and adapt, but he does not start from scratch. His old way of swimming is *displaced* to the new situation (p. 107).

When faced with seemingly intractable situations, humans have no recourse but to draw upon the partial meanings of prior knowledge to make sense of them. Better put, metaphors help "reorganize alien realms" (Burrell and Morgan 1979, p. 244) like the alien realm Schön tried to communicate with his child-swimmer-ocean metaphor. As we err in action, we discover that old meanings do not work well in explaining the way the world appears to us now, we reinterpret those meanings into something new and tentative. As time goes on, we elaborate on this temporary use of borrowed meanings and eventually adapt them into our more permanently accepted language that we believe reflects the way things are. We tend to lose touch with old meanings as they are displaced and the recontextualizations become part of our "normal" language; hence, the originating terms become dead metaphors. While Schön calls this process *concept extension and displacement*, we may also see the parallels to reified meanings inherent to the sedimentary stage of *institutionalization* discussed in Chapter 1.

Unlike the subscribers to modern military science, armed with Schön's approach to morphology, military designers can assess military knowledge structures more accurately (or ambiguously) as ephemeral elaborations and replacements of older structures. When new sciences emerge, such as those of late based on chaos and complexity (*chaoplexic*) (Horgan 1996; Bousquet 2009) theories, we can reconceive and replace old constructions with new imaginations. For example, when nineteenth-century war theorist Carl von Clausewitz (1984) introduced the metaphors of FRICTION[2] and

CENTER OF GRAVITY in his classic book *On War*, he was limited in his ability to extend and replace the metaphors drawing on the state of modern science of his time. Clausewitz extended his descriptions of FRICTION in war to his readers as images of trying to walk through water and CENTER OF GRAVITY as "the most effective target for a blow . . . the place where [victory] can be reached" (p. 120 and pp. 485–7).

Since then, many military theorists have published on the concepts of FRICTION and CENTER OF GRAVITY extending and displacing his original metaphors with new elaborations.[3] Like Clausewitz did in his time, contemporary military concepts draw upon the familiarities of their time. Compare, for example, Clausewitz's Newtonian metaphors to the post-Newtonian descriptions borrowed from complexity science and its derivative biological theory of self-organizing systems (a SWARMING BEES or HIVE INTELLIGENCE analogy). In a version of the US *Capstone Concept for Joint Operations* (Department of Defense 2009a), take note of how the concept writers extend the SWARM metaphor and create a displaced concept for military organizations operating without receiving orders from their higher-ups:

> Based on an underlying modular structure down to small-unit levels, joint forces will ROUTINELY and SMOOTHLY AGGREGATE and DISAGGREGATE into temporary joint formations of different sizes depending on the nature and scale of operations (p. 27).

On critical examination, units comprised of sophisticated, thinking, inculcated military members do not actually SWARM based on insect-like instinct; yet, one can envision how this ORGANIC logic can influence the way militaries would be trained and equipped to facilitate real-time mutual adjustments through NETWORK communications connectivity. Compare this with older, nineteenth-century concepts, based on the language of the science of the day, treating units more as COGS in a MACHINE where military maneuvers are ideally executed with MACHINE-like precision.

While Schön's theory of the adaptive language is in itself interesting, he cautions that analogy and metaphor are not synonymous terms. Critical reflection about our use of metaphor is an important check on the efficacy of new concepts extended from old ones. Sedimentary institutionalization is correspondent to becoming complacent in using only the analogous portion of metaphors (what I call the *zone of analogy*) and mindlessly ignoring the differences until the originating language is displaced (dead metaphor) and the resulting meaning becomes hypostatized. The reflective military designer, using analogous meaning to describe a novel situation, is mindful that the meaning is always underdeveloped because even the most elaborated metaphor contains irrelevant meaning as well as analogous meaning.[4] In other words, modern military institutions focus attention on the zone of analogy and miss both the incompleteness of transferred meaning. An attentive critique reveals that the institutionalization process has filled-in meaning to make the metaphor better fit to the new, unique situation, for example, through the next edition of a doctrinal manual. In other words, finding relational meaning as a zone of analogy and then extending that meaning even further are creative processes. Extension of meaning is the only way to communicate about novel experiences—past, present, or fictionally envisioned in the future. *Critical reflection* is about being mindful of the inadequacies of doing so (Figure 2.1, Frame Reflection), while sedimented institutionalization serves to block this reflexivity.

According to Schön's displacement theory, language shared in professional communities of practice can be imaginatively manipulated and purposefully recontextualized when discovered to be unsuitable for making sense of novel, perplexing situations as long as the professionals are mindful of the inadequacies of these conceptualizations. *All* language is metaphorical; hence, exists in a constant state of purposeful flux and creative renewal that will never be complete (Schön 1963, p. 48). How purposeful and effective that renewal is in the face of uniquely unfolding military interventions depends upon military designers being mindful of this analogous process of creative and critical thinking. Indeed, Schön presents such mindfulness as "removing the film of obviousness that covers our way of looking at the world" (p. 45) (i.e. the deinstitutionalization process).

Countless metaphoric variations can create frustration especially among those modern military institutions that seek to indoctrinate nascent members to their form of bringing clarity and nomothetic consistency of language to

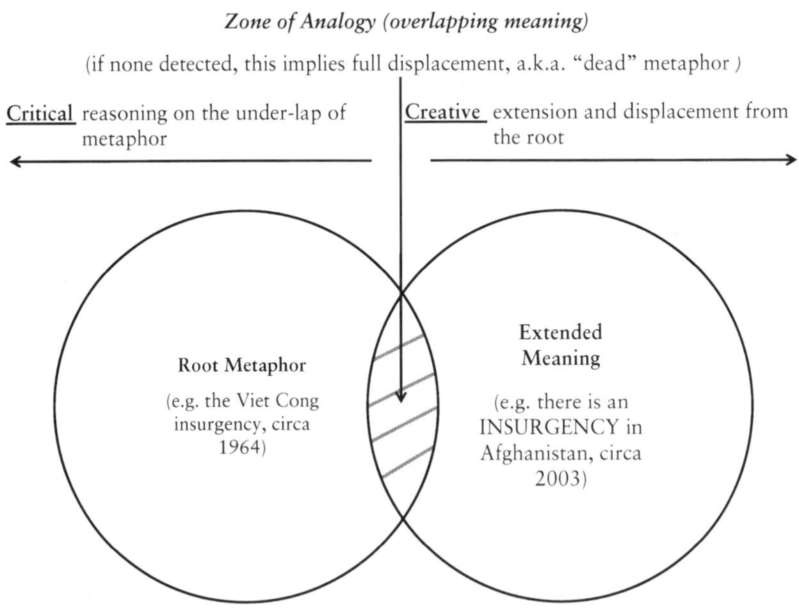

FIGURE 2.1 *Frame Reflection.*

bear on the framing of military interventions.[5] Brown's book criticizes this reification process and offers a counter process:

> To unmask metaphors that have become myths requires negative insight and circumspection; to create *new* metaphors is a leap of the imagination. It not only demands that we say "no" to the organization of experience as it is given to us in preordained categories; it also requires us to rearrange cognition into new forms and associations. The new metaphor, then, is not *merely* a substitution of a term from one frame to another. Quite beyond this, metaphor can create a new amalgam in our understanding. New metaphors, especially when elaborated into models and theories, are not merely new ways of looking at the facts, nor are they a revelation of what the facts really are. Instead, the metaphor in a fundamental way creates the facts and provides a definition of what the essential quality of an experience must be (emphasis in original, p. 85).

Multiple *reframings* (the essence of Military Design) involves metaphoric reasoning (discovering past assortments of concepts that can be extended and displaced into new, exciting meanings). This reasoning is coupled with a critically reflexive awareness of the limits of zones of analogy. While the creative morphological process of concept displacement can build enthusiasm and unleash creativity, institutional reflexivity demands that the military designer also look for disparities in metaphors that cannot carry all the meanings of the root metaphor. The extensions and displacements from root metaphors serve as theory-building logics for finding new meanings for action.

Institutional reflexivity demands that military designers recognize that these theories sociologically morph (meaning is extended and displaced) from limited zones of analogy and will never reflect "the truth." A postinstitutional approach to Military Design recognizes that no single source of metaphors can provide truth in the matter; hence, multiple frames of reference are required for analogical sensemakings. The next section proposes a multi-framing typology that can help military designers to both creatively use metaphoric reasoning and subscribe to institutional reflexivity to help shape a quest for reframing in important ways.

A multi-framing typology of metaphors

A worldview or sociological paradigm for explaining that worldview can be said to be a combination of ontology, epistemology, and methodology (Burrell and Morgan 1979, p. 3).[6] For example, those subscribing to the natural sciences sense the world as objective, accepting that knowledge is reduced to physical sensory perceptions and *nomothetic taxonomies*.[7] The "scientific method" is the standard process of validating that knowledge as both context- and value-free. Complexity scientists and chaos theorists also have an objective worldview, but have to rely on language or other symbols that reflect interdependencies and a more holistic, Gestalt-like *system of systems* and *complex adaptive systems*. Methods are just beginning to be found to model holism, attempting to represent how complex and chaotic systems uniquely work, as in the construction of causal-loop diagrams. These constructions comprise the epistemology of *choplexic science* (Horgan 1996; Bousquet 2009). Those who subscribe to the ideals of the humanities and fine arts have more of a subjective ontology, acknowledging that research is primarily based on symbolic interpretations—such as finding new meanings in "stories" or artifacts of human experience. Here, like the chaoplexic sciences, interpretive (or ideographic) methodologies are tied to the uniqueness of situations and would include hermeneutics, ethnography, archeological exploitation, idiographic research, and so forth.

Hence, there are at least three primary sources of metaphor at work in the context of postinstitutional military sensemaking:

- *Modern science* (e.g. the dominant influence portrayed by related knowledge disciplines of ordnance design, kinetic physics, engineering sciences, operations research, artillery-trigonometry, aerospace science, etc.)
- *Chaoplexic science* (e.g. concept forays into chaos theory and complexity sciences—*butterfly effects*, human systems ecology, meteorology, animal physiology, quantum physics, etc.) and the
- *Humanities and fine arts* (e.g. the "pocket heuristics" normally used in the field and involves finding analogies in military historic case studies, combat-as-a-team sport, etc.)

Each primary source of metaphor reflects a dominant *view* of reality and *knowledge* about that reality (*ontology* and *epistemology*, respectively). When taken into consideration together, these form synthetic reconstructions of reality—that of postinstitutional design. The resulting synthesis can be portrayed by crossing two continua, the *objective::subjective* (ontological continuum) and the *simple::complex* (epistemological continuum). The resulting quadrants reflect *objective-simplified* (drawing zones of analogy from modern science), *objective-complexified* (extending meanings from chaoplexic science), and *subjective-simplified* (searching for heuristics from the humanities and fine arts), and the most inventive of all, *subjective-complexified* (synthesizing extensions and displacements of meaning from those multiple sources) (Figure 2.2).

Although these sources of metaphors exist simultaneously, let us examine each type one at a time (more or less as Weberian ideal types[8]) and with examples of how they are employed.

The Modernist Quadrant. Already addressed in Chapter 1, modern military science is underpinned by objectivist ontology, stratified epistemology, and

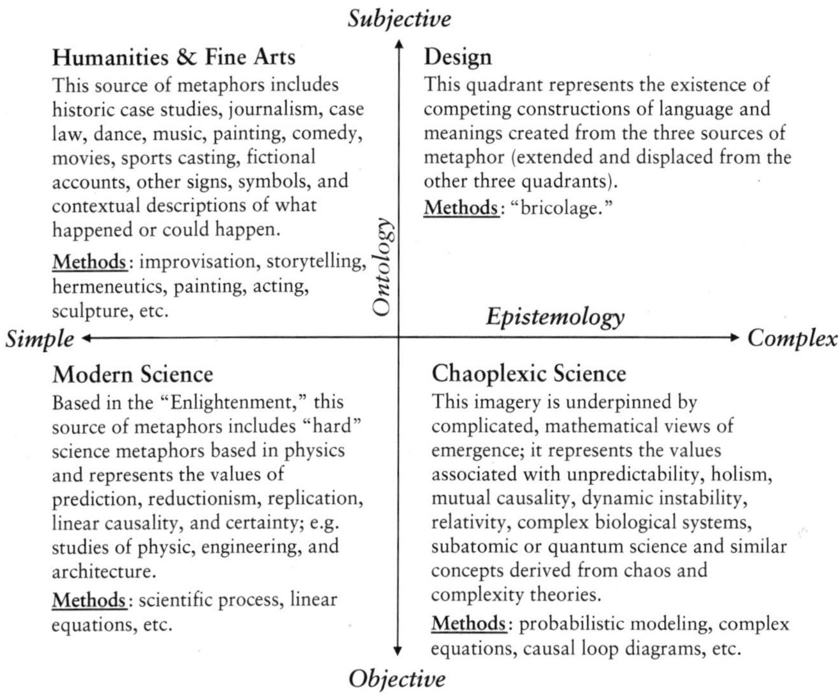

FIGURE 2.2 *Multiple Sources of Metaphors.*

the reductionist methodology of *positivism* (Burrell and Morgan 1989, p. 5).[9] Positivism is a belief system first described by French eighteenth-century philosopher, Auguste Comte. Comte argued that there is an objective truth to be found in the human social milieu that, up to that point, had been satisfied with theological or metaphysical explanations. Only through the strict scientific methods (i.e. isolation and manipulation of variables, hypothesis testing, objective experimentation, replication, and so on) can the truth be found. Positivists concluded that we can only communicate logic with language if it is accurately and precisely linked to the reality that exists through our objective five senses; hence, it is heavily based on the logic of numbers (*ratio-nality*). Hence, to understand the world through the *only* lens—objectivity—the method is to isolate empirical variables and reduce them to the point where we can label them, manipulate them, and measure the cause-and-effect relationships between them. Complicated problems (or multivariate phenomena) can also be isolated and addressed through this reduction process with the understanding that if we atomize its parts we can know the whole. The objectivist ontological critique applies in these other physical metaphors still used in modernist military discourse: FOG OF WAR, CULMINATING POINT, DECISIVE POINT, FRICTION, CONTROL MEASURES, CENTER OF GRAVITY, and so on. We will critique examples of the resulting epistemology in the paragraphs ahead.

In Westernized civilizations, modernists use this *objective-simplified* sense of reality that evokes the comforting positivistic images of employing context-free knowledge as in the applied sciences, rational planning processes, and ensuring more certainty in modeling the causal relationships between variables—the same comfort modern military institutions seem to seek in their body of knowledge.

Military modernists may speak to the SPREAD of democracy will CAUSE world peace; military schools may indoctrinate the troops to believe they are part of an INSTRUMENT of POWER and who will help solve the problem of rogue actors and terrorists by attacking their CENTERS OF GRAVITY. The extension of the term POWER, borrowed from physics, is a taken-for-granted ZONE of analogy in the military community so displaced to the point of losing touch with its metaphoric basis of meaning. Newton's second law of motion is extended in meaning by the military modernist—the related images of FORCE (as in "armed forces"), MASS (as a recognized principle of war), and ACCELERATION (as in the SPEED and DIRECTION of military maneuvers).

Contemporary US doctrine includes physical LINES OF OPERATION that describe the *geographic* line between the military force's base of operation and its objective or target. US joint doctrine of late has extended the meaning that now includes *metaphysical* LINES OF EFFORT referring to the need to change reified values to a more desirable state; hence, LINES OF OPERATION/EFFORT may now include actions to improve social constructions such as democratic governance, education, poverty, and so forth.[10] The same extensions apply to the modernist concept of DECISIVE POINTS which used to define CONCRETE aspects of turning the tide of battle and now include existential punctuated change as well (CHANGING the HEARTS and MINDS of the targeted populations).[11] Derivative abstract extensions include the relatively new theory of action, INFORMATION OPERATIONS, which reflect LINES OF EFFORT to create DECISIVE POINTS in changing the affective and cognitive frames of reference in TARGETED others.[12] Note how these extended concepts are drawn from an objective ontology and modernist epistemology—the world (assuming no differentiation between the physical and social) can be reduced to a precise language and causation can be measured, manipulated, tested, and repeated, treating human behavior (i.e. behaviorism that is delinked from any reference to metaphysical phenomena) as just another part of that objective world.[13]

We may find more subtle uses of the modernist metaphors as well. The Russian, Alexandr A. Svechin (1991/1927), who coined the "operational" level of war, provided this geologic to military planning in the late 1920s: "Actions will become ordered and coalesce into SMALL STREAMS flowing down to the GOAL and will form one BROAD STREAM as a result" (p. 74). Similarly, David Galula (1964), in his classic book, *Counterinsurgency*, uses modernist states-of-matter metaphors for describing the ASYMMETRY of the opponents: "The insurgent is FLUID because he has neither responsibility nor CONCRETE assets; the counterinsurgent is RIGID . . ." (p. 12).

Those who subscribe primarily to modern science root metaphors may treat complicated social situations as if they could be solved with something akin to increasing the intensity of the INDEPENDENT VARIABLE. This limited ZONE of analogy implies one-way causality, such as this POLICE-REDUCE-CRIME cause-and-effect analogy used by General Peter Pace, former Chairman of the Joint Chiefs of Staff, while attempting to communicate to the public on how to think about counterinsurgency operations as you would STREET CRIME:

> If you would use the analogy of a POLICE DEPARTMENT in a city, it's not that the city itself is without crime, but that the police department itself is capable of keeping the crime level down at a level below which the society can function (Pace 2006).

Perhaps the most widely (and mindlessly?) used sources of metaphors of the modern military science quadrant, particularly in the US Army, are drawn from the CONCRETE production sciences of ENGINEERING and BUSINESS MANUFACTURING. There are countless artifacts that demonstrate the dominance of these sources, many of them from the administrative side of the institution (i.e. the departments that reside in the Pentagon and assorted offices that make up the US Defense bureaucracy). Here is an extract from a 2011 PowerPoint slide from the Director of the US Army's School of Advanced Military Studies, attempting to communicate three focus areas of the program (again, I have attempted to highlight key ENGINEERING and BUSINESS MANUFACTURING metaphors with small capital letters):

- . . . DEVELOPING good leaders
- able to form a COHESIVE team
- have a FIRM understanding of peer leadership
- courage to lead from BEHIND, BESIDE and BELOW
- physical and mental TOUGHNESS counts
- . . . BUILDING effective operational PLANNERS
- GROUNDED in doctrine
- critical thinkers who assist in identifying problems
- clearly communicate recommendations verbally, GRAPHICALLY, and in writing
- . . . BUILDING great teammates
- able to be a PRODUCTIVE team member
- collaborates effectively
- does not care who gets the CREDIT
- a Leadership FACTORY

As another sample, here is a description of how a Defense Department manual seeks to frame the management of forces rotating into theaters of war into a kind of ARCHITECTURAL ENGINEERING problem:

> . . . the electronic documentation of organizational and force STRUCTURE data, military and civilian, be in a joint, HIERARCHICAL format. . . . To this end, . . .describes ARCHITECTURAL and behavioral aspects of organizational STRUCTURES. ARCHITECTURAL aspects describe the CONSTRUCTION of the different organizational elements. . . . Therefore, CHAIN of command is synonymous with CHAIN of leadership and command STRUCTURE is synonymous with leadership STRUCTURE. . . . The principle of using authorization data as BUILDING BLOCKS. . . (emphasis added, Department of Defense 2011d, pp. 10–14).

The modernist military designer, uncritically extending such concepts assuming the objectivist ontology and positivist epistemology may miss imaginative opportunities to draw from other sources of meaning that are recognized as more subjective and irreducibly more complex; the latter addressed in next quadrant, *chaoplexic*.

The Chaoplexic Quadrant. Economist Kenneth E. Boulding (1956) suggests that REVOLUTIONARY changes can occur when a new set of metaphoric meanings converts us, resulting in the reorganization of the image that can sometimes be spectacular. Others have also argued that such an exciting change in framing has come from a major paradigm shift—like from modernist to the chaoplexic sciences—stemming from revolutionary ideas in business, management, and organization design—through forms of modeling chaos and complexity (Hock 1999; Marion 1999; Weick and Sutcliffe 2001). Designers have called upon the language of these theories invoking *objective-complexified* images to create visions of chaotic or complex interactions. The assumptions are still that truth lies in the physical world; however, we are incapable of understanding the infinite number of causal interactions that create chaotic systems and unpredictable complex dynamics.

Instead of valuing the linear causal predictability associated with strict logical positivist beliefs (e.g. those associated with behaviorism), extended meanings from chaoplexic science may be helpful to readdress interactive, nonlinear, messy, social issues such as war, poverty, world hunger, and so on. Quantum science ideas associated with the Heisenberg principle,[14] for example, serves the logic, grammar and rhetoric of American military "concept developers" in their publication, *Capstone Concept for Joint Operations*. Here is a telling excerpt that reflects a chaoplexic zone of analogy:

> The operating PATTERNS of IRREGULAR enemies, for example, tend to be less easily discerned than those of REGULAR forces. Likewise, some SYSTEMS are simply less vulnerable than others to SYSTEM-level influence. NETWORKS of largely autonomous ELEMENTS, for example, tend to be less vulnerable to

> SYSTEM disruption than centralized hierarchies. Such SYSTEMS ultimately may have to be dealt with by dealing cumulatively with the individual ELEMENTS. Regardless of the approach, it is important to recognize that any action in a situation will change the situation. Operational DESIGN must always be alert to this, revising objectives as necessary (emphasis added, Department of Defense 2009a, p. 24).

Here is similar evidence of metaphorizing chaoplexity from US doctrine, the 2011 edition of Joint Publication 5-0, *Joint Operation Planning*, which draws meaning from an *objective-complexified* type of metaphor:

> To produce a HOLISTIC VIEW of the relevant enemy, neutral, and friendly SYSTEMS as a COMPLEX WHOLE within a larger SYSTEM that includes many EXTERNAL influences, analysis should define how these SYSTEMS interrelate. Most important to this analysis is describing the relevant RELATIONSHIPS within and between the various SYSTEMS that directly or indirectly affect the problem at hand (emphasis added, Department of Defense 2011c, pp. 3–10 to 3–11).

Indeed, there is a growing multitude of writings on the REVOLUTION in military affairs (RMA) that call to develop NETWORKCENTRICITY and SYSTEMS OF SYSTEMS that match the complexity of the environment and to look for patterns and clues in conducting EFFECTS-BASED OPERATIONS, using methods such as SOCIAL NETWORK ANALYSIS. RMA literature is replete with related terms and concepts such as OPERATIONAL NET assessment (ONA) which is associated with organismic views of STABILITY operations (analogous with stable organic compounds) in Iraq, the Horn of Africa, and Afghanistan. In at least one military publication, ONA has been reduced to these interrelating target SYSTEMS VARIABLES: Political, Military, Economic, Social, Infrastructure, and Information (PMESII) and how they might be affected by the interventionist's VARIABLES of diplomacy, information, military, and economics, (DIME) that should be manipulated in tandem, to achieve HOLISTIC PMESII EFFECTS. Look at the graphics on the left and note how it is similar to something out of an ORGANIC CHEMISTRY diagrams on the right (Figure 2.3, Conflict as a BIOCHEMISTRY Metaphor).

Indeed, academics in the business and public policy sciences are also beginning to write more using this chaoplexic imagery associated with DISRUPTIVE EVOLUTION, UNPREDICTABLE TRAJECTORY, and QUANTUM LEAPS. Examine this quote from two University of Colorado researchers:

> The terrorists attacks on September 11, 2001 demonstrated clearly the urgent need to develop the skills of COMPLEXITY thinking—to recognize changes in the LARGER CONTEXT; to take a BIG PICTURE approach to intelligence-gathering and national security; to develop a deeper

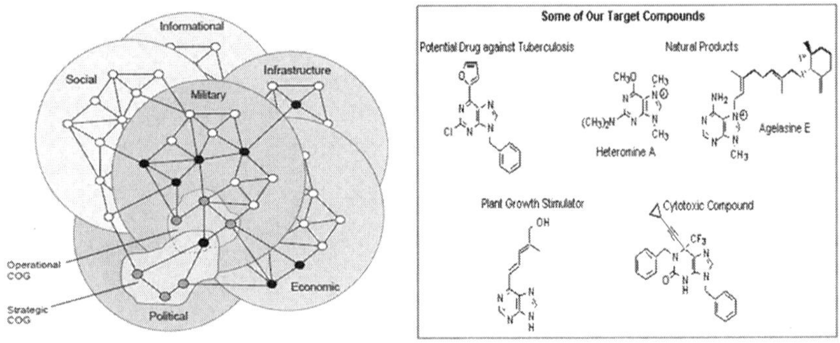

FIGURE 2.3 *Conflict as a Biochemistry Metaphor.*

> understanding of the SYSTEM DYNAMICS influencing regional politics and conflicts; and, most importantly, to enhance our understanding of COMPLEX SOCIOPOLITICAL HUMAN SYSTEMS (emphasis added, Sanders and McCabe 2003, p. 12).

The oft-used term, military TRANSFORMATION, popularized at the turn of this century, is borrowed from the logic of studying complicated BIOLOGICAL SYSTEMS and now permeates military discourse across many countries, to include NATO's "Allied Command, TRANSFORMATION," headquartered in Norfolk, Virginia. Simply stated, BIOLOGICAL TRANSFORMATION is when ORGANISMS, as COMPLEX ADAPTIVE SYSTEMS, adjust to the operational ENVIRONMENT by changing the way to TRANSFORM inputs from the ENVIRONMENT into outputs back into the ENVIRONMENT. Hence, the central idea behind military TRANSFORMATION becomes to continuously change from state-to-state dependent on ECOLOGICAL PRESSURES, as would a species over time or an individual ORGANISM responding to the SURVIVAL NEEDS of the moment.

The related complex PHYSIOLOGY of the human body can also be used by military designers to portray war and complicated operations. This 2001 quote is from Richard Haas, then Director, Office of the Policy Planning Staff, US State Department, where he attempts to indoctrinate his listeners to a TERRORISM-AS-DISEASE metaphor to convey the complexity at hand in the war on terror:

> Terrorism lives as part of the ENVIRONMENT. Sometimes dormant, sometimes VIRULENT, it is always present in some form. Like a VIRUS, international terrorism respects no boundaries—moving from country to country, exploiting globalized commerce and communication to SPREAD. It can be particularly MALEVOLENT when it can find a supportive HOST. We therefore need to take appropriate PROPHYLACTIC MEASURES at home and abroad to PREVENT terrorism from MULTIPLYING and check it from INFECTING our societies or damaging our lives (emphasis added, Haass 2001).

President Bush also alluded to a chaoplexic image of causality in the variables war when he reflected on the initial combat successes in Iraq:

> Had we to do it over again, we would look at the consequences of CATASTROPHIC SUCCESS, being so successful so fast that an enemy that should have surrendered or been done in escaped and lived to fight another day (emphasis added, Milbank 2004, p. A01).

The paradox inherent in Bush's explanation is that, given chaoplexic conditions, there was no way to "look at the consequences" ahead of time, but only in retrospect; hence, sometimes those that subscribe to the chaoplexic frame can mix the unpredictability associated with chaoplexic metaphors with the determinism that a modernist science would advertise.

The Humanities and Fine Arts Quadrant. The study of the humanities includes a wide spectrum from history, sports, fiction, journalism, news, etc. The fine arts include performing arts, music, painting, sculpting, dance, theater, and film. These "unscientific" communities of practice offer a plethora of useful metaphors for military designers. However, as with all metaphors, their use must be mindfully criticized. Starkey and Tempest (2009) recognize this:

> The design attitude encourages us to recognize that our ways of thinking and acting are encultured and that we need to consider, at every turn, which of our belief-habits are trustworthy instrumentalities. The role of the arts and the humanities is to remind us that there are other ways of thinking (p. 580).

In the following parts, we will explore (1) HISTORY, (2) PERFORMING ARTS, (3) SPORTS, (4) FICTION, (5) MUSIC, and (6) VISUAL ARTS as important sources of metaphors.

Part 1. History

. . . history is lived forward but is written in retrospect. We know the end before we consider the beginning and we can never wholly recapture what it was like to know the beginning only.

D. V. WEDGWOOD,
William the Silent

. . . the cause of the Roman Empire was the length of Cleopatra's nose: had her features not been perfectly proportioned, Mark Anthony would not have been entranced, had he not been entranced he would not have allied himself with Egypt against Octavian; had he not made that alliance, the battle of Actium would not have been fought—and so on.

ALASDAIR MACINTYRE (reminiscing on Blaise Pascale),
After Virtue

. . . we require a history that will educate us on discontinuity more than ever before; for discontinuity, disruption, and chaos is our lot.

HAYDEN WHITE,
Tropics of Discourse

The metaphoric extensions of historic cases are particularly pervasive, and I made a disproportional discussion on history in this chapter, because prospective military designers may be unaware of just how important experientially recorded metaphors are used to find a familiar frame for an otherwise perplexing, novel situation. While modern military science often focuses attention on deriving "principles," "lessons learned," and "best practices," that is, making historic precedent into a reliable science, the criticism that follows seeks to make these assertions implausible. In knowing how the STORY ENDS, modern military institutions can attribute causal relationships (illustrated by the CLEOPATRA'S NOSE metaphor in the above epigraph) that reify history as precedence. Indeed, this detailed knowledge of the past strengthens an ideological bent toward ends-based (*a posteriori*) rationality (making sense of what has already happened); hence, provides a fallacious justification of thinking and acting (*a priori*) toward making sense of an imaginary future. What results is the quest for the "vision thing" and what is actually a romantic view of the prescient military strategist—who arguably has no more than a kind of soothsaying, fantasizing, or performance as would a shaman rain dancer. The principal goal in this section is to expose the *mindless* use of institutionalized history as a source of positive, context-free, utilitarian knowledge.

The reason why there is confusion on the benefits of studying history is the expectation that history teaches us lessons we can use again; yet, the circumstances of history do not repeat. The use of interpretations about the past teaches us that, in our intellectual life, history is all we have. History provides limited familiarities (Schönian extended metaphors or, in psychological terms, heuristics) to sense-make about other situations. Hayden White proposes that "we require a history that will educate us to discontinuity more than ever before; for discontinuity, disruption, and chaos is our lot" (1978, p. 50). My argument that follows promotes the *mindful* use of history as a rich source of multiple, idiographic familiarities (i.e. a creative source of heuristics or frame resemblances) while stressing that its knowledge should be continuously criticized (to prevent hypostatization).

The military designer should be very suspicious of the espoused expectations envisioned by the limited philosophy of ends-based, rationalistic models promoted by modern military science uses of history. As the military designer struggles with making sense of volatile and ambiguous world events of the recent past, the "end game" rear-mirror view can produce false expectations. The hope of ends-based rationalism is vested in the belief that one can create effective strategies, plans, and decisions on the basis of a historic precedent to reach a desirable future end state. This belief is also linked to an overstated, *progressive* epistemology (i.e. things will continue in the future as they have in the past, so all learning is cumulative).

In that regard, the authors of the book *Thinking in Time*, Richard Neustadt and Ernest May (1986), describe how decision-makers (often mindlessly unaware) routinely use historic analogies to make decisions in the present. From their analysis of several important foreign policy situations involving US presidential administrations, they find three critical assumptions to the habitual use of history as metaphor:

> One is the recognition that the future has no place to come from but the past, hence [assumes] the past has predictive value. Another element is the recognition that what matters for the future in the present are departures from the past, alterations, changes, which prospectively or actually divert familiar flows from accustomed channels, thus affecting that predictive value and much else besides. A third component is continuous comparison, an almost constant oscillation from present to future to past and back, heedful of prospective change, concerned to expedite, limit, guide, counter, or accept it as the fruits of such comparison suggest (p. 251).

Nicholas Rescher (1998), one of our most prolific contemporary US philosophers, would find dispute with the assumption of predictive value. Rescher has written extensively on the fallacies associated with the study of history as a predictive endeavor.[15] He reinforces the dictum that "... the past is a different country—they do things differently there." He continues:

> For we can never adequately comprehend the past in terms of the conceptions and presumptions of the present. And this is all the more drastically true of the human future, and its cognitive future in particular. After all, information about the thought world of the past is at any rate available—however laborious extracting it from the available data may prove to be. But it lies in the nature of things that we cannot secure any effective access to the thought world of the future: its science specifically included, all its details are hidden from our view. *All that I know is that it will be different* (emphasis added, p. 177).

All metaphoric sources are at least linguistically rooted in history; that is, knowledge of history represents a socially constructed SUITCASE,[16] PACKED with past meanings that are extended and sometimes displaced beyond recognition. Without continuous critical examination, histories may become institutionally sedimented "dead metaphors" and mindlessly used as foreknowledge.

Yuen F. Khong (1992), writing from the international relations field, makes the claim that the uses of past wars as analogies for current ones are powerfully influential—and can be dangerously so—as to affect the way present wars are decided and fought. After pouring through many documents and communications among high-level members of the Johnson Administration, Khong traces the important decisions made in 1965 during the Vietnam War that were analogically argued based on reference to British appeasement, Munich, 1938, the Korean War, 1950–53, and the French debacle at Điện Biên Phủ in 1954. According to Khong, when used cautiously, historic analogies serve to help diagnose present situations in six important ways:

- They help define the situation in the terms of previous ones;
- They give a way to assess the stakes involved;
- They suggest prescriptions;
- They help evaluate the probability of success;
- They inform moral reasoning; and
- They serve as warnings of associated dangers experienced in like-situations (pp. 20–1).

Khong's theory of analogous reasoning is logically similar to Schön's (1963) concept displacement theory. Khong states:

> Analogical reasoning may be represented thus: *AX*:*BX*::*AY*:*BY*. In other words, event *A* resembles event *B* in having characteristic *X*; *A* also has the characteristic *Y*; therefore it is inferred that *B* also has characteristic *Y*. The unknown *BY* is inferred from the three known terms on the assumption a symmetrical due ratio, or proportion, exists.[17] . . . Consider [Henry Cabot] Lodge's use of the Munich analogy: appeasement in Munich (*A*) occurred as a result of Western indolence (*X*). Appeasement in Munich (*A*) resulted in a world war (*Y*); therefore, appeasement in Vietnam (*B*) will also result in a world war (*Y*). The unknown consequences of appeasement in Vietnam (*BY*) are inferred through the analogy to Munich (emphasis added, p. 7).

Robert L. Ivie (1997) claims the Cold War, "fought" often with rhetoric rather than bullets, links policy decisions to dominant metaphors and proposes the following (which is identical to the thesis of the present chapter):

> The motive for the Cold War, like all other human motives, is entangled in metaphor's linguistic web. The more we struggle to break free of figurative language in search of literal and true characterizations of ourselves and our adversaries, and the more we deny the inevitable

> ambiguity and constitutive force of our linguistic choices, the less likely we are to put metaphor to good use in search for practical alternatives. Thus, the critic is well advised to treat literalized metaphors as pragmatic fictions, exposing those that are no longer practical . . . and searching for others that may prove more functional as symbolic equipment for living (p. 72).

Ivie attends to the theory of history as metaphor:

> A perspective, or overall orientation, emerges from realizing the heuristic potential of a guiding metaphor; it leads to the formulation of motives or interpretations . . . [and] contains a "program of action" for responding. . . . We name one thing in terms of another, treat the name as a realistic perspective, and act as if it applies literally to a given situation (p. 73).

The consensus of these observers seems to be that the uses of history as decision justification will almost invariably misguide political decision-making (hence Military Design) efforts. Yet, there are contemporary commentators who insist there are lessons to be learned from history and that, in not doing so, one is incompetent. One is Army Lieutenant Colonel Paul Yingling, who, in his widely read *Armed Forces Journal* article, uncritically employs analogous reasoning to argue that generals are incompetent for failing to use history in the visioning process:

> America's generals have repeated the mistakes of VIETNAM in Iraq. First, throughout the 1990s our generals failed to ENVISION the conditions of future combat and prepare their forces accordingly. . . . America's DEFEAT IN VIETNAM is the most egregious failure in the history of American arms. America's general officer corps refused to prepare the Army to fight UNCONVENTIONAL wars, despite ample indications that such preparations were in order. Having failed to prepare for SUCH WARS, America's generals sent our forces into battle without a coherent plan for victory. Unprepared for war and lacking a coherent STRATEGY, America LOST the war and the lives of more than 58,000 service members (emphasis added, Yingling 2007).

Using Khong's (1992) logic to deconstruct Yingling's metaphoric weaknesses: the VIETNAM WAR (A) showed the generals FAILED TO PREPARE (X) the military for UNCONVENTIONAL WAR (AX); the US generals FAILED TO PREPARE the military to prosecute ongoing wars in Iraq and Afghanistan (BX); the US-supported counterinsurgent LOST (Y) in Vietnam (AY); therefore, it will LOSE (Y) the ongoing wars for the same reason (BY). This exposes the weakness in Yingling's analogous reasoning that we are yet again losing current wars for failure of generals to understand that history is knowledge (or in the modern military institution's vernacular, history is a science of "lessons learned").

Khong's theory would doubt conclusions such as Yingling's that claim senior officers are somehow flawed for their poor selection of historic analogies or using them incorrectly. The best we can hope for in the uses of history is for an array of heuristic "devices for suggesting and entertaining *tentative* interpretations of the nature of problems. . . . " and avoid using them as "dominant schemas through which much else" is viewed (p. 262). The best course of action for burgeoning Military Design practitioners then is to study history from a wide variety of perspectives, in both depth and scope with the purpose of increasing a BANK of heuristics that may be called upon in multiple, socially interactive, creative, and critical ways to inform later practice. All knowledge is historic—history is all we have.[18] R. G. Collingswood (1969) sums up the need for epistemological caution this way:

> . . . that historical knowledge is the only knowledge that the human mind can have of itself. The so-called social science of human nature or of the human mind resolves itself into history. . . . The historian has no gift of prophecy, and knows it; the historical study of mind, therefore, can neither foretell the future developments of human thought nor legislate for them, except so far as they must proceed – though in what direction we cannot tell – from the present as their starting point (p. 45).

While we would like to think predictability would come from a detailed sense of history, what we are stuck with are the taunts of *retrodictability* (Dray 1969, p. 124)—simply ideas of a future which are extended from the past as we imagine them now.

At this point, again from the Multi-Frame Typology of Metaphors, we will examine a few more metaphors from the humanities and fine arts quadrant, continuing next with SPORTS metaphors that have particular influence in enculturation of recruits and in framing military approaches to intervention.

Part 2. Sports

You are here today for three reasons. First, because you are here to defend your homes and your loved ones. Second, you are here for your own self respect, because you would not want to be anywhere else. Third, you are here because you are real men and all real men like to fight. When you, here, every one of you, were kids, you all admired the champion marble player, the fastest runner, the toughest boxer, the big league ball players, and the All-American football players. Americans love a winner. Americans will not tolerate a loser. Americans despise cowards. Americans play to win all of the time. I wouldn't give a hoot in hell for a man who lost and laughed. That's why Americans have never lost nor will ever lose a war; for the very idea of losing is hateful to an American.

GEORGE S. PATTON,
addressing his troops in 1944

It has long been noted that we understand war as a competitive game like chess, or as a sport, like football or boxing. It is a metaphor in which there is a clear winner and loser, and a clear end to the game. The metaphor highlights strategic thinking, team work, preparedness, the spectators in the world arena, the glory of winning and the shame of defeat.

GEORGE LAKOFF,
Metaphor and War

In her comprehensive study, Wanda Wakefield (1997) traces the military's institutionalization of SPORTS as a valuable metaphor intended for ideological indoctrination—linking participation in games (particularly boxing) to the masculine, highly competitive, warrior values of military training and combat. She reports that the US Army Service Forces' 1944 Technical Manual required all soldiers to box in company-level competitions:

> Despite the risk of injury and the anxiety such a requirement engendered in those who didn't want to get into the ring, those who wrote the Manual asserted that experience has shown "that boxing contributes greatly toward building a good soldier [as it creates] a sense of confidence and self-assurance [that] carry over to the bayonet and hand-to-hand fighting, the development of quick, decisive thinking and the practice of carrying on under physical stress and pressure . . . (p. 87).

In other words, the Army's zone of analogy included that the winning and personal endurance values required in boxing extended to actual combat. Artifacts of this metaphoric connection between masculine sports and the military still remain, according to Wakefield:

> . . . at the Super Bowl, fighter jets fly over the field; the national anthem is sung; red, white and blue are the colors of the day; and national unity is achieved through dedication to the game . . . . everybody is assured that it is men, not the girls, who are down there on the field (p. 139).

Likewise, the Associated Press reported that the George W. Bush Administration used sports as the dominant foreign policy metaphor to "run the White House:"

> Sports metaphors have become a pervasive way for Bush and his team to describe almost anything. Expressing ideas in terms of ATHLETICS is so

> routine in the highest levels of government — just as it is in more typical workplaces — that even people who do not follow SPORTS are used to it. Fairness means LEVELING THE PLAYING FIELD; focus is KEEPING YOUR EYE ON THE BALL. SEND IN THE HEAVY HITTERS if you want results. If sacrifice is called for, then TAKE ONE FOR THE TEAM. . . . When Secretary of State Condoleezza Rice was forced to answer critics of a plan to shut down North Korea's nuclear program, she needed a way to urge patience. So, naturally, the administration's top diplomat used the language of a FOOTBALL GAME. "This is still the FIRST QUARTER," she said. "There is still a lot of TIME TO GO ON THE CLOCK" (emphasis added, Associated Press 2007)

American FOOTBALL metaphors also conveyed the concept of operations for the 1991 offensive against Iraq during Desert Storm:

> The contingency plans were essentially OPTION PLAYS or "AUDIBLES" that corps commanders would CALL on the move to accommodate the enemy's reactions. Thus the precise intelligence on enemy movements was absolutely vital to MAKING THE RIGHT CALL. . . . the QUARTERBACKS [corps commanders] would be able to call exactly the right AUDIBLES to capitalize on successes. . . . Subordinate units studied their portions of the plans and RAN PRACTICE SESSIONS on makeshift sand tables to set the GAME PLAN more firmly in the PLAYERS' MINDS (emphasis added, Scales 1997, pp. 147–8).[19]

Former Chief of Staff of the Army, General Peter Schoomaker, employed this SPORTS analogy when he proclaimed his officers must be more adaptable and less specialized in their careers:

> We cannot afford, in my view, to specialize totally to units for single purpose any more, especially in this ambiguous environment, not only the contemporary operating ENVIRONMENT, but the one that we're going to face in the future. So what we're looking at here is going from single and DUAL EVENT ATHLETES to DECATHLETES and PENTATHELETE kind of formations that allow us to be successful in a variety of events (emphasis added, Schoomaker 2004).

Nathan Sassaman (who was officially reprimanded in command and retired early from the US Army) published a book using a SPORTS metaphor to justify his strong-handed use of force in Iraq:

> We clearly lost sight of our primary purpose—to destroy the enemy with overwhelming force at every opportunity—and somehow drifted toward a twisted policy that aimed to make the fight as FAIR as possible. . . . it was almost as if, rather than trying to WIN, we were merely trying to avoid LOSING. There is a difference (emphasis added, Sassaman and Layden 2008, p. 89).

The US Army today sees COACHING as a key skill in its leaders:

> In the military, COACHING occurs when a leader guides another person's development in new or existing skills during the practice of those skills. Unlike mentoring or counseling where the mentor/counselor generally has more experience than the supported person, COACHING relies primarily on teaching and guiding to help bring out and enhance current capabilities. A COACH helps those being COACHED to understand and appreciate their current level of performance and their potential, and instructs them on how to reach the next level of knowledge and skill (emphasis added, Department of the Army 2007, pp. 5–6).

Military designers should remain steadfastly mindful of the power (and limits) of the SPORTS metaphor in everyday military life, from the framing of foreign policy decisions are to be WON, influencing how a campaign is to be PLAYED, to how a soldier is COACHED to TEAM with others on the PLAYING FIELD against an OPPONENT.

Part 3. Performing arts

. . . all the world's a stage . . .

WILLIAM SHAKESPEARE,
As You Like It

Good drama is not about following a script according to existing tightly defined rules. It is, in part, about improvising to arrive at creative solutions to challenging situations, new interpretations rather than slavishly following a script. Good improvisation requires reciprocity.

KEN STARKEY and SUE TEMPEST,
Winter of Our Discontent

In military interventions, there are always tragedy, irony, and even comic relief, and DRAMATURGY provides an interesting frame for the military designer. Similarly, the fictional literature is an important heuristic. One of the more noteworthy sociologists of the twentieth century, Irving Goffman, developed a theory of the *dramaturgical* aspects of "everyday life"; that is, we act in ROLES that are SCRIPTED by sociological circumpressures.[20] Goffman theorizes that our social life is a theater—we PLAY on the STAGE before others oscillating between cynicism and sincerity depending on the degree our authentic self matches with our STAGE CHARACTER'S ROLE (the logic of Goffman's theory corresponds nicely with the institutionalization process discussed in Chapter 1). The military institution is the PLAYHOUSE, complete with REHEARSALS (training), STAGE (a THEATER of operations), SCRIPT (e.g. flag officer TESTIMONY before Congress), COMMAND PERFORMANCES, SET, SCENARIOS (described through doctrine, or tasks, conditions and standards of PERFORMANCE), IMPROVISATION (in military jargon, *Auftragstaktik* or mission command), and the AUDIENCE (outsiders or civilian government officials and the public) who WATCH, APPRECIATE, and CRITIQUE. The returning troops' parade-like celebrations are akin to a CAST STAGE BOW. Even nations and transnational wartime players are homogenized as unitary ACTORS—some rational, some heroic, and some are rogue.

Listen as General-of-the-Army Dwight D. Eisenhower (1948) reminisces after World War II:

> The number of infantrymen assigned to organized units in the Army had been reduced from 56,000 on July 1, 1939, to 49,000 on January 31, 1940. On the FACE of things, to the average foot soldier who could not foresee his ROLE in Europe or the Pacific, this reduction might with reason have been interpreted as a sign of his early disappearance from the military SCENE (emphasis added, p. 7).

Later in the same book, he makes these observations:

> . . . both Patton and I were confident that the corps was now ready to ACT aggressively and to take an important sector in the battle line. For one thing, the troops were at last angry—not only because of the rough handling they had received, but more so because of the insulting and slighting comments concerning the fighting qualities of the Americans, originated by German prisoners and given some circulation within the THEATER (emphasis added, p. 152).

Institutional ideals of military operations are encased deeply in assuring those with CHARACTER SET the example, PLAY or PERFORM appropriate ROLES, STAGE and REHEARSE their forces, and ACT in accordance with the plan (a kind of SCRIPT that tells the STORY).

Part 4. Stories

I haven't relieved many commanders, George, and I've never done it with malice. We've got a mission in this war, and anything which creates friction, slows down its accomplishment, has got to be eliminated. A commander who drags his heels is infinitely more dangerous to us than the VC.

MAJOR GENERAL GEORGE SIMPSON LEMMING,
a Vietnam War fictional character from Josiah Bunting's *The Lionheads*

Stories are narratives with heroes and villains, problems and solutions, tensions and resolutions. The most common are: stories of decline, including the story of stymied progress and the story of progress-is-only-an-illusion; and, stories of control, including the conspiracy story and the blame-the-victim story. Synecdoche is a small part of the policy problem used to represent the whole – for example, the horror story. Metaphor is a likeness asserted between one kind of policy problem and another. Common metaphors in politics include organisms, natural laws, machines, tools, containers, disease and war. Ambiguity is the ability of statement to have more than one meaning. Ambiguity is the "glue" of politics. It allows people to agree on laws and policies because they can read different meanings into the words.

DEBORAH STONE,
Policy Paradox

Dominant stories can affect military unit cohesion and influence actions over generations and across cultures, and the same themes in these dominant mythologies can reemerge in similar characters. In an interview with Public TV's Bill Moyers, Joseph P. Campbell asserts that, "A good way to learn is to find a book that seems to be dealing with the problems that you're now dealing with. That will certainly give you some clues." Campbell further maintains that movies have the same type of almost universally human myths:

> Bill Moyers: The first time I saw Star Wars, I thought, "This is a very old story in a very new costume." The story of the young man called to adventure, the hero going out facing the trials and ordeals, and coming back after victory with a boon for the community.
>
> Joseph Campbell: Certainly [George] Lucas was using standard mythological figures. . . . In the first stage of this kind of adventure, the hero leaves the realm of the familiar, over which he has some measure of control, and comes to a threshold, let us say the edge of a lake or sea, where a monster of the abyss comes to meet him. There are then two possibilities. In a story of the Jonah type, the hero is swallowed and taken to the abyss to be later resurrected—a variant of the death-and-resurrection theme. The conscious personality here has come in touch with a charge of unconscious energy which it has been unable to handle and must now suffer all the trials and revelations of a terrifying night sea journey, while learning how to come to terms with this power of the dark and emerge, at last, to a new way of life (Campbell 1988, pp. 145–6).

Dominant mythologies, such as these, influence individual reasons for joining, the development of recruiting advertisements, and even in decisions for making war.

The US service departments publish "official" readings lists about once a year. What may be surprising is that the US Army, Navy, and Marine Corps include fictional stories that seem to serve the normative views of leadership, the inevitability of moral dilemmas of war, ethics of the profession, and so forth. Here is a sampling of the listed fiction[21]:

- US Army Reading List[22] (Department of the Army 2011a):
    - *The Red Badge of Courage* by Stephen Crane
    - *Once and Eagle* by Anton Myrer
    - *Gates of Fire: An Epic Novel of Thermopylae* by Steven Pressfield
    - *The Killer Angels* by Michael Shaara

- US Navy Reading List (Department of the Navy 2011)
    - *The Caine Mutiny* by Herman Wouk
    - *Ender's Game* by Orson Scott Card
    - *Fields of Fire* by Jim Webb
    - *Master and Commander* by Patrick O'Brian
    - *Red Badge of Courage* by Steven Crane
    - *Run Silent Run Deep* by Edward Beach
    - *The Bridges of Toko-ri* by James Michener

- United States Marine Corps (2011a) Reading List
    - *1984 by George Orwell*
    - *Rifleman Dodd by CS Forester*
    - *Starship Troopers by Robert Heinlein*
    - *All Quiet on the Western Front by E. Remarque*
    - *The Killer Angels by Michael Shaara*
    - *Battle Cry by Leon Uris*
    - *Once and Eagle by Anton Myrer*
    - *The General by CS Forester*

This "official deviation" from the modern science metaphors that dominate most official military doctrine may seem surprising. Although not well explained why these works of fiction were important at the websites where I found them, these novels seem intended on serving as powerful cultural expressions for institutional members to call upon to frame the desired (often heroic) attributes of mythical figures and richly describe the "trials and ordeals" of military life. Shibboleths become proverbs, such as, "Remember the Alamo!" (meaning that even against all odds one should be ready to die for a higher purpose). "No more Task

Force Smiths!" (signifying the unpreparedness of the US military at the start of the Korean War). "Leave no comrade behind!" (the brotherhood-of-war storyline). In Vietnam, "We the unwilling, led by the unknowing, doing the impossible, for the ungrateful . . ." (the story that soldiers are at war and the rest of society is not).[23] These represent the larger and recurring stories of what to do or not do, how to think or not think, and the paradoxes of sardonic patriotism—all in the face of the similar trials and ordeals surely ahead.

Interestingly, the US Marines are the only service to use fiction to illustrate doctrinal concepts. For example, the Marine Corps Doctrinal Publication 6, *Command and Control* (United States Marine Corps, 1996) states:

> "Operation VERBAL IMAGE," the short story with which this publication begins, offers a word picture of command and control in action (done well and done poorly) and illustrates various key points that appear in the text. It can be read separately or in conjunction with the rest of the text. Chapter 1 works from the assumption that, in order to develop an effective philosophy of command and control, we must first come to a realistic appreciation for the nature of the process and its related problems and opportunities (Preface).

Note the use of the terms "short story," "word picture," "philosophy," and "appreciation" in this paragraph. Chapter 1 is indeed a novelette, richly describing the fictional characters and events in combat situations, particularly where higher-level headquarters have a completely different understanding of unfolding events from their subordinate units. Here is a telling excerpt from the 32-page narrative that comprises the story, where a Marine platoon leader took action in the absence of any specific orders to do so:

> Takashima called it "a world of hurt for the bad guys." Damn if those bastards didn't walk right into it, he thought as he scampered forward to get a better look at the situation at the crossroads where first platoon had just sprung an ambush on the leading elements of the enemy column. *I owe Knutsen a beer when this is all over.* He couldn't explain how he knew, but just from the sound of things he could tell that first platoon had caught them pretty good. . . . *Thank goodness for staff officers, pilots, and subordinate commanders who exercise initiative and quickly adapt to changing situations* (emphasis in original, pp. 17–18).

Here, the Marines demonstrate that they value good storytelling to convey meaning and to institutionalize ideals. Through effective storytelling the Marines are able to explain an otherwise complex concept of *command and control* through the use of creative writing.

What makes FICTION an effective source of metaphor? Some interesting and prolific qualitative research has been done on this subject. One representative study by Patricia Bradshaw (2002) suggests that the following qualities help judge whether a story is good (and I think they apply to the Marine's story approach to doctrine):

- Describes a sequence of actions and experiences done or undergone by a certain number of people, whether real or imaginary.
- People are presented either in situations that change or as reacting to such changes.
- In turn, these changes reveal hidden aspects of the situation for thought, action, or both.
- This response to the new situation leads the story toward its conclusion.
- Deal with emotional and relational or expressive tasks.
- Power comes to those who tell the story if others believe the story or the definition of reality that the storyteller creates.
- Legitimacy in the act of storytelling comes from shaping the story to fit the needs of the particular audience.
- Appreciates the criteria of effectiveness that various stakeholders apply.
- Constructing a reality about the organization to influence follower perceptions and expectations.
- Artistry in deciding how cohesive and how loose the story needs to be (pp. 471–84).

By no means a "silver-bullet," Bradshaw goes on to warn of the dangers of inappropriate contextualizations: the story may become hegemonic (i.e. overly institutionalized or inculcated) to the point where it may become a taken-for-granted grand narrative of "how things are around here"; the one who holds power may silence alternative perspectives and perhaps superior frames; hence, the organization may lose its "strategic fit" with the environment (because it fails to recognize compelling alternative meanings). She concludes:

> Scholars will find it useful to undertake research to test this approach and to reveal the dominant stories of various different organizations. They may find common plots that are increasing in frequency of use. Qualitative and inductive field studies can reveal the dynamics of reality construction processes in various organizations. Such research can generate new ways of accessing stories and achieve a better understanding of how stories are developed. By exploring the storytelling metaphor as a way of better understanding key functions, the goal of this article is to encourage nonprofits to be more creative and hence more resilient (p. 481).

Part 5. Music

Welcome to the Jungle, We got fun 'n' games.

GUNS and ROSES

I remember, in mid-1989, watching in awe, from across a parade field on an Army post in Panama, an infantry battalion of soldiers doing physical training to the rhythm of a very loud, heavy-metal beat of Guns and Roses' "Welcome to the Jungle." Many of us stationed there were pretty sure that it was just a matter of time before we were to use military force to remove Manuel Noriega and his cronies from power. The young soldiers I watched that morning were indeed destined to participate in Operation Just Cause combat operations. I could not help but be motivated from the hard-hitting tune and I often thought back as to how hard rock perhaps affected the soldiers' group "warrior" psyche. I speculate that music as a metaphor has also had profound impacts on Military Design efforts.

Should generals ORCHESTRATE operations (i.e. generals are CONDUCTORS, plans are SHEET MUSIC) or should they be more like JAZZ IMPROVISATIONALISTS who allow the MUSIC to FLOW more freely, permitting other MEMBERS OF THE BAND to assume the LEAD PLAYER where it feels right (i.e. military officers are JAZZ CLUB owners, who provide the ATMOSPHERE where MUSIC can FLOW)? Once moving the frame from the ecological frame to the musicological frame, the military designer may seek to study how JAZZ IMPROVISATION works and perhaps can be used as an extended metaphor for the conduct of military interventions in a particular case where the ORCHESTRATION metaphor does not seem to work.

Organization theorist Karl E. Weick (1998) studied IMPROVISATIONAL JAZZ with this purpose in mind: "To improve the way we talk about organizational improvisation" using the jazz metaphor. Weick asserts that studying this source of metaphor will improve the "source of orienting ideas" about "creativity and innovation in organizations" (p. 543). I summarize his major points in the following clip:

- *What is improvisation*? "Improv" is dealing with the unforeseen and unexpected that may include "flexible treatment of preplanned material." Other qualities include playing extemporaneously, making a difference with ongoing action, spontaneity, novel activities, creation of something while it is being performed, is linked to intuitive processes, requires a "disciplined practicer" (p. 544). "Wade in and see what happens." or it's a matter of "composing on spur of the moment" (p. 548).
- *There are Three Properties of Improvisation.* (1) *Degrees.* Improvisation lies on a continuum: *interpretation* (paraphrasing, where taking minor liberties in redefining music [meanings] as the novelty of the situation is apparent)—*embellishment* (ornamentation or imaginative

"rephrasing")—*variation* (modification, where new melodies/notes are inserted that relate to the original melody)—*improvisation* (all of the above blended—"full spectrum improvisation") (pp. 544–5); (2) *Forms*. Like chaoplexic science proposes, small changes in initial conditions can be radically shifted into amplified effects, we can detect only in retrospect "from elapsed *patterns*;" (3) *(Re-) Cognition*. Looking behind (interpreting through retrospection) while creating new possibilities (*sensemaking*, not to be confused with decision-making) and memories are enhanced with new or improved meanings (*bricolage*) (emphasis added, pp. 544–8).[24]

- *The Metaphoric Aspects of Improvisation are Important (making links to what we must do)*. Jazz metaphor permits new images and the *paradox* of simultaneity of *control with respect to innovation* (if it can happen in jazz why can't it happen in my institution?). Can be related to "non-jazz" metaphors that resemble the process (cuisine, journey, language, and so on). Also allows rethinking what you originally thought (i.e. extended metaphor or *creativity*). Leader activities in combat are like playing jazz: discovering goals, creating/changing procedures/rules, mixing the expected with the novel, and so forth. Improvisation is like reflecting-in-action . . . . "when managers deem an environment to be unanalyzable, they seek information by means of strategies that are 'more personal, less linear, more ad hoc and improvisational'" (emphasis added, pp. 548–50).
- *Conclusions Helpful to the Military Designer*: "To understand more about improvisation undoubtedly will help us get a better grasp on innovation" during military interventions (p. 555). For example, if ones views counterinsurgency operations as improvisation, then military actions are viewed as songs: "The song can be played exactly as scored or with improvisation, but one would not expect an improvisational [military practitioner] to play one song over and over . . . ." Does the unit "authorize improvisational rights" to its members as an operational imperative? Are military designers intellectually capable of holding opposite thoughts (e.g. control::improvisation) necessary to make sense in the face of complex and chaotic situations (p. 549)?

Part 6. Visual arts

A silver and enamel badge 1 inch in height and 3 inches in width, consisting of an infantry musket on a light blue bar with a silver border, on and over an elliptical oak wreath. The bar is blue, the color associated with the Infantry branch. The musket is adapted from the Infantry insignia of branch and represents the first official U.S. shoulder arm, the 1795 model

Springfield Arsenal musket. It was adopted as the official Infantry branch insignia in 1924. The oak symbolizes steadfastness, strength and loyalty.

US Army Official Website Describing the Combat Infantryman's Badge

Visual art can create and represent quite passionate meanings-for-action. Two researchers, also organization theorists, Mary Jo Hatch and Dvora Yanow (2008), propose that PAINTING can offer rich metaphor to stir new imaginations and possibilities when it comes to artistically dealing with situational uniqueness:

> Scholars paint theoretical canvases, using words, without always making transparent the logic of inquiry embedded within their writing. This is especially so when writing for their own epistemic communities, whose members share a set of usually unspoken methodological presuppositions concerning the 'reality status' of what they study and its 'know-ability'. When research topics engage scholars across epistemic communities, as in organizational studies, arguments may be difficult to parse precisely because these presuppositions remain implicit, unnoted and, perhaps, unnoticed. By enabling new ways of seeing familiar things, metaphors can facilitate such encounters by making the implicit less so (p. 23).
>
> From its source, our metaphor brings to its TARGET attention to the elements and processes of painting a canvas – what one paints, tools for and modes of painting, etc. – and how what artist sees influences what the painting (re)presents.
>
> . . .
>
> Used as a supplement to verbal argumentation, the visual, ARTISTIC MATERIAL opens the discourse. . .not only to other avenues of understanding complex philosophical ideas, but to also to greater AESTHETIC APPRECIATION of its phenomena and to acts of theorizing about them (emphasis added, p. 36).

FIGURE 2.4 *Combat Infantryman's Badge.*

The article continues, and I substitute "Military Design" terms here for "painting," "researchers," and "social scientists" (which, for all intents and purposes, are the alter egos of military designers):

> . . . The painting metaphor lends a new vision to the argument that [designing] itself is a method of inquiry, a way of looking at worldmaking. If [Military Design is] part of how [military designers] "see" their phenomena, then methodology becomes central to the question of what [military designers] produce, and the painting metaphor, being a means of rendering methodologies visible, has an important role to play . . . (p. 36).

Major Ben Zweibelson, an active-duty US infantry officer who majored in graphic art in his undergraduate work, created this image of Mexican drug cartel and its problematization with respect to the United States as part of a design effort. Note that he uses a TECTONIC PLATE (signifying slow-moving change) AIR PRESSURE AND CURRENTS (representing more rapid ENVIRONMENTAL changes) metaphor to base his graphic (Figure 2.5) (Zweibelson 2011).

I asked Ben to describe his creative approach to making the graphic in a story. As I hope you will note, his description is unique to himself and the group of students he was working with, that the creative heritage and "knack" is not provided as something to emulate or replicate (as a modernist approach would demand), but to *appreciate*:

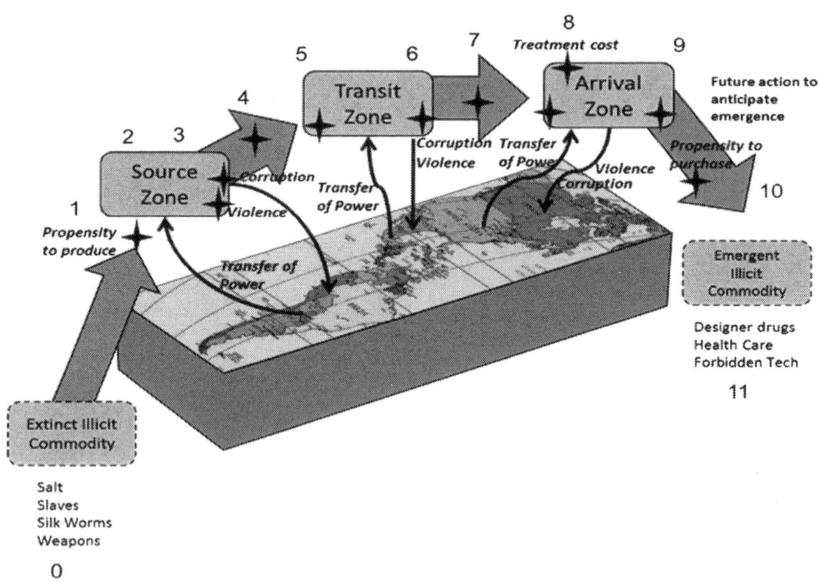

FIGURE 2.5 *Example of Metaphoric Graphic Design.*
(Artwork Courtesy of Major Ben Zweibelson).

At first, my small group (five US Army School of Advanced Military Studies – SAMS – students) researched Mexico mostly on our own. I think this is how we bound our interiority [what we knew and what was available in our source materials] knowledge – we map-out what we know, and know we know. I developed, on my own, through trial and error, a 50 slide presentation I built- it really showed graphically my evolution from learning about Mexico (phase 1- understand and bound what your organization "knows" and "knows it knows") and this set me up for exploring and designing our "illicit commodity cycle" later on. Next, I briefed the slides to my small group prior to the exercise starting. Their input and the guidance from my instructors really made me think critically at a level well beyond anything I had done before in planning. Those first attempts at understanding were, in the words of my professor, 'descriptive and what-centric.' After several hours of struggling through this, I broke through some mental barriers and began to seek the 'explanation and why-centric' instead. This prepared me for the design exercise.

The first two days of the exercise, our student leader tried to have all five of us work together to brainstorm collectively. I already knew that I do not work well this way with design approaches. Creativity is, in my opinion something often occurring individually instead of in group settings. This is based on a lifetime of being an artist, plus four-and-a-half years of college education as a graphic designer and fine arts major, along with my over 18 years in the military. One might enjoy inspiration in a group setting, but for me, creativity is an internal function of intelligence, experimentation, visualization, inspiration, and creation and destruction. In other words, except for large mural projects and eccentric artist teams, most every work of art (paintings, regular sized sculptures, photos, etc.) are individually done by one creative human at a time. Collaboration does help, but it does not work in the forced manner that military planning and design doctrine demands. This is my own theory, but it has served me quite well in my career thus far. The interesting thing is that this runs quite contrary to military institutional concepts where we are expected to emphasize teamwork, groupthink, and collective agreement. Creativity does not function in that environment. When I consider the broad range of examples of military creativity, the majority of them appear to reduce down to the thoughts of one individual, be it a general discovering the applications of deep penetration, an innovative staff officer wrestling with existing doctrine and a complex problem, or a special forces operator out on a *foreign internal defense* or *unconventional warfare* operation adapting to a unique environment.

I broke from the group and "white-boarded" on my own, and then pulled the group in to show them my own creative discoveries on why (not what) Mexico was doing what we were seeing with relation to cartel violence, envisioned as a complex system. I started with large Mary Jo Hatch [referring to her 1997 book, *Organization Theory*] cycles for the United States and Mexico separately. This drove some initial discussions, which I also wrote into narratives to capture our appreciation of the system. At this point, the appointed student group leader took me aside and had a little chat with me about how he was a little concerned that I was not being a team player and I was going "rogue" too much. I needed to work with the team. At the same time, he agreed that the vast majority of the day's deliverables were entirely mine, to include the graphics, drawings, and narratives. So, he seemed a little frustrated that I was breaking with what the Army and SAMS' faculty wanted us to do, and at the same time, I was not conforming within the institution's preferred approach for staff work by single-handedly producing the vast bulk of work—work that meant something, work that perhaps had deeper explanation than the other four team-members that continued to circle the "this is what we know" zone where description and reductionism reign supreme. This is not a critique of their work, which was quite useful for detailed planning-but it did not seem to *explain* anything about the system. They were, to use a trendy design phrase, "admiring the problem" and draping details over it. Spending hours building slides on describing and analyzing the major cartel networks or the Mexican political system never seemed to get us beyond the narrow applications of military action within a closed system. Our design approach needed to break past those self-imposed barriers, to reveal to us some of the larger phenomenon at work.

That Friday (the third day of the exercise), I had a creative breakthrough. We were chatting as a group, I was thinking about the bulk of work already produced, and I was challenging myself on what our products so far were *not* explaining. What was a higher level of abstraction I could push to, where a logic, a pattern existed- awaiting discovery. That high-abstraction of "why?" jumped out at me, and I walked to the white board in a corner and drew out the new concept that addressed the core phenomenon of illicit commodities in general—this went far beyond cocaine and Mexico, but seemed to be timeless and embrace any illicit commodity across human existence. The holistic nature of this concept was both abstract, yet explanatory in appreciating the cycle of violence, power, and application of societal values to tangible things. Once done, I turned to the group, drew them in, and explained the logic while trying to have them discover the concept themselves instead of briefing it to them as if I were administering the new knowledge to them. Not as a teacher instructing students, but as a fellow "traveler" that saw some strange weather, pointed it out, and then speculating with the group why the weather was behaving as it seemed to be doing. We were in the "fog," and eventually they seemed comfortable with the uncertainty and high abstraction where we were talking about not just cartels, but ANY illegal enterprise; not just cocaine, but ANY item that humans associate with value and legality (valued and legal, valued and illegal, not valuable and legal, not valuable and illegal). This drove the illicit commodity cycle that I drew out for the group, and we began discussing the tensions of each phase of the endless processes of adaptation and entropy, prosperity between nations, and criminal enterprises.

Once our faculty instructor saw the concept and stated he liked it, the hierarchical military structure of the student group asserted its top-down approval, and the, now-legitimated process continued. Despite this symbolic action, which is an unfortunate necessity in virtually every military school, unit, etc., I was confident that it felt right. It was the right direction . . . and I took every effort to encourage the group to break away from military conformity (i.e. "let's do a slide with lines of effort, and a desired end-state, like we always do!")—and this worked better when I addressed the concept of problematization—to critically think about how you think. Why do we need an end-state? What does that mean? Will the illicit commodity cycle ever extinguish? Or will it merely evolve, adapt, and transform as we enact in the system? If so- is the concept of "end state" even useful right now at the conceptual planning level, or is it a reminder of the detailed planning logic that is pervasive in all aspects of military form and function?

My proposed concept progressed through several more iterations as the group began to accept the logic and embraced at least some of it. Later, we had extensive discussions on the operational approach. I once again broke away, made my non-linear approach concept with the thermal drafts metaphors for short-term action and Hatch cycles as tectonic plates for long-term cultural change, and I pitched this to the group. There was sharp division- some liked it, some were uncomfortable with a design deliverable that did not "check the block" on traditional lines of effort leading to clear end-states and decisive points. There was a general fear in some that if we briefed something that "did not look like what the other groups were doing" or "did not look like the examples in doctrine," we would fail.

Another student came up with another abstract concept using the cycles, but using a 'steam pipe' concept where valves and mixtures of "gases" (representing different actions from each instrument of power) was selected as the group's "design deliverable." When briefed our design, the senior leader present stated that he liked the abstract concept, but wanted "more detail." Perhaps he meant, ". . . more explanation about why the system behaves as it does, and what we can do to influence it with deliberate action."

Because my final design approach concept was not selected, I developed it on my own further and wrote the subsequent Small Wars Journal article featuring it and other concepts. In the end, it was a journey where I

> wandered into the fog, made observations and created things, and walked "back to base camp" to talk by the fire with my fellow travelers. They helped me make sense of whether I was on the right track, but then I went back out into the mist, alone, to continue to create. Each time, I would return to the fire (our organization, and the associated logic and cultural institutionalisms), get feedback, share, exchange, and continue to advance the ideas. Creativity was in the fog, but confirmation of good progress versus ineffective or erroneous progress occurred in the group. And at times, "around the fire," I noticed that because others did not explore in the fog the places I visited, they could not realize by the fire due to how strong the light of the fire might be blinding them from things one could only discover with a fog-light. Since I had seen it with my fog-light, I could also see that sometimes, my camp-mate (or mates) were blinded by institutionalism and the pervasive blaze of the fire; it burned too bright to allow the subtle and novel elements visible only in fog-light to be understood. To discover, they had to leave the fire and join me in the fog . . . learn with me- I could not 'teach it'- nor could I guide them in the fog if they carried a torch with them from the campfire. The torch represented a resistance (field assumptions, in-house assumptions, and root metaphors) to breaking from institutional core tenets and preferred logic.
>
> In the end, the group took some of the ideas, and rejected others. The final group exercise 'deliverable' represented a struggle between the military hierarchy and artistic expression that potentially threatened one another. Creativity battled groupthink and institutionalism, and made some headway in some respects, but failed in others. The final article represented my individual work and creativity, and presented perhaps another narrative that could further drive an organization's subsequent detailed planning process as a template—an appreciation of a complex system that appreciates the self-organizing and adaptive reality which reacts poorly to deliberate and sequential actions by a hierarchal structured organizations that emphasize uniformity, collective action, and repetition (Personal correspondence with author, September 6, 2011).

Ben continues to richly describe his creative growth, from childhood, as follows:

> My father was a child psychologist in the 1950s and 60s. He was also an artist, a lifelong painter, sculptor, and writer. My earliest memories of our laundry room were the large kiln in the corner- and making stuff out of clay with him. This was very odd for most kids- but normal for me. My father did not let my mother buy us coloring books because "you will condition them to draw within someone else's lines." Instead, we only got blank paper. Blank canvas- to craft our own work, our own ideas . . . essentially, as Jacques Rancière (1991) explained in *The Ignorant*

Schoolmaster- so that the ignorant could learn on their own, without a master; to discover the creativity that exists within all humans; it just needs to be stimulated- not taught. You do not give someone creativity like you give them a shirt to wear. But we try to do that all the time. The vast majority of people I went to art school with in college were already pretty talented folks but only a very small handful of them, in my opinion, were in touch with their true creative potential- for those few, they went on to excel in their own endeavors. The rest hold down jobs where they might go through the motions, but they are still just coloring in coloring books. They approached new problems the same way, seeking to apply solutions that were either directed by the institution, or were previously successful for them- and these are artists I am describing!

I knew from a young age that I was a very visual thinker. In the 7th grade, I was getting unusual grades- half were very high, the rest were rather low, and they were not tied to subjects. Eventually the school did a few intelligence tests on me. It turns out that I was an extremely effective visual learner, but a weak auditory learner. In other words, I did well in classes where the teacher used pictures or drew on the chalkboard, but poorly in those where they orally discussed lessons with no visuals. Since then, I have tailored much of my learning to play to my visual strengths through words and graphics over listening to lessons or information in auditory venues.

I think that visual concepts help convey information better than narratives if you are doing it right. They can also complement each other. But we often make very busy PowerPoint slides- is the logic that because a topic is complicated of complex, the slide has to be? Can a simple slide convey deep explanation? I think so- in fact, I think that is the best way to do it. Can a slide use a graphic in a way the group has never seen? Air currents and tectonic plates instead of the doctrinal lines of effort and centers of gravity? Why not? How about tornados and a narrative about the horse carriage industry? Or must we use a Civil War battle and some maps with graphic control measures everyone is familiar with? Does a graphic demonstrate a new or different way of looking at something complex? Perhaps another metaphor-as-story could work here:

> Imagine a building with a center courtyard; it is sealed off, and there are windows you can look through around the inside of the house to gaze into the courtyard to make sense of some statue in the middle. It is dark, and tough to figure out what the statue is. The front window is the preferred window – we all use it, and our leadership wants everything to be framed with that view. But, for this statue, that view is not enough. In fact, it is misleading. We need to walk around to other parts of the building, perhaps even something as wild as climbing out onto the roof and peering down from the skylight to

> GAIN DIFFERENT PERSPECTIVE. IN THE END, WE WILL PROBABLY USE THE "FRONT WINDOW"' VIEW BECAUSE OUR ORGANIZATION RESPONDS BEST TO THAT, BUT WE CAN PRODUCE A GRAPHIC THAT RICHLY BLENDS OTHER PERSPECTIVES WHILE DELIVERING IT IN THE PREFERRED FORMAT, BUT STILL NOT A SLAVE TO ALL THE PROBLEMS WITH JUST LOOKING THOUGH ONE WINDOW ONLY (Zweibelson, personal correspondence with author, September 6, 2011).

My idea to present Ben's work-narrative here is not to point out a developmental scheme for future military designers as fine artists (representing the modernist approach would be to try and replicate or find those with the requisite backgrounds and experiences of "successful" designers) but to highlight the uniqueness of how Ben approaches design in a "Ben-only" way. Ben's uniqueness illustrates the Claude Bernard famous line, "Art is I, science is we."

Military Design Quadrant: Amalgamated Metaphors. Human nature is more complicated than to ascribe meaning based on a single source of metaphor. The *subjective-complexified* view (the HEART of design) represents a hybrid of types of metaphor discussed. From this perspective, the design of language is a form of sensemaking and reflects how designers seek to construct the reality of others by drawing on metaphor from multiple sources (Figure 2.5, Concepts for Military Design); hence, making sense often becomes the MIXING BOWL of metaphoric creativity.

Equipped with this virtual VEGETABLE SOUP of language, we can portray how designers aspire to influence and borrow from others' sense of the otherwise uninterpretable, incoherent, or disorderly messes "out there" in the world. Designers create new frames derived from political rhetoric, psychological schema, opinions, arguments, judgments, and amalgamate other heuristics as they attempt to affect meaning and enact. All sources of metaphor are at work in promoting social constructions of reality. One or more sources may dominate over others at various points in time and may vary across and inside various knowledge communities (i.e. these MIXTURES have important cultural overtones). These dominations may become institutional PSYCHIC PRISONS and should be revealed and challenged by the military designer (Figure 2.6).

From a postinstitutional perspective, the basis of professional military knowledge may now seem more malleable. A major conclusion is that concept texts seldom reveal what other modernist communities have built as rather clear roles, norms, and values of intellectual argument that we would find, for example, in their applied scientific journals and textbooks (that include rigorous peer reviews, attributing authorship to prior researchers, adhering to a custom of making citations, documenting a rich "audit trail" of documented intellectually rigorous discussion, and socializing a revulsion toward plagiarism, etc.). These absences should underscore that approved military concepts are supported only by a façade of modernist and chaoplexic

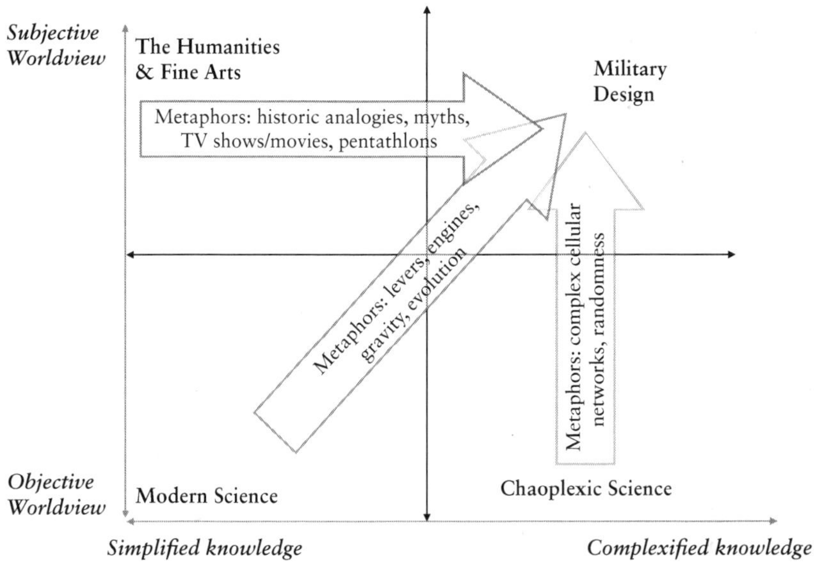

FIGURE 2.6 *Sources of Metaphors to Aid Military Design.*

metaphors and cannot be subject to the rigor of knowledge assimilation demonstrated in the natural sciences.

Armed with the proposed Multi-Frame Typology of Metaphors, to recognize and discern metaphor, one can be more reflective on the influencing process of Military Design. Hence, one might conclude that exposure to modernist and chaoplexic metaphors serves only as a *pretense of knowledge* because these sources imply a prognosis on events and "environments" that are neither predictable nor explainable without them. A case in point is the three LEVELS OF WAR (tactical, operational, and strategic) metaphors produced under the tutelage of 1970s, post-Vietnam senior Army officers, Generals William E. DePuy, Donn A. Starry, and Creighton Abrams. The LEVELS OF WAR present a metaphoric façade of ecological niche science—that biological phenomena are investigated from the individual ORGANISM to the ECOLOGICAL whole-of-SYSTEM perspectives (from the microscopic view to the macroscopic view). These displaced concepts eventually became the taken-for-granted, "best ways" to investigate the nature of complex military interventions—reified as "levels of analysis."

The more reflective military designer now may center the debate on the efficacy of the metaphor, for example, WAR AS AN ECOLOGICAL HIERARCHY (extended from the biological theories). Perhaps the more reflective military designer can examine war with a more nontraditional and more aesthetic metaphor borrowed from the humanities and fine arts—through interpreting historical accounts, creative processes of painting, composing music, poetry, and so on.

Some final thoughts on metaphoric reasoning

To employ these ideas of amalgamated metaphors,[25] advice to military designers would have to include:

> . . . negotiate meaning . . . and become aware of and respect both the differences in your backgrounds and when these differences are important. You need enough diversity of cultural and personal experience to be aware that divergent world views exist and what they might be like. You also need patience, certain flexibility in world view, and a generous tolerance for mistakes, as well as a talent for finding the right metaphor to communicate relevant parts of unshared experiences while deemphasizing others. Metaphorical imagination is a crucial skill in creating rapport and in communicating the nature of unshared experience. This skill consists, in large measure, of the ability to bend your world view and adjust the way you categorize your experience (Lakoff and Johnson 1980, p. 231).

I propose a framework in this chapter that can assist institutional reflexivity and help designers find and negotiate sources of meaning, being ever mindful of when and how metaphors are being used. The designer continuously recognizes and challenges metaphoric reasoning, particularly those that would seem to otherwise mindlessly dominate modern military science. Modernist metaphors are so prevalent that it is easy to robotically treat them as the truth rather than as Platonic, shadowy images of truth. Unawareness of language as metaphor can grow and work to "anesthetize" military designers against the worst effects of assumed truth. The danger of hypostatization is that such simplification can seductively serve to reduce the anxiety and confusion of institutional members who otherwise face the ambiguity prevalent in military interventions. My proposed framework seeks to expose a more open philosophy that has been suppressed by a longstanding façade of modernism.

Multiple sources of metaphor should include modern science, chaoplexic science, stories and images associated with a sense of retrospection (of what has happened in the past), aesthetics (of what is beautiful), context (literally "with text," that creates a mental image), and fiction (what could happen, could have happened or what is perceived as happening right now or in the future). The emergent debate on postinstitutional Military Design should now center on critical and creative inquiries about whether prevailing metaphors can be modified, diminished in use, or discarded for some other form of sensemaking that works better to convey new or altered shared meaning. Barring such reflection, the military designer can easily become too comfortable by framing situations with the use of hypostatized metaphors. That critical reflection can also serve to motivate imaginative ways to generate and explore exciting metaphors and invent breathtakingly rich eloquence in postinstitutional Military Design. In the next chapter, as part of this exploration, I will attempt to deconstruct "the usual suspects" in modern military science: *strategy*, *leadership*, and *planning*.

Notes

1 It is reasonable to accept, then, that *all* communications and representations are ambiguous to some degree.

2 Henceforth through this chapter, I use SMALL CAPITAL LETTERS indicating that I am highlighting the principal metaphors at work.

3 When I used "advance search" (all text) for articles on Ebsco Host Research Data Bases, under the "Military and Government Collection," and used the phrase "center of gravity and war," I received 1,471 article hits. This gives some idea of the magnitude that this metaphor has been displaced into military science. For a discussion on how translation (from German to English) can interfere with the original intent of the metaphor, see Joseph Strange and Richard Iron (2004).

4 In that regard, paraphrasing Richard H. Brown (1977), the paradox of metaphors is that they are meant to be understood while misunderstood (pp. 82–3). Brown does not see metaphors merely as heuristics. They constitute *all* theories (explanations) of reality in both the natural and social sciences. I must say here that Brown's book, particularly his chapter on metaphor, is a must-read for those interested in metaphoric bases of framing.

5 It is interesting that both the US Army's War College and Command and General Staff College use the proclaimed "Universal Intellectual Standards" proffered by The Foundation for Critical Thinking (Paul and Elder 2004). The Foundation offers the "scientific method" (i.e. modern science) as the only way to legitimate knowledge. This is more evidence of an ideology at work. I will further criticize Paul and Elder claims to "universal intellectual standards" in Chapter 5.

6 Gibson Burrell and Gareth Morgan (1979) also added *human nature* as a fourth dimension of worldview or paradigm, defined as the relationship between humans and their environment, expressed along a continuum of voluntarism::determinism. I did not include this continuum in my model (below) as this will be manifested in the selection and attribution to volunteerism::determinism in institutionally favored metaphors.

7 Nomotheticism is the search for general laws of nature. By *nomothetic taxonomies*, I am referring to the categorization of these "laws" into parsimonious and useful cause-and-effect relationships. Modern military science strives to replicate nomothetic taxonomies found in the "hard sciences," for example, through levels of analysis (strategic, operational, and tactical levels) and the programmed or planned tasks associated with each level. I will discuss more on this modernist quest for task certainty in Chapter 3.

8 Don Martindale (1959) (quoting Weber 1949) speaks to Weberian ideal types. "Ideal types are not stereotypes, averages, or abstract concepts. 'An ideal type is formed by the one-sided *accentuation* of one or more points of view and by the synthesis of a great many diffuse, discrete, more or less present and occasionally absent concrete individual phenomena, which are arranged according to those one-sidedly emphasized viewpoints into a unified analytical construct, in its conceptual purity, this mental construct cannot be found anywhere in reality'" (emphases in original, p. 68). Martindale concludes, "Ideal types are not methodological expedients but transempirical form of constituting a kind of heaven of Platonic ideals in which events participate; one must assume that any given ideal type is destined to be surpassed. It must also be assumed, however, that ideal types will continue to be employed as long as sociology or any science relies upon the comparative method" (p. 88).

9 Also known as *logical positivism*, the latter is a term coined by a multidisciplinary conference of scientists convened in the 1920s, nicknamed the *Vienna Circle*. According to Gibson Burrell and Gareth Morgan (1989), positivists "seek to explain and predict what happens in the social world by searching for regularities and causal relationships between its constituent elements. Positivist epistemology is in essence based upon the traditional approaches which dominate the natural sciences" (p. 5). This modernist paradigm is linked to definitional-operationalism, microeconomics, and behaviorism.

10 The obvious ethical question then becomes who gets to choose the valuation goals? Are there universal ethics, such as those claims that there are universal human rights? Is poverty a relative state of mind? Unfortunately, US doctrine does not address these sorts of existential issues which are germane to a postinstitutional approach to Military Design.

11 The US Department of Defense (2011a) *Dictionary of Military and Associated Terms* is well populated with these extended and displaced (i.e. dead) metaphors borrowed from the hard science of war. The two definitions of LINE OF OPERATIONS are: "A physical line that defines the interior or exterior orientation of the force in relation to the enemy or that connects actions on nodes and/or decisive points related in time and space to an objective(s)"; and, "A logical line that connects actions on nodes and/or decisive points related in time and purpose with an objective(s)." DECISIVE POINT definitions include a similar epistemology: "A geographic place, specific key event, critical factor, or function that, when acted upon, allows commanders to gain a marked advantage over an adversary or contribute materially to achieving success." INFORMATION OPERATIONS, a derivative extension of LINE OF OPERATION metaphor, is defined as, "The integrated employment, during military operations, of information-related capabilities in concert with other lines of operation to influence, disrupt, corrupt, or usurp the decision-making of adversaries and potential adversaries while protecting our own."

12 Those involved in the relatively new military specialty of information operations metaphorically use artillery and attack aviation terms and processes such as TARGETING.

13 I will address in more detail later in this chapter how behaviorism has affected modernist military science.

14 The *Heisenberg Principle* (developed from investigations into what light is) includes the notion that once you pay attention to the complex system, you are then part of the milieu. The inherent paradox is that in military interventions you cannot hope to understand the situation before you act in it (the Napoleon maxim *On s'engage et puis on voit*) (Mannheim 1936, p. 127).

15 It is interesting that as a young man, Nicholas Rescher worked for the RAND (an acronym for "research and development") Corporation—an organization devoted to forecasting.

16 Hence, it is the metaphoric use of the French word, *portmanteau* (large suitcase) to describe how language serves as a collection of *meaning containers* with combinations of words like SMOG (smoke and fog).

17 Again, I refer to this overlap as a *zone of analogy*. Yuen F. Khong's "Y" is referred to by Schön as an "extension" and furthermore adds that eventually the original analogy may disappear into a dead metaphor. So, the meaning then morphs, over time becoming independent of the original "Y" and the current situation has a conceptualization of its own (fully displaced or sedimentary institutionalization). Resurfacing this lost fallacy (or mindfulness) is a key aspect of postinstitutional Military Design.

18 In early 2012, I attended a US Army-sponsored conference where some participants insisted that creativity in envisioning a future is essential to "strategic thinking in command." In other words, a burgeoning strategist should seek to create a desired future by first inventing knowledge about it. I would argue (employing Schön's 1963, concept-displacement theory) that one can only extend and displace from concepts already "known" (no matter how clear or distorted the knowledge of past and current experiences). The extensions of "known" concepts into fantasized ones are themselves a kind of historic (albeit, perhaps more recent) knowledge. Such ideas of "prospection," described as a kind of visioning, will always be misleading. To be prospective is a process of reflection on- (retrospective) and in- (during) action and not some sort of hallucinogenic, mystical foreknowledge. Projecting on the current (or a past) situation is perhaps better stated as an exercise of "retrospection anticipated in fantasy" (Schütz 1962, p. 87).

19 I was present in his command post when, just before the ground attack, Lieutenant General Gary Luck, then Commander XVIII Airborne Corps, explained it to his staff using similar words (I recall Luck's reference to football-style "audibles" distinctively and now, twenty years later, I can attribute the power of sports metaphor to convey a military concept of operation).

20 In one discussion of social pressures, Erving Goffman (1959) uses a military example: ". . . in the raw recruit who initially follows army etiquette in order to avoid physical punishment and eventually comes to follow the rules so that his organization will not be shamed and his officers and fellow soldiers will respect him" (p. 20). He also wrote a related book about *framing* which is equally germane to the present book (Goffman 1974).

21 The US Air Force list does not include fiction (Department of the Air Force 2011).

22 These lists change usually upon appointment of new chiefs of staff. For example, the Army changed its list in March 2012, from the above listed fictional books, adding Fra Elbert Hubbard's 1899 classic *A Message to Garcia* and removing Steven Pressfield's *Gates of Fire*.

23 I have heard from my students the recent (in the wake of US interventions in Iraq and Afghanistan) version as: "The Army is at war while everyone else is at the mall."

24 *Bricolage*, from a linguistics design point of view, is akin to the purposeful mixing of metaphors, familiar meanings, and alternative paradigms to create a new, richer idea of what is happening. I discuss the professional Military Design role of *bricoleur* in Chapter 5.

25 Karl Mannheim (1936) refers to this relationist perspective *dynamic* (in other words, *dynamic relationism*) (p. 88).

3

A Critique of "The Usual Suspects" for Military Design

... meaning is dependent upon reflexivity—the process of turning back on oneself and looking at what has been going on. Meaning is attached to actions retrospectively; only the already-experienced is meaningful, not that which is in the process of being experienced.

attributed to ALFRED SCHÜTZ by GIBSON BURRELL and GARETH

Morgan, *Sociological Paradigms and Organizational Analysis*

Reification implies that man is capable of forgetting his own authorship of the human world, and further, that the dialectic between man, the producer, and his products is lost to consciousness. The reified world is, by definition, a dehumanized world. It is experienced by man as a strange facticity, an opus alienum over which he has no control rather than as the opus proprium of his own productive activity. ... The basic "recipe" for the reification of institutions is to bestow on them an ontological status independent of human activity and signification.

PETER L. BERGER and THOMAS LUCKMANN,
The Social Construction of Reality

This chapter is based on the premise that actions-to-solve problems are framed by institutionalized meanings. In other words, institutionalized meanings are housed in an organization that can be described as

> ... a collection of choices looking for problems, issues and feelings looking for decision situations in which they might be aired, solutions looking for issues to which they might be the answer, and decision makers looking for work (Cohen et al. 1972, p. 2).[1]

In many ways, institutions are composites of ordained solutions. Particular to modernist military institutions are, among others,[2] what I call "the usual suspects" for designing military interventions: *strategy*, *leadership*, and *planning*.[3] These hypostatizations represent powerful beliefs that affect Military Design frames of reference. I will attempt to deconstruct and reconstruct them in order to demonstrate that otherwise institutionalized meanings can themselves be redesigned.

In fact, this is a good place to pause and reflect on the morphology of the meaning of the word "design" itself. The root prefix "de" is from Latin and means "of." "Sign" has Latin roots, meaning "image." Hence, the meaning design is metaphorically related to the processes and products of human imagination. Interestingly, Webster's *Third New International Unabridged Dictionary* has dozens of definitions for the word. Those who have imported the term to identify it with professional practice seem to borrow meaning from the field of architecture; signifying design is concerned with "the art and science of building." It is no wonder that those who have used design to speak to professional practice borrow related meanings from architectural design. One such metaphor is "framing"; after all, how can one construct a building without frames? Several images come to mind: structural frames (blue-printed plans); roof frames (to protect against adverse weather); window frames (to understand the outside world and allow light in); and door frames (to walk out onto the right pathway). These could easily transfer to traditional military staff work concepts: planning, protection, intelligence, and positioning. Frames are important to the ways humans socially construct reality, analogous to how architects use them to structure a building.[4] However, and this is the point of this chapter, we should recognize that even the words "design" and "frame" can be critically deconstructed, particularly with their limited "zones of analogy."

So, an important aspect of institutional criticism is *frame reflexivity* (Schön and Rein 1994). Frame reflection is being mindful that institutionalized solutions are man-made conceptions that may be critically deconstructed and analyzed; thereby creating opportunities for radical pathways to *re*frame by purposefully changing the usual meanings (Goffman 1974). Frame structures are often expressed as schema, metaphoric narratives, and causal stories (each presenting a different view of reality) (Stone 1989), but in any case, they represent *institutional programmed courses of action* (Berger and Luckmann 1967, p. 62).

In that vein of thought, I will continue to promote this sort of institutional reflexivity on some interesting language that may otherwise seem matter-of-fact to military modernists. Defining problems of a modern military become conformational problems of strategy, leadership, and planning. These frames provide the habitualized logics, grammars, and rhetorics to construct a cultural reality much like the engineering sciences are called upon as technical solutions that "look for" architectural design problems. We shall speculate as to how these three taken-for-granted frames can be criticized in three parts: Part 1. Frame Reflection on "Strategy"; Part 2. Frame Reflection on "Leadership"; and Part 3. Frame Reflection on "Planning." Our critical inquiry shall be oriented on this question: How can these otherwise hypostatized concepts be deconstructed and/or reconstructed to encourage more creativity in Military Design?

Part 1. Frame reflection on "strategy"

Brasidas . . . took up a defensive position on Cerdylium. . .on high ground across the river . . . with good views in all directions, so that no move made by Cleon and his army could escape notice.

THUCYDIDES,
History of the Peloponnesian Wars

The word strategy has been institutionally reified to the point that it serves as the unquestioned *raison d'être* of Western-styled war and general staff colleges. So pervasive is the term that I could not find a single military English language journal article attempting to challenge the expression as anything but quintessential to the professional of arms. This section first seeks to deliteralize the word—theorizing that its meaning has been morphologically displaced from an ancient Greek wartime phenomenon.[5] The goal here is to emancipate thinking about strategy by surmising multidisciplinary conceptualizations—that is, "strategy as perspective" (Mintzberg 1987, pp. 16–17).[6] Somewhere along the line, strategy became a dormant (if not dying or dead) metaphor. Indeed, with the backdrop of Donald A. Schön's theory of displaced concepts, one can postulate about the morphology of strategy—a word that, through cross-institutional networks of exchanged meaning, has been recontextualized since the ancient Greek phenomenon appeared.[7] Strategy can be investigated as a dead metaphor spurring critical and creative inquiry about how its meaning structure came about and its conceptual limitations.

Only a handful of writers have attempted to linguistically unravel the military sensemakings we have built around the phenomenon of war (e.g. Ferrari 2007; Mutch 2006; Stickle 2004; Talbot 2003; Brendler 1997; Medhurst et al. 1997; Windsor 1996). Some provide morphological insight by examining how others have borrowed meaning from the context of war. For example, cognitive linguists have marveled at the daily use of terms normally associated with the logics, grammar, and rhetoric of war (Lakoff and Johnson 1980, pp. 4–7). The uses of war as a framing metaphor seem endless:

- *Muster* support for the war on poverty
- NFL team's *offensive* line
- Apple *outmaneuvers* Microsoft

- The leadership qualities of *General George S. Patton*
- Bureaucratic *infighting*
- The *tactics* of partisan politics
- The *attack* on American family values
- A Madison Avenue marketing *blitzkrieg*
- A political *campaign*
- A *defense* attorney

Equally intriguing is the way other knowledge disciplines have influenced the frames of war through what has become a "metaphoric network" (Ricœur 1977, p. 244)[8]:

- The *fog* and *friction* of war
- Military professionals practice the *management* of violence
- Department of Defense *business* processes and *enterprises*
- Iraq and Afghanistan *surges*
- The *Cold* War
- *Psychological* warfare
- The enemy's *center of gravity*
- *Irregular* warfare
- Military as an *element* of *power*
- *Fourth generation* warfare

How did these extensions and displacements of the concept, "strategy," happen?

The linguistic context of the word strategy seems to stem from an ancient Greek military officer responsible for the outcome of a battle or war—*stratégos* (hence, the Greek root word "*stratos*" or army and "*agos*"[9] or leader).[10] How high-level military beings literally directed their forces in war is encapsulated in the original meaning of the word strategy as the praxis of the military leader.

One can only speculate how the subjective meanings we derive today were extended and displaced from the objective reality of a senior officer of a Greek archipelagos' city-state army, standing on the high ground, able to physically see, hear, and smell the Peloponnesian battlefield as the

FIGURE 3.1 *Cartoon of Ancient Greek Scene.*

Thucydides epigraph to this section indicates. Perceiving the flow of the battle with his senses, the general was tactically able (the meaning of modern-day *tactics* is morphologically derived from the related Greek word *taktikós*, which translates to "orders") to bring some order to the battle, of course to his advantage. The army's purpose (or *telos*—Greek for "goal") was set by his employer—the city state. The original meaning of strategy, then, was the general who literally sensed the events unfolding from a vantage point, created favorable conditions through tactics, and was teleologically motivated by his city-state's wartime goals.

These and other associated meanings of strategy have since been projected into other knowledge disciplines, such as business, international relations, public administration, and, sports, connected by transdisciplinary logic: "strategic studies." In time, when motivated with the demands of new, unfamiliar situations, other disciplines engaged in searches for heuristics, finding logical resemblances to the origin of the word that include having the hierarchical authority level ("level" is rooted in the Latin word *stratum*) that comes with "high" rank; developing a vision toward the future, as one would sense from a vantage position; finding ways to bring order to their institution; and setting goals that define success. These extended meanings continued into far-ranging derivative theories for action in the particular field. The resembled "war logics" of strategy were projected into other knowledge disciplines, recontextualized, and projected back.

From the Schönian perspective, the morphological process affecting the meaning of strategy seems to be connected to the displacement of theories of action through contextualizations and recontextualizations of how and what to do when faced with important novel situations.[11] In plainer English, knowledge communities adapt and reconstitute the meaning of strategy as they reflect in and on the new situations they face. Situations have no meaning inherent to themselves; people structure situations into what they refer to as "problems." The emergent contexts warrant further displacement of the meaning of strategy and dynamically shared meaning among the disciplines (various contexts), and layers of new associated metaphors are themselves extended and displaced in the emergent metaphoric network. The displaced ideas of strategy that took on elaborated meanings in other fields are projected back and forth with military studies. Extended language constructions (e.g. the noun, strategy, becomes an adjective, "strategic") emerge in the military and other communities of practice, such as "strategic leaders," "strategic vision," "strategic end state," "strategic deception," and "strategic planning." These extended and displaced meanings of strategy are today found in the highest-level conceptualizations of all US Defense Department war and staff colleges and are elaborated to the point that all curricula are designed around them.[12]

Strategy can be framed as a morphological amalgam of *generative metaphors* (Schön 1993) that eventually become mutually referencing in the emerging of a relatively insular, interdisciplinary web of strategic studies. There are at least three important and overlapping implications: (1) The resulting *epistemological frustration* (lack of closure) is continuously generated through the metaphoric network of strategic studies; (2) The potential emancipation that postinstitutional forms of *reflexivity* afford; and (3) The challenge of *reframing* in problem settings.

Epistemological Frustration. The interdisciplinary exchanges of meaning that occur in the face of novel or emergent situations (in the context of business, international relations, public administration, sports, military, and so forth) represent what may be for some a disconcerting appreciation for the fluctuating and transforming view of the meaning of strategy. Evidence of epistemological frustration about "what strategy is" is widespread in various disciplines that entertain the concept.[13] Schön's (1963) theory of concept displacement teaches us that there can never be an answer to "what strategy is" as it is socially constructed and reconstructed to suit the needs of culture. It is not situations that are novel; it should be the meanings we ascribe to them. To the modernist, this conclusion would be exasperating (e.g. Martineau 1853, p. 5); hence, hundreds of journal articles have been published to attempt to reconcile a precise definition and process for strategizing. These efforts were and always will be inconclusive.

Alternatively, the interdisciplinary extensions of meaning that occur in the face of novel or emergent situations (in the context of business, international relations, public administration, sports, military, and so forth) represent a fluctuating and transforming, social constructionist view of strategy. Situations that are volatile, uncertain, and complex defy a stable causal science of military intervention, so the demands of modernism and the modernist's hope for progressive knowledge can never be met. To the constructionist, the epistemology of strategy is and always will be fluid and ambiguous. This admission, that the word strategy is always equivocal, becomes the constructionist's pathway toward frame reflexivity. Its ambiguity is embraced as this quality of equivocality permits circumstantial design of strategy's meaning.

Institutional Reflexivity. To reiterate, Schön (1963) offers that theories are rooted in the logics that metaphors provide. In institutions, base metaphors have widespread "rhetorical control" over the theoretical framing of situations as problems (Kilduff et al. 2011, p. 308). For institutions, "the origin of the confusion may lie in the inadequacy" of the metaphors by which they try and order phenomena (March and Olsen 1989, p. 12). Hence, the reflexivity process would explore the assumptive connections between the nonliteral logics imbedded in extended and displaced metaphors that drive theory construction in the institution. Military institutions that also link to metaphoric networks that Thomas S. Kuhn (1996) conceptualized as a "community of practitioners," cannot easily "step outside" the logic of the modernist-based metaphors that drive those paradigms (p. 5).[14]

What Oswald Spengler (1939, p. 238) calls "historical pseudomorphosis" blinds the institution to alternative paradigms—spirally referencing, reifications eventually create a narrow, homogeneous form of reasoning and what follows are the associated pitfalls of cognitive dissonance (Festinger 1957), groupthink (Janis 1991/1971), single-loop learning (Argyris and Schön 1980), the collapse of sensemaking (Weick 1993), and so forth.[15] The proposed cure is reflexivity—". . . an awareness of the situatedness of scientific knowledge and an understanding of the researcher and research community from which knowledge has appeared" (Hardy et al. 2001, p. 554). Institutional reflexivity is related to the idea of community members exercising practical skepticism about the esoteric knowledge and values that the institution would otherwise hold dear. A reflexive, postinstitutional, collective consciousness requires not only suspending belief in what may be dogmatic assertions but also admitting (humbly) that the institution can never know how to obtain positive knowledge. Initially frustrating to institutions that have been culturally situated in a positivistic epistemology, this more critical view may serve to emancipate the collective mind and stimulate searches for linguistic frames outside the otherwise assumed *esoteric boundaries*.[16] In the present case, the logic displaced from the literal work of the ancient Greek general has served as the metaphoric foundation for large-scale educational institutions of strategy, namely, the US war colleges.

As detailed in Chapter 1, without reflexivity, institutions tend to reify meanings—they objectify their perception of reality mindless of extended and displaced (i.e. dead) metaphors (Burrell and Morgan 1979, p. 266). In the case of US war colleges, the idea that education about war can be addressed at levels (or its Greek-rooted synonym, *strata*) feeds the reification of "levels of war" which are presently explained as tactical (lowest), operational (mid-range), and strategic (highest). Hence, entry-level officer education is molded around instruction in tactics, mid-range officer education is oriented on operations, and the more senior officers attend war colleges to study strategy. Logics related to levels also emerge and *Piagetian* constructs such as "officer development" follow the logic of strata—enlisted and junior officers (babies and children), mid-grade officers (adolescents) and high-ranking officers (adults and seniors).[17] The logic includes this sampling of taken-for-granted, Social-Darwinistic assumptions that a more reflexive institution may want to challenge:

- One cannot think strategically without advancing through the lower levels of development (i.e. the *recapitulation theory* of tactics and operations)[18];
- Only the senior-ranking officials who make it to the top of the food chain are empowered as "strategic leaders"; and

- The hierarchy of learning objectives that makes up military educational curricula needs to follow both the promotion system of "survival-of-the-fittest" and the levels of war.[19]

The assumption of the "ontogenetic pattern of cognitive development" is a modernist's fallacy that demands critical reflection (White 1978, p. 10).[20]

The Art of Reframing (and the Aesthetics of Appreciating the Frame). In that regard, Ray Holland (1999) defines "transdisciplinary reflexivity" as going beyond the traditional view of "unidisciplinary" logics and into multilevel reflexive analysis in order to fend off self-fulfilling prophecies and other confirmation biases (p. 466). Hence, paraphrasing his method, transdisciplinary reflexivity on the idea of strategy may include the following:

- Assume the knowledge of strategy is not subject to "scientific methods" (e.g. subject to rigorous natural science methodologies, such as reductionism and levels of analysis).
- Explore the interpretations of strategy-like terms from the view of other cultures, institutions, and/or knowledge disciplines (outside "strategic studies") and consider these other interpretations and symbolic meanings.
- Observe how disagreement with one's own institutional view of strategy (or arguing the view that "strategy does not exist" outside the institutional reification of the term) may result in social alienation of those who express those disagreements.[21]
- Notice when and if the practice of individual or rogue-group reflexivity about strategy is oppressed/suppressed by those more powerful members of any and all institutions that study strategy. After all, their positional power and rank may be an inseparable part of the hypostatized term (i.e. strategic concepts recapitulate and reinforce the existing organizational power distribution in the hierarchy) (p. 474).

As the institution becomes more receptive to institutional-reflexive activities, the critical and creative searches for alternative frames become more favorable in light of insider power politics (Schön and Rein 1994).[22] Openness to new meaning constructions across other, less familiar, knowledge disciplines may be a key to solving "the poverty of words available" when faced with unfamiliar or alien situations (Ricœur 1977, pp. 106–7). When members of the institution accept that "their" science of strategy involves the critical mindfulness of how the displacement of concepts works, a Kuhnian *paradigm shift* becomes not only seen as possible, but can be rigorously pursued and rewarded.[23] The meaning of strategy (now viewed, postinstitutionally, as an adaptive "meaning container") can be redesigned at will by projecting other frames of reference into it (Lakoff and Johnson 1980, p. 6). Alternatively, the word can be subjugated to other useful partial meaning-carriers (base metaphors) that can help frame or reframe problem settings.

A more reflexive military designer may concentrate efforts at finding creative ways to construct sensemakings about messy situations at hand and critically dismiss (at least temporarily) the institutionalized linguistics of strategy in search of other frames—even those that may be available from other cultures. For example, one promising extracultural view of Military Design is provided by French sinologist François Jullien (2004). Jullien carefully portrays the Greco-Western dominant contextualization of strategy as quite foreign to the logic, grammar, and rhetoric of Chinese Confucianism. In lieu of ends-based rationality, typically associated with a Greco-teleological view of strategy, the Chinese developed a very different way of reasoning that is opportunistic (reminiscent of a Heraclitean "in-the-flow" ontology) and reflects the dynamic "competing balance" (e.g. *ying* and *yang*) view of time, space, and knowledge.[24] Whereas Clausewitz illustrated the metaphor of "friction" as walking in water, the Chinese perspective contextualizes very differently: "[Water] has no constant shape. There is nothing softer and weaker than water, yet nothing is more penetrating and capable of attacking the hard and strong" (Lai 2004, p. 4). The idea shifts from struggling against the power of water and learning to flow with its power. Eastern cultures tend to find more meaning in verbs (balancing, flowing, time as a stream) than Westerners who think in terms of nouns (categories, generalizations, and a point-in-time sense of stability) (Nisbett 2003, pp. 148–53). Perhaps "strategizing-in-action" may reflect the same contrast to the idea of *having* a strategy (the noun).

Institutional reflexivity may also seek sources of reframing outside a reified metaphoric network of meanings, outside the normal participants that have otherwise exchanged and fed each other extensions and displacements of the root metaphor of strategy. For example, the Santa Fe Institute (SFI) is expressly founded for "multidisciplinary collaborations . . . of complex adaptive systems [that are] critical to addressing key environmental, technological, biological, economic, and political challenges" (Santa Fe Institute 2011). Here, the dominant metaphor is derived from the logics and rhetoric of subatomic sciences which spawned the relatively new interdisciplinary science of complexity. At SFI, strategy is hardly a mentionable idiom and instead the concepts of "perpetual novelty" and "endlessly unfolding surprise" are key extensions of the original complex subatomic phenomena that serve as base metaphors (Waldrop 1992, p. 147 and p. 165). At SFI, rather than focusing on the romantic hope of the empowered "strategic leader" who, with "strategic vision and strategic planning", achieves the nation's "strategic end state", attention may shift to extended metaphors of complexity—such as those associated with "emergence" and "self-organizing systems".[25]

The purpose of the more reflexive, design-of-meaning approach,[26] involving searches for multidisciplinary and multi-institutional frames is not to seek "the best answer". Ideally, the military designer stays open to multiple frames, triangulating on the novel situation at hand and never expecting closure (Woolgar 1988). Some traditional military practitioners and researchers may complain that this openness to designing frames with multiple metaphoric bases is an impractical eclecticism and is the prerogative of college professors who observe intractable social messes from a safe distance and produce this kind of academic solipsism. After all, how can one extract a utilitarian art associated with institutional reflexivity and the continuous search for multiple metaphoric frames such as from humanities, the fine arts perspectives, or chaoplexity?

Two researchers, Haridimos Tsoukas and Mary Jo Hatch (2001), compare what they refer to as the *logicoscientific* frame, to strategizing with a reframing method using the verisimilitude of *narratology*—the art of storytelling (recall a similar approach from the Chapter 2 part addressing "Stories"). From this perspective, strategy-making would involve interpreting situations by generating multiple "in equivalent descriptions":

> [A] narrative approach to complexity theory suggests our understanding of complex systems and their properties will always be grounded in the narratives we construct about them. When we characterize initial conditions as perturbations of a system, we construct the beginning of a plot (the system is a character or protagonist and the perturbation is a situation or antagonist) that may conclude with the system moving off in a direction that is surprising. As with unpredictable characters in other stories or in life, the complex system is interpreted as volatile or capricious. When the multiple interactions of systemic behavior in complex systems produce emergent (new) modes of behavior, in narrative terms the plot thickens, the characters develop. To put this more reflexively, when we theorize about complexity, we narrate (p. 1007).

Conceiving of "strategy as storytelling" could lead to a qualitative renaissance in military science and offer a way to explore frames toward postinstitutional Military Design. The idea is to produce more skepticism in debates over applications of modernist views of strategy and reflect more critically on the emergent phenomena associated with military interventions. The same can be said of the value of deconstructing the military modernist conceptualization of leadership (that would include the institutionalized, modernist view of leadership).

Part 2. Frame reflection on leadership

Gen. John Allen, the top U.S. commander in Afghanistan . . . told Pentagon reporters that he is reviewing the command climate of Staff Sgt. Robert Bales' unit in southern Afghanistan. Bales has been charged with 17 counts of premeditated murder, accused of walking away from the base on possibly two occasions on the same night, and gunning down [local Afghan] men, women and nine children while they slept in their beds. . . . Allen said that . . . there may have been leadership failures during this and other recent incidents. . . .

LOLITA BALDOR, 2012,
Associated Press Release

This concept of leadership is founded in the feudal touchstone of citizenship: one's relationship with one's king. This relationship implies several assumptions: (a) that the king deserves allegiance by virtue of rank, (b) that there is a natural, hierarchical difference in status, intelligence, and ability, (c) and that the subject's role is to serve the king's wishes. Consequently, leadership scholars tend to assume that anyone who holds a supervisory position is a leader, that supervisors necessarily have abilities and traits that set them apart from subordinates, and that moral behavior is defined by productivity.

RICHARD A. BARKER,
"How Can We Train Leaders if We Do Not Know What Leadership Is?"

Gary Gemmill and Judith Oakley (1992) sum up their critical review of research on the modernist leadership paradigm as follows:

> We further argue that the major significance of most recent studies on leadership is not to be found in their scientific validity but in their function in offering ideological support for the existing social order. The idea of a leadership elite explains in a Social Darwinistic manner why only certain members of a social system are at the apex of power and entitled to a proportionably greater share of the social wealth. So-called leader traits are woven into a powerful social myth, which while serving to maintain the status quo, also paradoxically sows the seeds of its own destruction by accentuating helplessness, mindlessness, emotionlessness, and meaninglessness. The social myth around leaders serves to program life out of people (non-leaders) who, with the social lobotomization, appear as cheerful robots. It is our contention that the myth making around the concept of leadership is, as [Warren] Bennis asserts, an unconscious conspiracy, or social hoax, aimed at maintaining the status quo (p. 115).

While I do not wholly reject these writers' rather nihilistic conspiracy theory about leadership, I do advocate taking a multiple-views position (as I did with the concept of strategy) in that leadership is a socially constructed concept that has evolved from a (now) dead metaphor. Schön (1963) brings his theory of displaced concepts to light in his example of how the Western theory of leadership evolved. Originally, leadership was "displaced from theories of travel, passage, or directed movement from one place to another" and not just limited to the human species (p. 66). Note how transpositions of the travel concept take us to conceptually link the following concrete intimations of human leadership in the abstract: go first, destination, location, guide, path, road to, sidetracked, direct, indirect, follow, explore, point-A-to-point-B, and so on. Abstract extensions from the travel metaphor may include answering these sorts of questions:

- Is it better for a leader to *sail* the organization or *powerboat* the organization on its journey?
- How can we *change the direction* of the organization?
- What is the desired *end*?
- Can we publish a *road map* to get to our destination?
- Should "strategic" leaders have a *vision* further out than their followers can see (to the point that followers succumb to their *super-vision*)?

These questions have become hypotheses that countless modernist-oriented theorists have used to replace the original, concrete idea of leadership as a function of purposeful travel. Today, the modernist institutionalization of military leadership continues to be extended and displaced in the ways of an illusory positive science to the point leadership (like strategy) has become hypostatized.

As Western institutions that extended and displaced leadership from the concept of follower dependencies in traveling through unknown territory, they may miss the important metaphysical extended meanings (aesthetic and emotional) of social relationships. This linear view of leadership shaped how the modernist institution developed a metanarrative (Lyotard 1984) that prejustifies actions (as would a manipulated "independent variable" to affect "dependent variables" in an empirical science experiment). When faced with novelty in military interventions: figuratively "line up" behind the leader as s/he leads the rest forward in time and space through an undesirable start of a complex military intervention and path-find into a more desirable end. Leadership becomes synonymous with officers-in-charge (commanders, platoon/section "leaders," etc.) with the institutional heroic expectation that those in positions of authority "lead the troops." There is perhaps no better cultural artifact to demonstrate this belief than the US Army Infantry's "Follow Me!" statue located in Fort Benning, Georgia (Figure 3.2).

With this Schönian metaphoric displacement in mind, we can pay some attention to the potential impact of the postinstitutional view of military leadership with respect to design philosophy; rephrased, what is a more flexible leadership model in the context of a more reflexive philosophy for Military Design? Here, I would like to again invoke the multiple viewpoints approach and speak to the social construction of leadership. Several authors

FIGURE 3.2 *"Follow Me" Statue at Fort Benning, Georgia* (Department of the Army photo by John D. Helms).

have attempted to reconstruct leadership—offering an existential challenge to traditional views. The purpose henceforth is to summarize alternative frames of leadership by three noteworthy authors, which are arguably very important to the postinstitutional pursuit of mindfulness: Ron Heifetz of Harvard University, Donna Ladkin of Cranfield University, and Keith Grint of Warwick University (and formerly of the Shrivenham Defense Academy). The remainder of this section will explore the impacts of leadership reframed by these authors with the intent to spur institutional reflexivity.

Interestingly, Ron Heifetz, in his 1994 book *Leadership Without Easy Answers*, does not use any version of the word "follower" throughout his 348 pages of text. His thesis is that *leaders help others lead themselves* through difficult, complex, and even life-threatening circumstances—leaders beget self-leaders and coleaders. His principal argument is that leadership is not about knowing where to go (as the root metaphor suggests), but is adaptive work that occurs where technical definitions and known solutions are inappropriate. The implications are clear for the institution: if one is not dealing in adaptive work when faced with unique, novel, and complex situations, one is engaged in something else other than leadership.

Adaptive work, according to Heifetz, involves influencing others away from learned dependence on formal authority or what he calls *authoritative response* (p. 87).[27] An undesirable feature of the more traditional way of framing leadership is that it creates inappropriate reliance on formal sources of authority where others are not motivated to discover or create solutions because they are inculcated to rely on the superordinate to lead them. In other words, the military modernist view is that leadership is a kind of technology that troops rely on for dependable guidance. Here is an extract from a US Air Force doctrine on leadership epitomizing leadership as a "force-development process" (i.e. technology is the underpinning logic):

> Leaders do not appear fully developed out of whole cloth. A maturation must occur to allow the young leaders to grow into the responsibilities required of senior institutional leaders and commanders. This force development process provides leadership focus at all levels in an Airman's career. The expeditionary Air Force requires leaders who can take warfighting to the highest possible level of success in support of our national security objectives. Those leaders can only be created through an iterative process of development involving education, training, and expeditionary operations seasoned with experience and ongoing mentoring by more experienced leaders. The end result is an individual capable of successfully operating as a leader at all levels anywhere, anytime (Department of the Air Force 2006, p. iii).

This learned dependency serves as a constraint when adaptivity is needed. Heifetz's alternative view challenges the values, attitudes, and habits that comprise the modernist's proclivity to see leadership (much like Gemmill and Oakley 1992) as a socially demanded fostering of follower dependency. Heifetz argues that the preferred purpose of leadership is to lessen dependence (i.e. to devolve dependency), promoting more freedom of action in individuals, groups, and organizations especially when faced with novel, highly complex, and uncertain situations.

Instead of authoritative response being the currency of leadership, reorienting the attention of others on *creative deviance* becomes the important aspect of leaders' work. Hence in a postinstitutional reframing, deviating in spite of formal authority displaces the modernist, technical mindset of following the leader with formal authority (Heifetz 1994, p. 187). From this perspective, leadership is provocative in nature—spurring the debate while not resolving it ("with no heat, nothing cooks") (p. 106). Postinstitutional leadership is about helping change the meaning for action in others (Pondy 1978; Pfeffer 1981; Smircich and Morgan 1982; Hunt 1984; Fairhurst and Sarr 1996). In Heifetz's terms, a "sense of purpose is not the same as a clearly defined purpose", and the former (purposeful sensibility) is more efficacious under complex conditions than the modernist ethic that leaders are supposed to provide clarity of purpose and clear guidance (1994, p. 274). While the difference may first appear subtle, on deeper reflection, this argument reflects the paradigm shift demanded by novelty (leadership draws attention to the unsurely) that is, away from modernism (where leadership is expected to authoritatively provide surety).

Figure 3.3 presents my modified version Heifetz's situational typology, designed to consider the military context.[28] Note the continuum between

Situation Type	Frame	Course of Action	Primary locus of action
TYPE I (seen this before)	Modernism	Clear	Commanders, Officers, or Noncommissioned Officers
TYPE II (there is some resemblance to the past)	Somewhat novel	Perhaps Knowable, but Requires Learning	More Participatory
TYPE III (cannot make sense of this situation)	Multiple Frames	Requires imaginative deviance	Group-Discursive

FIGURE 3.3 *Heifetzian Leadership Situations.*

technical work (associated with "Type I" situations) and adaptive work (with Type "III" situations). In Type I situations, it is possible for the commander to employ institutionalized knowledge (or "competency mapping", further explored in the next chapter) that includes the authoritatively decisive, rational-analytic decision-making models (e.g. incorporating the ORSA process described in previous chapters—that are replicated in the US Marine Corps' Decision-Making Process, US Army's Military Decision-Making Process and Troop Leading Procedure, and the US Joint Operations Planning Process) to define the problem and decide the best course of action.

Type II situations may offer partial familiarity in problem definition while designing approaches to them seem indeterminable—they call for more critical inquiry, creation of divergent knowledge, and contextual development. Type III situations defy both problem identification and the quest for preplanned courses of action. As we move along the scale from Type I to Type III, authoritative direction must shift away from relying on those in formal military positions of authority to a more dispersed power arrangement. The troops who are immersed in the complexity of the situation must craft ways while *reflecting-in-action* (Schön 1983). Reflection-in-action differs from a modernist's technological view of leadership. In the postinstitutional military, reflection would connote an effort to creatively deviate from top-down attempts to centralize actions called "theater strategies" or "campaign plans" or "specified tasks" contained in orders sent down from the higher headquarters.

Juxtaposing this (the idea of reflection-in-action), modern military science assumes readiness to act is a function of *knowing-in-action* (efficacious only in Heifetzian Type I situations). Postinstitutional Military Design would involve more creative than technical approaches for Type II and especially for

Type III situations. The leadership context requires emergence of *craftwork* (open to aesthetic appreciations, get a feel for, or tacit, or intuitive, learning) and less so modernist preconceived theories of action (a.k.a. doctrine). This differentiation again highlights the postinstitutional ethic: "Humbly, I may have to act to creatively deviate from assimilative knowledge about what to do" as differentiated from the modernist's: "I know authoritatively what we must do."

To create situations for honest and open dialogue (required by the Heifetzian design approach to epistemology, where new sensemakings are explored), commanders and others given formal authority should refrain from an angry reaction from their annoyance by such deviant actions. In that regard, creative deviance can come across as insubordination characterized by the uncomfortable ethics of questioning or ignoring calls for authoritative response. Particularly in Type III situations, Heifetz asserts that "Deviants may become the best source of leadership" (p. 271).

The military modernist institutional form of authoritative response may be ineffective and even *iatrogenic*.[29] The proposition of adaptive work may serve the shared sense of purpose with troops in the field who are acting, crafting, and being inventive about their learning in what constitutes smaller, unique, localized military interventions (i.e. they engage in creative deviance). Traditional forms of campaign planning (higher headquarters' top-down efforts to link and orchestrate large-scale military interventions among subordinate units) may actually squelch the necessarily unique learning strategies going on in these localized interventions. In Type III situations, a postinstitutional design philosophy at the local level better serves the *emergent* nature of the complex intervention effort than would attempts to integrate design efforts at the traditional, authoritative, higher-level headquarters.

Ironic to the modernist military institution, nonconformism becomes the postinstitutional ethic of leadership. From this perspective, leadership is dispersed, heterarchical, and linked primarily by common values and a sense of committed purpose. Instead of directing operations, those in positions of formal authority would instead seek to provide resources to these diverse and disperse localities of *action learning*.[30] For example, in dealing with a wide diversity of localized settings, the combined-joint task force headquarters orients on supporting the many divergent activities of troops operating as adaptive leaders in various locations. The work of deviant leadership in each locality is uniquely adaptive to the context at hand. This point provides a good segue to Donna Ladkin's (2010) reframing of the leadership concept.

Complementary to Ron Heifetz's view of this sort of emergent leadership, Ladkin's phenomenological approach to leadership is nontraditional, at least with respect to the modern military institution.[31] In her book, *Rethinking Leadership: A New Look at Old Leadership Questions*, Ladkin presents leadership as a social phenomenon that cannot be separated from the unique context from which it emerges. Her argument may startle those who have framed leadership around desired qualities usually sought from those institutionally endowed with authoritative rank and position (e.g. the modernist model). With her framework, people and purpose (what is leadership for?) interact with the socially interpreted *historicity* (i.e. the context). These create unique dynamic and treat undesirable conditions as a *leadership moment*.

For Ladkin, the essence of leadership is a socially relational undertaking especially in highly complex situations where purpose may be fuzzy; hence, reality is created through a social-interactive process.[32] When context and purpose are sensed to be "right" for the situation at hand (negotiated by parties involved), this constitutes the leadership moment, implying that "right" may be ephemeral (p. 178). As with Heifetz's argument, the traditional roles of leader-follower become blurred as more participants are interactively involved. The meaning-making becomes more networked, with the leader role shifting around the group, serving as a hub for facilitating co-constructed meanings-for-action (p. 181).

The implications of such an alternative view of leadership with respect to complex military operations could serve postinstitutionalism. For example, this perspective may also call into question the traditional oligarchic military organizational values associated with positional authority and military rank. As with Heifetz's explanation, knowledge displacement and creation of new knowledge are viewed as critical to reframing situations in a much more democratic fashion. The idea of an inverted campaign (the upside-down hierarchy) seems well supported by Ladkin's phenomenological version of leadership. Leadership is reframed away from authoritative values and more toward decentralized and participative values (those most closely linked with a postinstitutional approach to Military Design). Operational strategies emerge from localities. Yet, this should not preclude the situationally driven need for other forms of officership that may call for central direction and hierarchical accountability—as suggested next by Grint (2008).

Keith Grint is a prolific writer who advocates multiple views of leadership and often uses military historic case studies as the basis of his reconceptualizations of leadership. In one of his books, *Leadership, Management and Command: Rethinking D-Day*, he presents a circumstantial framework in the military context largely based on what leadership is not—that is, it is neither command nor management. As with Heifetz's and Ladkin's, Grint's view is a hard departure from the military modernist convention that sees the commander as a synonym for leader. For one thing, Grint sees command, management, and leadership as representing different sources of authority.

As a relationalist, as are Heifetz and Ladkin, Grint tries to flesh-out leadership based on the meaning of the context at hand. Leading takes place when commanding (ordering others what immediately needs to be done) and managing (the efficient allocating of resources) not only do not work but may interfere with effectiveness especially under very complex and ambiguous circumstances. Grint's argument, based on a historic case study of the Allied invasion of Europe in June 1944, is that when undertaking complex military interventions it takes all the three factors (command, leadership, and management) to be successful. The trick is to intuit what is the proper balance while not given the advantage of time and geography of one's choosing. Hence, Grint's argument is supported through retrospection on perhaps one of the most complicated campaigns of World War II—the June 1944 invasion of Normandy.

According to Grint, Command is something associated with *speed* of decision-making and the *critical* need to do or not to do something even if the commander is likely to be wrong. The source of power for command is *fear*—through the legitimization of coercion and compliance. Command is politically *autocratic* (hierarchical and coercive) in that it requires obedience (in its most extreme form, execution of tasks without question).

Grint's view of management (or what the modernist military may term "logistics and administration") is associated with deliberate planning (note the meaning of the term when hyphenated: "de-liberate"), rule-setting, process engineering, and rationally derived resource allocation decisions to handle *tame* or recurrent problems that have been solved before (similar to what Heifetz calls Type 1 situations). Keys to management are institutionalized bureaucratic and technocratic political values believed to govern order and efficiency of military readiness and the sustainment of military interventions. The source of power for management is regulated by legal-rational rules and procedures.

Leadership, according to Grint, is associated with wicked (in Heifetzian terms "Type III") situations that make command iatrogenic and managerial forms of technical rationality problematic. Whether the situation is diagnosed as time-critical, tame, or wicked should drive whether to exercise autocratic command, technocratic management, or leadership and, as Grint concludes, the complexity of the situation may demand elements of all the three—and it is an art form to properly blend them. The key source of political power for leadership is democratic in nature in that it comes from those who, through intellect, intuition, and emotion, choose to act and reflect-in-action when faced with indeterminacy. Figure 3.4 is my hybrid adaptation of a combined (Heifetz-Ladkin-Grint) model.[33] Note that the situation drives which values should dominate; hence, whether to exercise authoritative response (command, manage) or facilitate creative deviance (leadership) would be based on *appreciative judgment* (Vickers 1965).[34]

This part has argued that three authors (Heifetz, Ladkin, and Grint) offer a nontraditional view of leadership that is complementary to postinstitutional Military Design. The implications of Grint's view on Military Design are not quite as radical as Ladkin's or Heifetz's; yet, these views permit

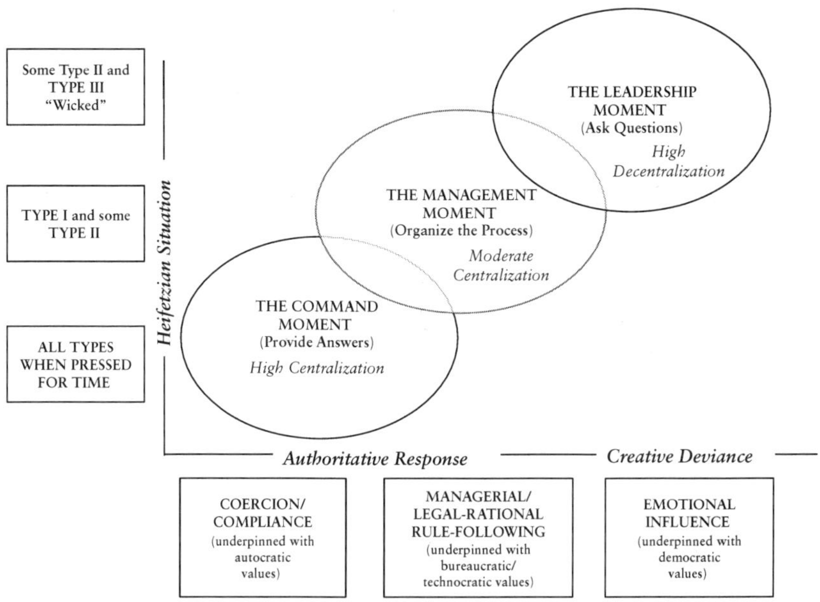

FIGURE 3.4 *A Hybrid Model of Situations and Sources of Authority.*

multiple, simultaneous perspectives. While Heifetz's and Ladkin's existential constructions of leadership are compatible with Grint's model, Grint adds two other important militant forms of social control—command and management. Synthesizing their views, there are several considerations for furthering a postinstitutional Military Design agenda.

Given the opportunity to reframe the concept of leadership, I speculate that a postinstitutional response to modernist views of leadership may be either rare or hidden. Consider that leadership (framed around *sui generis* and democratic values) is often overpowered by structuring obstructive dependencies on institutional forms of authoritative command and management. Postinstitutional reframings of leadership can be flexible enough to challenge autocratic and technocratic values associated with *authoritative response* and seek to equalize them with more plural values that guide organizations-in-action and more associated with *creative deviance*. A postinstitutional reframing would also recognize that dialogical sessions inherent to the professional practice of Military Design require innovative forms of knowledge creation—where rank and positional authority associated with command and management may have to be "left at the door." Leadership is not defined in a plurality, but by individual aesthetics, as a personal relationship in the moment and in context—***leadership is "I"; command and management is "we."***[35] The need to reframe military situations as *problems of decisiveness* (associated with command) and/or *planning problems* (associated with management and addressed in the next part) should be extended to include framing them with less traditional emphases—as problems of postinstitutional forms of Military Design (associated more with the uniqueness of human relationship and the appreciation for creative deviance).

Part 3. Frame reflection on planning

Planning concerns man's efforts to make the future in his own image. If he loses control of his own destiny, he fears being cast into the abyss. Alone and afraid, man is at the mercy of strange and unpredictable forces, so he takes whatever comfort he can by challenging the fates. He shouts his plans into the storm of life. Even if all he hears is the echo of his own voice, he is no longer alone. To abandon his faith in planning would unleash the terror locked in him.

AARON WILDAVSKY,
If Planning is Everything Maybe It's Nothing

In this apparently postmodern age, planning seems to be entering its post-rational period: Rationality has become a bad word. Rational planning is commonly associated with misplaced scientism, overweening technocracy, and self-serving professionalism. Rationality is said to mean a narrow instrumental focus on means, unwarranted empiricism, and spurious objectivity based on purported facts that deconstruction reveals as either foolish class- or culture- based prejudices or manipulative partisan deceit. Linked to specialized expertise, rationality seems to reject nonscientific or subjective knowledge: personal, societal, or human values, individual intuition and common sense, socially and culturally constructed cognition, and imaginative vision.

ERNEST R. ALEXANDER,
Rationality Revisited

The origin of the word, plan, comes from Latin *planus*, which means flat surface or table-like platform. The word (both a noun and a verb) evolved from the original meaning associated with a drawing made on that flat surface; hence, plan signifies the man-made image, sketch, or diagram devised for future action that leads to something desirable. Indeed, imbedded in the logic and rhetoric of planning is the causal assumption derived from modern teleology of architectural engineering—the more detailed the design (the blueprint), the more likely one will have a quality, purposeful result (the future product).[36] In modern military science, the art of planning has come to represent the architectural-like process and product of Military Design. The belief (PLAN = DESIGN) is so institutionalized as to become the *raison d'être* of modern military staffs. In the military context, the zone of analogy extended from architecture includes the art of design for a future "construction" (in modernist terms, tactical, operational, or strategic art) as well as a detailed and complicated schedule of requisite tasks (that are the ingredients of a tactical, operational or strategic plan) that will lead to the completed, aesthetically pleasing "building" (i.e. the tactical mission, operation, or strategy accomplished).

Displacing the architectural metaphor into the military context, the "materials" (logistics) and "subcontractors with tools" (differentiated military units) for "construction" (operations) of the "building" (the ends of the military plan) are designed by the "chief architect" (the commander). Also contained in the displaced metaphor of architecture, the principal design focus of modern military science is *mission analysis*, that is, the breaking down of military interventions into *tasks* (to-do lists). Once identified, the tasks are phased over eventual time into a military plan and their forecasted synchronized performance serves as the blueprint for success.

The borrowed architectural logic of mission analysis appears quite rational to the modern military mindset as commanders and staffs can face difficult military interventions by (1) deconstructing them into smaller, definable problems; (2) figuring out what tasks need to be performed to address each of them; (3) dividing those tasks among subordinate units who, in turn, do the same down the line (from the "strategic" level to the individual trooper); and, (4) by controlling and the performance of linkages among these units (the "plan"), the overall goal is reached.

Modern military doctrinaires have named these cumulative linkages of tasks *logical lines of operation* or *lines of effort* signifying that the intermediate levels' (such as theater and joint task force headquarters) job one is to manage linkages between the allocated tasks at lower echelons of command and higher-order tasks that ultimately comprise the highest national and coalition policy agendas (e.g. Department of Defense 2011b). On its surface, the architectural logic is quite seductive, especially to those who like to measure their way to success as would architects, building contractors, landscape designers, and civil engineers (using degrees of completion, performance metrics, and so forth). The entire modernist approach to planning is metaphorically based on the architectural design of tasks (Alexander 1986).[37] Figure 3.5 illustrates how the architectural design metaphor has dominated modernist infatuation with planning—as if tasks were children's building blocks.

Indeed, one version of this *Universal Joint Task List* (UJTL) is an astonishing 1,080-page document describing thousands of pre-engineered tasks, each with standards of performance (similar to building codes in American cities) (e.g. Department of Defense 2002). The purpose of the proclaimed "authoritative" list is stated as follows:

> The Universal Joint Task List (UJTL) serves as a menu of tasks in a common language, which serve as the foundation for capabilities-based planning across the range of military operations. The UJTL will support

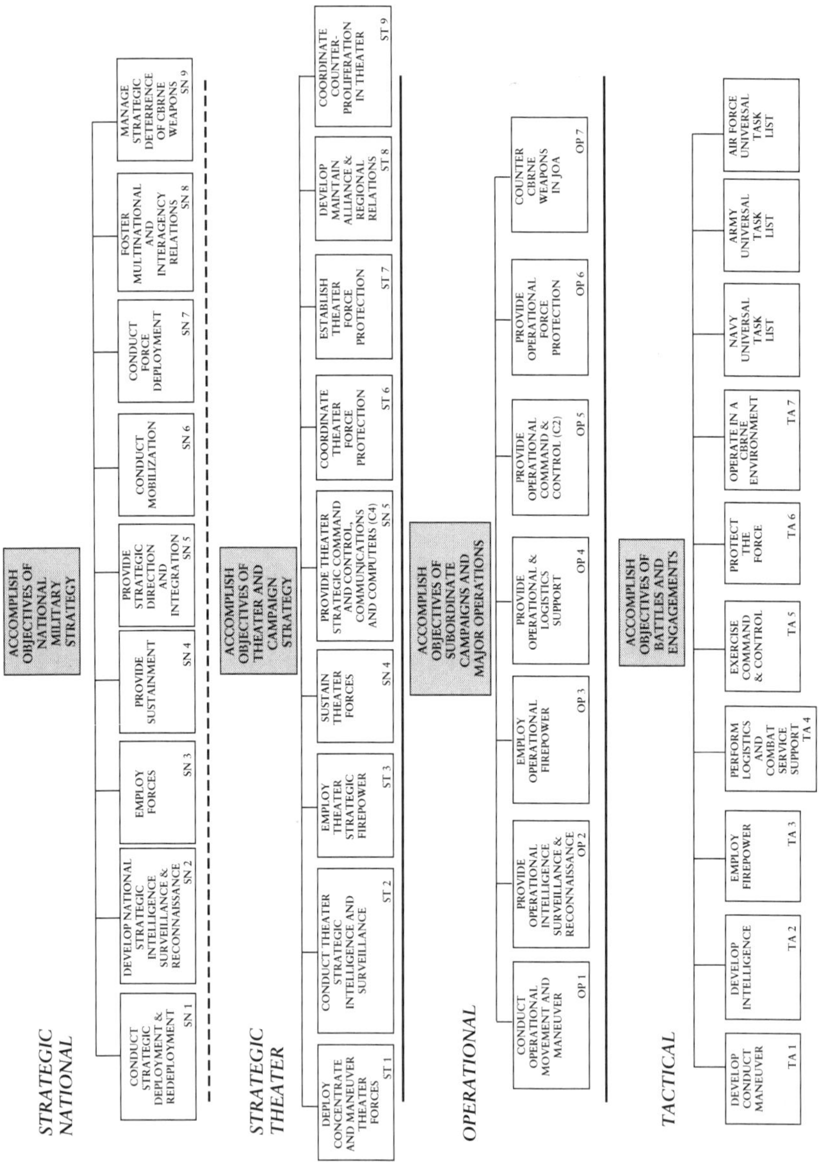

FIGURE 3.5 *The Architectural Structure of Joint Forces Tasks (Department of Defense 2002, p. B-A-3).*

DOD in joint capabilities-based planning, joint force development, readiness reporting, experimentation, joint training and education, and lessons learned. It is the basic language for development of a joint mission essential task list (JMETL) or agency mission essential task list (AMETL) used in identifying required capabilities for mission success (paraphrased from p. A-1).

The list has been incorporated into a web-based computer program from which Defense agencies may use to develop their individualized lists of tasks, complete with preordained measures of performance (a.k.a. metrics). Each service department is required to publish a more detailed accounting of tasks that support these tasks (in the US Army's case, down to the soldier level). There is a classified version as well. In my terms, this represents an incredibly elaborate "architectural rationalization of military intervention," and my intent is to criticize this *modern-extremist* approach hopefully to the point of revealing the myths at work.[38]

The first teleological myth is that all human work is of the same nature, that is, work can be broken into tasks and are a matter of scientific technique.[39] Charles Perrow (1967, 1986) developed a typology of tasks that challenges this assumption. Comparable to the tasks performed by auto assembly line workers, Perrow (1986) calls the first kind *routine tasks*, characterized by the bureaucratic ideals of "specialization, formalization of authority, standardization, and hierarchy" (p. 274). Next are the more complicated *engineering tasks* that involve planning organized capabilities over time and in various, tightly coupled combinations. Some tasks are somewhat unpredictable and require some improvisation; hence, Perrow called these that address the third-order of complexity, *craftwork*, characterized by the creative use or artful modification of already available routine or engineering tasks. The most complex tasks (unpredictable and radically improvisational) are those that are *nonroutine*. Here are more specific descriptions of each kind of task:

- *Routine*: These are tasks that technology has solved and can be judged to a decided standard. They have to be observable, reproducible, and improvable—like a manufacturing assembly line. In the military context, conducting a marksmanship range is a good example. For routine tasks, process engineering and performance metrics work very well (e.g. did you hit your target or not?).
- *Engineering*: These tasks are more complicated in that they involve detailed planning as would development of an architectural blueprint for a building and all the required materials, construction workers and their tools that come together, synchronized in time and space. A good military example is a Military Design developed in steps derived from ORSA science: (1) The *definition of the problem* and the determination of the

means of measuring its critical elements; (2) The *collection of data* (either by direct observation, the use of historical data, or the use of computer-generated data); (3) The *analysis of the collected data* (using both mathematical and nonmathematical methods); (4) The *determination of conclusions* based on the analysis of the collected data; and (5) The *recommendation* to the military decision-maker of a course of action [compete with tasks listed] designed to correct or improve weapons and equipment, organization, doctrine, strategy, or policy (Shrader 2006, p. v). Here, analysis and metrics (that serve as standards for judgment for a particular operation) work relatively well (you'll know when you are "winning" by measuring task effectiveness), but can be spoiled by unforeseen variables (such as weather, etc.); hence, contingency branch plans and phased sequels are also planned as hedges against uncertainty.

Routine and engineering tasks are developed as listed in the US Defense Department's UJTL described above and in the ORSA planning process described in Chapter 2. The following two types of tasks are unique and unpredictable—not conducive to planning:

- *Craftwork*: This sort of task involves artful actions and the accompanying aesthetic qualities of doing something rather new, unique, or novel within the same general category of work. Technical standards are not possible and the adage "I'll know it is 'right' when I feel it" applies. For example, a mixed context (say the US military in support of the Federal Emergency Management Agency) may involve on-the-scene investigative work in addressing something that has not quite been seen before but looks relatively familiar—like a previous disaster relief operation. For these sorts of tasks-in-progress, analysis and use of metrics can become quite problematic because each situation is so unique and morphs over time; hence, if task performance can be measured, it is done so in retrospect and that measure will not apply in future craftwork (so standardization of metrics is implausible).
- *Nonroutine*: Here, the troops are faced with something so novel that we do not have a standard language structure to "frame" the situation into a definable problem, so even craftwork is not sufficient. These usually involve complex, appreciative judgments, action learning, and generative metaphors. In military contexts, this may call for dealing in situational ethics as very complex situations may be characterized with a multitude of "competing values"—such as whether to detain an Afghan poppy farmer and whether to burn his crop. The situation may involve highly contextual and localized activities that the institutional skill set one has developed is not appropriate and may be in fact iatrogenic. These situations are "wicked" and hence a planned task structure is unknowable and is usually made sense of in retrospect (not

with prospective theories of action). Yet, with respect to leadership-as-deviance, the troops must reflect-in-action as the situation emerges, and command-like and management-like authoritative responses are not able to tell them what to do. The collectively exercise appreciative judgment as they act, finding new meaning in the situation. The troops immerse themselves in the moment and act in order to inform their next act (a.k.a. *muddling through*) (Lindblom 1959). Performance metrics are nonsensical in these cases and participants must rely on *successive limited comparisons* to gain a sense of accomplishment or failure in small increments. Adapted from Lindblom's (1959) view of muddling through, the successive limited comparisons characteristics for military interventions are very different from the ORSA approach and would include: (1) one cannot separate political values from the needed actions in military interventions (they are "closely intertwined"); (2) the means and ends dichotomy usually used in military planning yet they are not distinct so it is inappropriate to think they are; (3) The test of a "good" military course of action is that flag officers and their civilian political superiors may agree on what to do without agreeing that it is the most appropriate means to the agreed objective; (4) Analysis is limited as alternative values, courses of action, and outcomes are neglected; and (5) Small, incremental actions greatly reduce reliance on theory, hedge against being wrong, and focus attention on what is happening now in comparison to what was recently before.

Armed with Perrow's typology of tasks, one can envision "what to do" only through preordained framings of military campaigning primarily oriented on the machinated design of routine and engineering tasks. Here, the architectural model of military tasks for planned intervention is an appropriate theory of action fallaciously based on the architectural metaphor imbedded in the modern military science of planning. Mission analysis, a modernist reductionist process to determine the hierarchy of routine and engineering tasks that, when well defined and well controlled, is believed to encompass the whole mission. Under this modernist paradigm, even national policy is envisioned with unsupportable clarity as the synthesis of rolled-up routine and engineering tasks to be performed by "task forces" to achieve them; hence, individual and tactical tasks can be rolled up into operational tasks which can, in turn, be rolled up into the superset of strategic tasks.[40] Interpret this narrative describing the routinized and engineered planned tasks of Military Design using the 1942 Allied invasion of North Africa "Operation Torch" plan (Eisenhower 1948)[41]:

In modern war, battle areas frequently extend over hundreds of miles of front and are equally extensive in depth. Throughout such a theater are combat troops, replacement camps, hospital centers, lines of

> communication, repair shops, depots, ports, and a myriad of service organizations, both air and ground. . . . All these units, individuals and activities must be carefully controlled, so that everything is coordinated toward the achievement of the commander's strategic plan . . . The military methods and machinery for making and waging war have become so extraordinarily complex and intricate that high commanders must have gargantuan staffs for control and direction . . . the teams and staffs through which the modern commander absorbs information and exercises his authority must be a beautifully interlocked, smooth-working mechanism (pp. 74–5).

Compare this machine-like image to the perplexing narrative of the 1964–65 Vietnam War pacification planning which assumed the many hallmarks of the desirable routinization and engineering of tasks. Note how "metrics" served as a sort of anxiety reduction mechanism, mimicking an ideal objective "truth," never acknowledging this was an exercise in wishful planning (FitzGerald 1972):

> Of course there were always new approaches, new "concepts" in pacification. This year it was a "rethinking" of the [Civil Operations and] Revolutionary Development program. After the failures of 1966, the CIA decided to call back the RD cadre to give them a month more of retraining: a month more, but this time, so the officials said, the program would succeed. To measure the success more accurately, Robert Komer, now chief of the entire RD program, developed, with the help Secretary McNamara, a new evaluation system using computers and multiple choice questionnaires. After explaining with logic and clarity how the Hamlet Evaluation System worked, he said modestly that it was not a perfect system, but that it was an improvement over its predecessors. And he was undoubtedly correct: the only uncertainty was what was being measured. . . . It was enough, perhaps, that the new system convinced the American public that 67 per cent of the Vietnamese population lived under government control, and that figure represented a gain of 4.8 per cent over the year before. . . . When Ambassadors Porter or Komer announced that x per cent of the population was pacified, the New York Times reporter . . . never once asking what "pacification" meant or whether indeed it was the right thing for the United States to be doing in Vietnam (pp. 340–1).

Craftwork and nonroutine tasks are developed in *local contexts* and *each is unique*.[42] Here, institutional hierarchies associated with authoritative response are incapable of commanding or managing tasks at the local levels because neither the commanders nor managers can know what needs to be done. In such complex conditions, tasks are better typed as craftwork or emergent because these types require higher echelons of command (or better said "management") to admit ignorance. Listen to this testimony from a US Army planner during his tour in Afghanistan:

> In order to do a real Design effort we would have had to have brought in some practitioners and asked them for input (as well as become practitioners to some extent ourselves- and put practitioners on our Design team), then asked them to go out and try a few of our ideas, shaped some kind of feedback mechanism, and then re-shaped our views and future activities based on those mechanisms. And we would have had to be constantly adapting both our own structure as well as recommending changes to the command's structure and the structure of the teams we were sending out. In other words, a "full" Design effort would have meant action—not just "planning" (Martin 2011, p. 12).

At best, the institutionalized hierarchy serves to provide values-based context and the resources in support of the localities (what historian Robert Wiebe 1967, called "island communities").[43] Postinstitutional approaches to Military Design are based on localized action learning and are inherent to a dynamic, action-learning practice. Troops artfully invent tasks in small increments as they become immersed in situations requiring the appreciation of craftwork or nonroutine work to deal with the novelty at hand.

Tasks that are effective in complex operations are those that are not prospectively analyzable (i.e. not subject to mission analysis and its related architectural engineering of tasks). Traditional mission analysis, a hallmark of reductionism, is ineffective except perhaps for assuring that routine and engineered type tasks are performed in support of localized craftwork and emergent tasks. Military Design is reframed to signify this upside-down nature of the task structure for the required dispersed strategies and improvisational operations that are developed through situational immersion and action learning. Craftwork and emergent tasks are improvised-in-action and changed-in-action as the local situation morphs and as those immersed in the moment can better make appreciative judgments. In this view, Military Design is not a methodology toward *understanding* (the hope of task-based reductionism). Postinstitutional approaches to Military Design are more about designing-in-action while acknowledging of knowability of tasks in military interventions.

Some final thoughts

The concepts—strategy, leadership, and planning—have become reifications in modern military institutions to the point where they seek to attach meaning-for-action to virtually any Military Design situation. Normally uncriticized, these frames stream through time alongside situations that have not yet drawn sufficient attention and inside believers-of-the-frame that flow in time with them. A window of opportunity for situational framing opens when sufficient attention the believers link the frames to the situation that now has the attention of those with institutional power. This is when the streams come together in terms of habitualized "problem framing."[44] My purpose here is not to dismiss these "usual solutions" but to demonstrate how a design undertaking can be used to deconstruct and reconstruct them with alternate meanings. In summary, my essential purpose in this chapter has been to advocate the process of designing language around the situation rather than designing the situation around our existing language. The metaphoric equation is derived from sociologist Max Weber's descriptive theory of social action: ACTION = BEHAVIOR + MEANING. The modernist military usually focuses on behavior. Framing, on the other hand, is about finding particular meaning in the uniqueness of the situation at hand. The next chapter shall address still another mode of critical inquiry that enables such reconstructions across paradigms: *relationalism*

Notes

1 Said in a different way, "Despite the dictum that you cannot find the answer until you have formulated the question well, you often do not know what the . . . question is until you know the answer" (March and Olsen 1989, p. 13). For this chapter, I propose that when one "frames the problem" one calls upon solution sets to do so (past solutions become heuristics or metaphors for framing the newly presented situation). So, the problem is defined by the meaning content of past solutions. Frame reflexivity is acknowledging that this can and is happening and, through that awareness, members can become more *postinstitutional* (seeking energetically to reframe beyond the reified frames).

2 There are other categories of ordained solutions in the US Defense Department: doctrine, organization, training, materiel, personnel, and facilities. I am addressing three of what I consider the most hypostatized based on my own, emic perspective.

3 John W. Meyer and Brian Rowan (1991) would call these legitimated "vocabularies of structure which are isomorphic with institutional rules [and that] provide prudent, rational, and legitimate accounts" (p. 50). I speculate that the US military experiences what I would call *existential instability* after wars like the recent ones. It has the "usual suspects" (a rush to icons) that seem to recur (e.g. my list for this chapter includes: *doctrine*, *strategy*, and *planning*). For the next chapter, I will add: *military profession*. After the American demise of the Tet Offensive in Vietnam in1968, there seemed to be a similar existential moment for the institution (e.g. see Bradford and Murphy 1969).

4 Even the meaning of "institution" has its roots in a building metaphor.

5 For a detailed discussion on cultural frames of reference from an anthropological view, see William I. Thompson, 1971. Thompson links the meaning

extensions of tribal *shaman*, *headman*, *clown*, and *hunter* to later societal concepts of *religion*, *state*, *art*, and *military*, respectively.

6 Henry Mintzberg (1987) proposes that one can conceive of strategy in at least five ways: as a *plan* (course of action); a *ploy* (deceptive actions that mislead the competitor); a *pattern* (a plethora of activities that may not be deliberate, but may *emerge* consistent with dominant values); a *position* (of relative advantage to a competitor); and a *perspective* (consistent with the way an institution frames the situation). The latter, in my view, also explains the other four; hence, I use it as an inclusive concept that would recognize all of the above.

7 In the present chapter, I am taking a *semasociological* approach to the linguistics associated with the "language of strategy." For an *onomasiological* approach to the evolutionary meaning of strategy, I would commend exploring the approach taken by Beatrice Heuser (2010, p. 3).

8 Interestingly, Paul Ricœur (1977) subtitled his book, *Multi-disciplinary Studies of the Creation of Meaning in Language*, which is precisely the ideal I strive for in the present book.

9 From the Greek verb *agein* (to lead).

10 According to Rich Horwath (2006): "The ancient Greek equivalent for the modern word 'strategy' probably would have been *strategike episteme* (a general's knowledge) or *strategon sophia* (the general's wisdom). One of the most famous Latin works in the area of military strategy is written by Frontius and has the Greek title of *Strategemata*. *Strategemata* describes a compilation of *strategema*, or 'strategems', which are literally 'tricks of war'. The Roman historians also introduced the term *strategia* to refer to territories under control of a *strategus*, a military commander in ancient Athens and a member of the Council of War. The word retained this narrow, geographic meaning until Count Guibert, a French military thinker, introduced the term *La Strategique* in 1799, in the sense that is understood today" (p. 1).

11 According to John G. Mitchell (1990), contextualization is akin to the Husserlean practice of ". . . a subjective intuitive, reflective method to analyze and interpret things which are given to our consciousness; it is a way of getting at the nature and meaning of the phenomena which are being experienced and examined" (p. 2).

12 The word and its derivatives are all but worshipped. All of the US War College mission statements (from their home websites), the word strategy or some derivative is included (emphasis added): National—". . . conducts a senior-level course of study in national security policy and *strategy* . . .;" Army—". . . prepares selected military, civilian, and international leaders for the responsibilities of *strategic* leadership . . .;" Naval—"Develop *strategic* and operational leaders"; Marine—"Graduates are prepared to assume senior leadership positions of increasing complexity through the study of national military *strategy*, theater *strategy* and plans . . ."; Air—"To prepare students to lead in a joint environment at the *strategic* level"; and Industrial—"future executives will be better prepared for leadership and success in developing national security *strategy* and policy . . ." (emphasis added, United States War Colleges 2011). Paraphrasing Aaron Wildavsky (1973), *if strategy is everything, then perhaps it is nothing*.

13 Examples of written works from different disciplines expressing this frustration include Evered (1983), Mintzberg (1994), Marcella (2010).

14 Thomas S. Kuhn defines paradigms as "universally scientific achievements that for a time provide model problems and solutions to a community of practitioners (1996, p. 5)." Perhaps the most used textbook in US military staff and war colleges would be the edited work, *Makers of Modern Strategy*, in which the editors' introduction claims the writers therein "did not compromise . . . scholarly objectivity" (Paret et al. 1986, p. 5). I reject such claim to objectivity (one of the sub-theses of the present book).

15 Oswald Spengler (1939) borrows the word *pseudomorphosis* from the science of mineralogy—in essence, he uses a metaphor to explain metaphors.

16 Note that I use a geographic metaphor to create the syllogism. My intent is to use the syllogism, "esoteric boundaries," as shorthand to explain the claims of professional knowledge and assuming laypersons do not know how to apply it. If, for example, military science is claimed to be the purview of military members to apply it, the military institution would assume "esoteric boundaries."

17 Jean Piaget was a renowned psychologist (also a self-professed epistemologist), well known for his theory of human cognitive development—from baby to adulthood (e.g. Piaget and Inhelder 1958).

18 At the turn of the last century, Ernst Haeckel (1900) developed *recapitulation theory* (e.g. in biology, *ontogeny recapitulates phylogeny*) that serves as an (often objectified) heuristic for all things human (to include social and intellectual development). The idea that all things (even answers to existential questions) evolve is a form of scientific progressivism. Interestingly, Haeckel's confidence in modernism led him to write the following: "The atheistic scientist who devotes his strength and his life to the search for the truth, is freely credited with all that is evil; the theistic churchgoer, who thoughtlessly follows the empty ceremonies of Catholic worship, is at once assumed to be a good citizen, even if there be no meaning whatever in his faith and his morality be deplorable. This error will only be destroyed when, in the twentieth century, the prevalent superstition gives place to rational knowledge and to a monistic conception of the unity of God and the world" (p. 291). Clearly he is referring to the eventual "science of everything" that I discussed in Chapter 1.

19 Beatrice Heuser (2010) makes this connection: "Social Darwinism was inappropriately named after Charles Darwin, owing much more to Herbert Spencer's Principles of Biology published in1864, where he coined the famous notion that only the fittest race/nation would survive a colossal struggle for resources against all others in a world that was getting too small for all of them" (p. 123). Social-Darwinism is arguably the logic that dominates the modernist military promotion system and the correspondent ecobiological view of strategy in war.

20 I will cover this issue in more detail in Chapter 5.

21 Steve Woolgar (1988) characterized this danger of institutional alienation as a political risk. The pathway to reflexivity to Woolgar is "to describe and expose the politics of explanation" (p. 165). The ethic of military designers

would have to include making "a promise not to stay within your academic boundary" (p. 175). Fictional storytelling is not out of the question when it comes to framing, claims Woolgar.

22 Donald A. Schön and Martin Rein (1994), addressing the nexus of science and art, emphasize efforts to "reframe" away from anything resembling the Greco-Western, ends-based-rationalistic construction of idioms (in this case, *strategy* is the idiom). In the face of intractable social messes, Schön and Rein further emphasize a paradigm shift toward the art of "reframing" and "reflection-in-action" and moving away from "the policy-analytic movement" (pp. 11–13).

23 Thomas S. Kuhn posits further that "shifts" occur when "an existing paradigm has ceased to function adequately in the exploration of an aspect of nature to which that paradigm had previously led the way" (1996, p. 92).

24 See also Frans P. B. Osinga (2006) who links Boyd's "OODA-Loop" theory to Chinese philosophy (pp. 37–42). OODA is an acronym for Observe, Orient, Decide and Act—Boyd's rapid decision-making cycle that allows for situational fluidity.

25 The logic of this metaphor is that order (*taktikós*) does not come from a high-ranking official. It *emerges* from "matter's incessant attempt to organize itself into ever complex structures, even in the face incessant forces of dissolution described by the second law of thermodynamics" (Waldrop 1992, p. 102). The epistemology of war extended from this base metaphor would result in very different, extended conceptualizations from that of *stratégos*.

26 In other words, *bricolage* (discussed more fully in Chapter 5).

27 *Authoritative response* is quite similar to what Donald A. Schön (1987) called *technical rationality*. In my words—this is the belief that all problems recur and, over time, one can solve these problems with solutions that worked before. So, based on experience with problems that are expected to recur, military officers are promoted into higher positions of authority and hence expected to be able to respond better than those less experienced. The logic falls apart if one shifts into an alternate belief that each situation is so novel that such experiential learning (i.e. "authoritative response" that is based on prior successes and failures) may actually interfere with the ability to reframe or practice more reflexively.

28 I modified Ronald A. Heifetz's table in his book that used his frame (physician-patient) instead of "Officer/NCO-Troops." Where he had Solution and/Implementation, this author substituted "courses of action." This table substituted "tasks" for his word "work," added the term "craftwork," and linked "doctrine" to technical tasks (1994, p. 76).

29 I borrow and extend the meaning of *iatrogenic* from the medical profession. The term means intervening with good intentions, yet inadvertently causing more harm than good. This is a valuable idea for promoting mindfulness in postinstitutional Military Design efforts.

30 Action learning is a concept developed in the 1950s by MIT professor Kurt Lewin (1958). He turned away from a modernist *best practices* approach (the idea behind military concept development, doctrine, and lessons-learned programs) to solving complex social problems to a dynamic, real-time, and pragmatic method of theorizing-while-practicing, resulting in continuous

personal and organizational development. His ideas have been further developed by a host of students of social psychology and organization theory. Prosecuting the full range of military interventions requires action research as an effective professional military methodology. Variations on this concept include action science, collaborative inquiry, action research, and interactive social science.

31 Phenomenology is interpreted by Donna Ladkin as a philosophical viewpoint primarily based on philosopher Alfred Whitehead's (1968/1938) version of process metaphysics (the Heraclitean idea that the world is in constant flux and transformation and hence so is our knowledge of it). John Mitchell (1990), another writer on phenomenological approach to leadership, described it as a "radical shift in perspective away from logical and empirical evidence and toward subjective, intuitive, personal, symbolical, and hermeneutical interpretations as they appear to the consciousness" (p. 51).

32 Donald A. Schön (1987) called this having a "reflective conversation with the situation" (p. 76).

33 I took several liberties to blend additional military terms into Keith Grint's model, hoping not to lose the wisdom of Grint's (2008, p. 16) original diagram. Added were references to design (not mentioned in Grint's book) as well as calling these three aspects of effectiveness "officership." "Wicked situations" is borrowed from Horst Rittel and Melvin Webber (1973).

34 Geoffrey Vickers (1965) describes appreciative judgment as making intuitive, aesthetic, qualitative decisions about the "state of the system," both internally and in its external relations (p. 40). Anthropologist Gregory Bateson (1979) described appreciation as "looking at life through a big enough *macro*scope" (p. 229). John Dewey (1934) described this sort of critical appreciation as very different from "judicial judgment" (a kind of once-and-for-all legalistic decision) (pp. 314–15). Dewey claims in the process of critical judgment one cannot use "standardized 'objectivity' of ready-made rules and precedents" (p. 316) to criticize art as masters of the art "do not follow models or rules but subdue both . . ." (p. 314).

35 I am, of course, rephrasing Claude Bernard's famous "Art is I; Science is we"; signifying that leadership can be reframed away from a science into a more situationally unique concept—an art form.

36 The fallacy of the metaphor is, of course, that military planning cannot be assured that the "blueprint" will result in the planned design. While architect's practice may result in something aesthetically pleasing, conceived in advance, with the precision of the blueprint, no such prediction or precision is possible in the social milieu of military interventions. Yet, the commitment to planning is extremely strong in the modern military institution.

37 Ernest R. Alexander (1986) explains: "The first planners came from the ranks of the other 'design professions': architecture, landscape design, and civil engineering. One concept they brought with them was utopianism: the idea that you can 'design' an ideal end state and use it to change the world to conform more closely to the utopian ideal" (pp. 4–5).

38 By extremist, I mean beyond the belief of someone from outside the institution who is critically examining these practices. I think many Americans, for

example, would find this sort of detailed planning tool, in Freudian terms, "anal retentive" and perhaps use the related metaphor "obsessive compulsive disorder" to describe the institution. There is some evidence in culture studies that find such preference for detail and control as a dominant characteristic of the modern military institution. James G. Pierce (2010), for example, found that the US Army "may be inhibiting performance and unconsciously perpetuating a cycle of caution and an over reliance on stability and control" (p. 112). The Universal Joint Task List (e.g. Department of Defense 2002) and its derivatives reflect, in my view, "standardization on steroids."

39 This is the logic of Frederick Taylor, circa 1910, that he called "scientific management" (Merkle 1980).

40 In modern military jargon, these are called *specified tasks* (dictated from higher headquarters) and *implied tasks* (derived by the local commander that higher did not specify but need to be accomplished).

41 This operation is used by the Joint Forces Staff and the US Army Command and General Staff colleges as a case study in joint military "operational art." I believe this case was popularized not only because it is well documented but also because it so well exemplifies the planning approach to military interventions—how designing them around routine and engineering tasks actually works. I note that there are no messy Vietnam case studies used in the core curricula.

42 I am not saying all military planning is hopeless as history bears some fruit to some degree. I agree with W. H. Walsh (1969) with his assertions that: ". . . if it is absurd to look on history as a series of deliberate movements, it is equally absurd to ignore the truth that men do sometimes pursue coherent policies" (p. 69). My issue is that we will not know if policies are "coherent" ahead of time; only in retrospect (i.e. we may only reflect in- and on- action) shall we have that knowledge. Was NAZI Germany's *lebensraum* policy coherent in retrospect? Was the post-WW II US policy of *containment* coherent in retrospect? (Note that both words are metaphors.) All planning is based on degrees of conjecture, soothsaying, etc. based on interpretations of past experiences be they phenomenological (one's own meaning) or vicariously interpreted (e.g. through institutionalization meanings about history).

43 One can find evidence that decentralization is at work from artifacts such as General David Petraeus' 2010 memo, to his troops that emphasized immersion: . . . "Consult and build relationships. . . . Earn the people's trust, talk to them, ask them questions, and learn about their lives. Inquire about social dynamics, frictions, local histories, and grievances. . . ." Also he indicated his ethics-guidance: "Stay true to the values we hold dear. This is what distinguishes us from our enemies. . . ." (Petraeus 2010) (Petraeus served as Commander of international forces in Afghanistan, 2010–11). Also from his experience in Afghanistan, Mathew Hoh, the US Department of State official who resigned in protest in October 2009, called this island community phenomenon "valleyism." In a Washington Post interview (Hoh 2009), he said, "The [Afghan] terrain is formidable to put it in an understated manner. The societal makeup to include the interaction of village to village and valley to valley, is such that allegiances seem to be to family and then to

village/valley above and beyond anything else. This is why I use the term 'valleyism' to explain the reasons why local populations are fighting us and the Afghan central government." Also see Giddens (1987) where he points out that, "Communication became distinct from transportation only with the invention of the electromagnetic telegraph" (p. 172). In other words, towns and villages become more socially integrated as they become able to communicate physically or electronically. This is the thesis of Robert H. Wiebe (1967) in his portrayal of how the United States transformed from 1877 to 1920.

44 Similar concepts and theories in psychology and social psychology include: *self-fulfilling prophecy*, *single-loop learning* (discussed in Chapter 5), *bounded rationality*, *cognitive dissonance*, *social habituation*, and so forth.

4

Relationalism

Paradox involves – contradictory yet interrelated elements . . . that seem logical in isolation but absurd and irrational when appearing simultaneously.

MARIANNE W. LEWIS,
Exploring Paradox

. . . simplicity is not an inevitable hallmark of truth . . . but merely a methodological tool of inquiry. . . . We need not certainly presuppose that the world somehow is systematic (simple, uniform, and the like) to validate our penchant for the systematicity of our cognitive commitments.

NICHOLAS RESCHER,
Philosophical Reasoning

If people have multiple identities and deal with multiple realities, why should we expect them to be ontological purists? To do so is to limit their capability for sensemaking. More likely is the possibility that over time, people will act like interpretivists, functionalists, radical humanists, and radical structuralists. . . . Sensemaking is not an individual process, it is a social process. . . . Language is action: Whenever people say something, they create rather than describe a situation. . .

KARL WEICK,
Sensemaking in Organizations

Here, we reconsider the mathematical metaphor:

ACTION = BEHAVIOR + MEANING

suggested by D. C. Phillips and Nicholas C. Burbules (2000, p. 70).[1] The equation symbolizes that human action[2] must include meaning and not just behavior. Does a group find meaning before action, during action, or after action; or, all of the above? There are at least two philosophies that

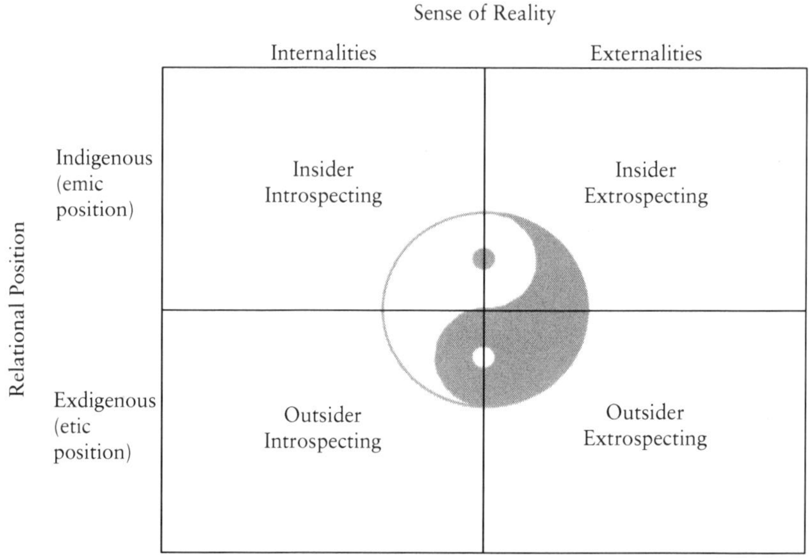

FIGURE 4.1 *A Quadigenous Model of Relationalism.*

deal with the constituents of action: *rationalism* (acting ideally based on unemotional facts, positivist assumptions of means-ends causality, and with the precision of measures of performance) and *relationalism* (acting based on consideration of paralogical,[3] comparative, competing and/or blendings of meanings that may include rationalism, art, aesthetics, emotions, cultural traditions, and paradoxical values) (Weber 1994, p. 31; Wolff 1974, p. 249; Lyotard 1979, p. 60).[4] Rationalism (the prevailing logic of the modernist) is not possible without a monistic, emic position complete with simplifications and reified categorizations of meanings to create a nomothetic, realist approach to inquiry (Rescher 2001a, p. 204). The following model of relationalism (that subordinates rationalism to but one way of framing meaning-for-action) presents four philosophical perspectives that permit exploration of simultaneous meanings. The model recognizes simultaneous opposites – "Ying::Yang" juxtapositions – to include those indigenous (from an insider position, looking inward and outward[5]) *and* exdigenous (from an outsider position, looking inward and outward[6]). My proposed neologism to describe the model is: "quadigenous" to reflect these opposing positions that produce multiple and simultaneous frames of reference (Figure 4.1).

Let's examine these perspectival modes of framing in more detail in the context of Military Design.

Rationalism. The US Army publishes standardized tasks—lists of behaviors it expects soldiers and Army organizations to execute during military interventions by design (i.e. Military Design is a "science project").

Here, meaning-for-action is *pre*scribed in the form of doctrine, directions from higher authority (memoranda, regulations, plans, orders, etc.), and as directed verbally by appointed officers and noncommissioned officers. In rationality's purist form, the average soldier is hardly expected to contemplate or discover new meanings-for-action other than that of fear and fear for others in their group.[7] Units are also conditioned in the same manner (e.g. compliantly or unconsciously practicing lists of standardized individual or collective behaviors). These represent the rational ideal type inherent to bureaucratic (unquestioned rule-following) forms of Military Design.

Rationally derived meaning-for-action in Military Design also calls for an explicit objective "end state." The reasoning goes this way: Break the desired end state (the prescribed meaning for action) into intermediate, contributing meanings-for-action (like tributaries would form rivers and lakes). The rationalist assumes that the contributing meanings for action add up to the overall meaning for action (called a campaign or strategy). Classic examples of the rational approach to Military Design can be found in artifacts from the American involvement in Vietnam. From archival reports from the US Army 9th Infantry Division, which operated with the US Navy along the waterways of the Mekong Delta, the following chart (Figure 4.2) reveals the institutionalized operationalism of military intervention. This chart was extracted from a report (Ewell and Hunt 1974, p. 71)[8] that showed US Army 9th Infantry Division ratios of enemy eliminated compared with US soldiers killed in action, July 1968 to May 1969. In this case, the independent variable was "airmobile operations," believed to serve the overall end state of defeating the Viet Cong insurgency and the North Vietnamese communists.

Similarly, contributing missions throughout the Vietnam area of operations were assumed to add up to the meaning of "victory," that is, the desired end state must be operationally defined with rolled-up, quantitative data. The definition of "end state," then, was assumed systematically coherent with the accumulation within that 9th Division data regional collection toward an overall, theater-wide Military Assistance Command, Vietnam campaign objective. Simplification through statistical aggregation (codified in the science of ORSA), earnestly designed to provide logic and grammatical clarity to subordinates, was not considered problematic until later in the war as the United States was pulling out.[9] Even decades after the US involvement ended, some dyed-in-the-wool rationalists argue that the reason for the Americans losing the war was that the political-military actors were not rational enough in their design of the lower-level missions, tiers of intermediate objectives, and collective grand end states (e.g. Summers 1982; Krepinevich 1986; McMaster 1997). Rationalism relies on a fallacy: the statistical aggregation of meaning (Rescher 1998, p. 152). As such, the rationalist relies on a kind of stereotyping into simplified, microeconomic meanings. Terms such as the "United States' foreign

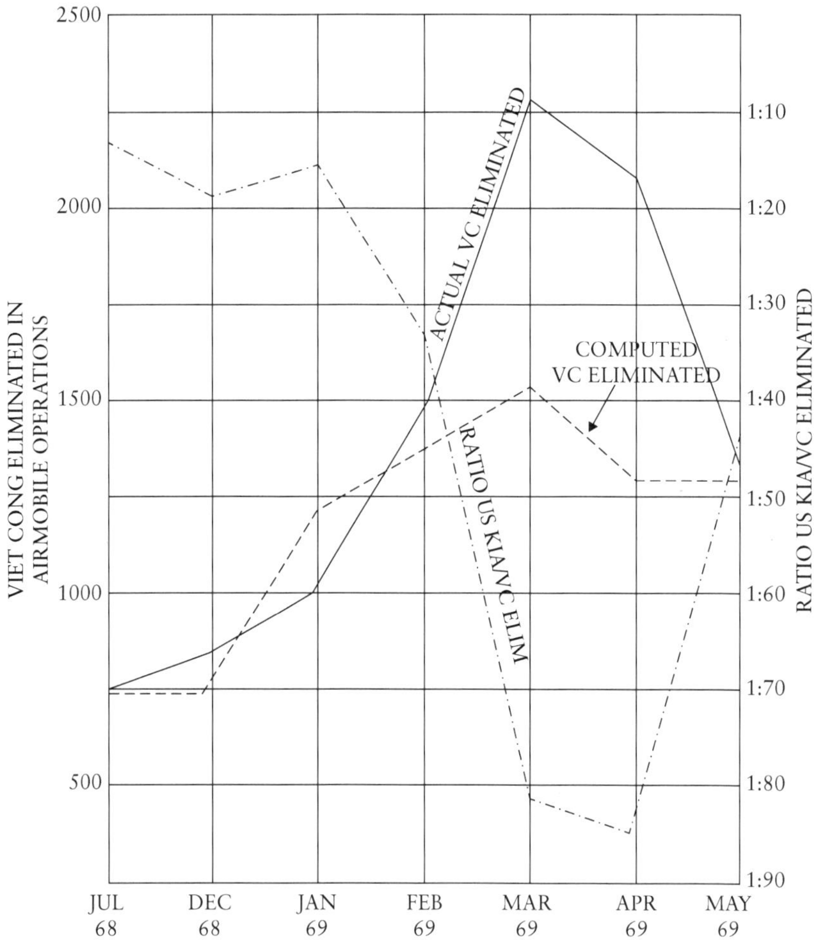

FIGURE 4.2 *Ninth Infantry Division Ratios of Enemy-Eliminated-to-US-Soldiers Killed-in-Action, July 1968 to May 1969 during the Vietnam War.*

policy," the "The Battle of Waterloo," "Patton's Army," and so on are used as if these historical complex (at the time, seemingly incoherent) activities and organizations are single, homogenous, and orderly unities. The policy process is ambiguous, battles are fought by thousands of individually acting participants, and sophisticated armies cannot be represented by a single general. The commentator who takes this amalgamated point of view of history, then, legitimates it through the ". . . prime directive of rationality [that is] to restore consistency in such situations" (Rescher 2001b, p. 9). The futurist (often labeled the "strategist" in modern military science) merely extends that illusion of the singular rational actor of the past continued into a rationalized future.

Relationalism. A relationalist would argue that to capture the messiness of the situation one must reveal the paradoxes and ambiguities (i.e. Military Design is more of a "meaning project"). As an alternative to rationalism (that demands the single best point of view), relationalism seeks multiple points of view; therefore, it accepts paradoxes and ambiguities as "normal" to the processes of inquiry.[10] To inquire relationally is to reflect on multiple points of view, acknowledging that social phenomena are not homogenizeable. Richard H. Brown (1977) makes the point this way:

> . . . the textual existence of persons studied by a statistical positivist is at the discretion of their author – he may not acknowledge them at all, instead insisting that his study is of forces, attitudes, or variables. Even if he gives them voice, it may be audible only through the screens of chi-squares and standard deviations; that is, as a way of illustrating the method by which the subjects' "naïve" voices were coded into the authoritative voice of the author (p. 65).

Brown continues: "Instead of attempting to reduce all worlds to the world of science, the [relationalist] seeks to illuminate each in light of the others, and to examine the purposes each most effectively serves (p. 228)." For illustrative purposes, listen to the principled words of social-psychologist (who is arguably a paralogist) Jonathan Haidt:

> Individual reasoning is not reliable because of the confirmation bias. The only cure for the confirmation bias is other people. So, if you bring people together who disagree, and they have a sense of friendship, family, having something in common, having an institution to preserve, they can challenge each other's reason. And this is the way the scientific world is supposed to work. And this is the way it does work in almost every part of it. You know, I've got my theory, and I'm really good at justifying it. But fortunately there's peer review, and there's lots of people are really good at undercutting it. And saying, "Well, what about this phenomenon? You didn't account for that." And we worked together even if we don't want to, we end up being forced to work together, challenging each other's confirmation biases, and truth emerges. . . . They're encouraging us to be more modest. . . . Wisdom comes out of a group of people well-constituted who have some faith or trust in each other (Moyers 2012).

Needless to say, relationalism involves a rather dramatic shift from the rationalist commitment to hierarchical forms of decision (concentrating on the rationality of the single decision-maker).[11] Relationalism seeks eclectic methods of inquiry and exposes both paradox and equivoques inherent to military interventions. This philosophy explores ever-shifting patterns of meaning from multiple points of view. Whereas rationalism seeks clarity of meaning through simplification, relationalism seeks appreciation of multiple meanings and *complexification*. This is not meant to be a form of pessimism as the modernist may claim; rather, the difference supports a more critical philosophy—toward wisdom in practice. Ming-Jer Chen and Danny Miller (2011) present a definition of relationalism that I subscribe to in this chapter:

> . . . a thought system in which concepts and entities enjoy no final definition, but are constantly redefined by their context. In such a system, paradox is not an irrational state; that is, a paradox need not be rendered rational through the cancellation of one or the other of opposing entities of which it is composed. Instead. . .entities simply exist with respect to and within the context of another (p. 7).[12]

Note the importance of *paralogy*[13] and other relational forms of reasoning. Another illustration follows. Let us take the issue of American competing values as a case study from a paralogical view. Deborah Stone (1997) examines the paradoxes and ambiguities involved in political decision-making by juxtaposing values and looking for relational patterns. She presents the paradoxical values of *equity*, *liberty*, *efficiency*, and *security* in her book, *Policy Paradox*. She defines these values concisely:

> Equity is defined as "treating likes alike." Efficiency is "getting the most output for a given input." Security is the "satisfaction of minimum human needs." Liberty is the ability to "do as you wish as long as you do not harm others" (p. 37).

Taken one at a time, these may seem like rational goals in the context of a Western-style democracy. From a rationalist point of view, each seems to signify a worthwhile "end-state" for causal actions toward these ends for both domestic and foreign policy. When considering each value in isolation (as an ideal type), there are countless internalities to consider in defining and achieving them. When considering the four values at the same time, the externalities are paradoxical. Both forms of paradox contribute to ambiguity vested in a relational perspective; hence, the impossibility of rational meanings-for-action can be appreciated. I will next examine the internality of each paradox and then comment on the externality of these values.

Equity. "Treating likes alike," for example, requires categorical definitions that make "alike" ripe for debate (e.g. the vagueness and multiplicity of group identities, like "privileged" and "underprivileged") (e.g. Marshall 1999) and debates about governing "who gets what, when, how" (Lasswell 1936). On a world population scale, arguing from the equity frame, there are already espoused "universal" equity goals such as those developed by the United Nations' declaration, Article 25:

> Everyone has the right to a standard of living adequate for the health and well-being of himself and of his family, including food, clothing, housing and

> medical care and necessary social services, and the right to security in the event of unemployment, sickness, disability, widowhood, old age or other lack of livelihood in circumstances beyond his control (United Nations 1948).

The internal paradoxes associated with equity coincide with ambiguities when it comes to defining contributory action on behalf of them. How does one party agree with others to what the meaning of an *adequate* standard of living, for example? Even if agreed to, at what point do violations of such universal equities justify a military intervention?

Efficiency. "Getting the most for a given input" does not address what it is that should be produced (i.e. accentuating the ambiguity of "end-states") (e.g. Cohen and March 1986, pp. 195–6). If efficiency were an unequivocal goal, the US Army would still be driving M4 Sherman instead of the M1 Abrams tank and the Air Force flying F4 Phantoms instead of F22 Raptors given that "the most" is a matter of valuation. At the same time, there seems to be efficiency limits as to the monetary costs of military interventions—how does one define "the given input" that is not relational to the enemy's? When are high-tech military organizations and a military intervention "worth it?" Commenting on approaches to rationalizing combat actions in Vietnam, Julian J. Ewell and Ira A. Hunt (1974) point to internal paradox and ambiguity of the meaning of efficiency:

> The process of analysis and improving efficiency while desirable tended to confine one's thinking in a set framework. This could be prejudicial to change and innovation. The Communists were fairly clever at eventually devising defensive measures against a new tactic and as a result it could be expected to be less and less profitable as time went on. This placed a premium on changes to keep ahead of the Communists and to retain the initiative. The Communists' reaction to continuous changes and innovation was relatively slow and uncertain so the cumulative effects of many innovations was [sic] quite productive. In sum, while using analysis, one should foster change and innovation (p. 234).

Security. The definition of what qualifies as "human needs" becomes a conundrum when physical and existential well-being are equivocal (e.g. Maslow 1943). For example, qualifiers such as "economic-security" may be paradoxical when considered with "physical-security." The Vietnam adventure was full of such paradoxes illustrated by the side effects of American valuations of population economic-security coupled with a rapid build-up and draw-down of US forces that interacted with population physical-security in complex ways:

> . . . as the American troops depart and the supply of dollars declines, along with the shooting, many of the refugees will return to their villages and to agriculture. But for many the return will not be so easy. It is not

> merely that the population has grown and some of the arable land has been permanently destroyed. It is a social problem. Some millions of Vietnamese have now lived in the cities for five, ten years or more; a half generation of their children has grown up without ever watching a rice plant harvested. A certain number are used to the luxuries of the Western-dominated city. The life of the peasantry is almost as foreign to them as it is to Americans, and yet they lack the very foundation upon which American society rests. These new city people have no capital – most of the money the United States invested in South Vietnamese officials and businessmen has flown to safer investments abroad – and they have no industrial skills. They are not producers, but go-betweens who have engaged in nothing but marketing and services. The American war has altered them and rendered them helpless (FitzGerald 1972, p. 434).

Liberty. Lastly, how does a society or an interventionist define "harm" as in "do not harm others?" Here, the internal paradox of involved in judging what constitutes the "commons" cannot be a rational, either-or debate; it is a relational debate (Ostrom 1990). The familiar phrase "provide for the common defense," in the US constitution, may collide with expected liberties afforded by the same document. The classic juxtaposition of the US National Security Agency's ability to tap into phone conversations has led the American Civil Liberties Union to press charges. Strange bedfellows such as members of the American Libertarian party (usually considered one of the most conservative political parties in the United States) may lock arms with the far left leaning ACLU; hence, more evidence of paradox and ambiguity. There is more than one intervention where US troops collected weapons from foreign village populations (as in Vietnam) while in their own American home town, citizens may own and carry weapons.

Externality, Paradoxes, and More Ambiguity. Stone's (1997) approach to appreciating the paradoxes in political decision-making demands that these values be considered even beyond their already confusing internality of meanings. There are also ambiguities interacting among them. Each of them seems to represent opposing, incommensurable ends with respect to each other. Societies may have to find "balance" among equity, security, liberty, and efficiency without ever being quite satisfied when considering even just one of them.[14] These make the modernist quest for disambiguation—such as rationalizations that permit illusive "understanding" in a particular situation in American interventionism—impossible. Figure 4.3 demonstrates how the use of a quadigenous chart can help the apprentice designer "see" some of the relational paradoxes (internalities and externalities of meanings) involved in unique and shifting contexts.

Militaries and military interventions designed around internal ambiguity of meanings respective to externally interactive meanings associated with

Equity
- Intervention frame: "who gets what, where, and when?"
- Internal Paradox: equal and unequal are subjective points of view.

Liberty
- Intervention frame: "why should government intervene at all?"
- Internal Paradox: government controls and individual choice are subjective points of view.

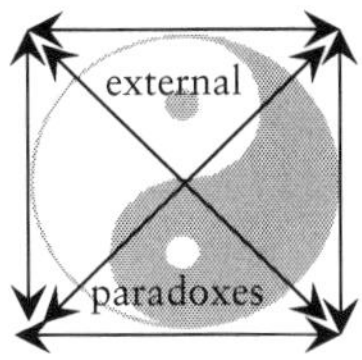

Security
- Intervention frame: "what are basic needs?"
- Internal Paradox: physical and socio-emotional needs are subjective points of view.

Efficiency
- Intervention frame: "what are the 'commons'?"
- Internal Paradox: monopoly and competition are subjective points of view.

FIGURE 4.3 *Values Paradox (based on Stone, 1994).*

security, equity, liberty, and market will always have surprising, paradoxical side effects when reflected in- and on-action.[15] The ambiguity of action within and among just these four values would become even more so by adding additional competing values (e.g. timeliness and patience) and their situationally specific interactive meanings from various points of view (e.g. the politics of *jus ad bellum*, *jus in bellum*, etc.).

The permutations and interactions of these conundrums are endless and fleetingly situational, making all meanings-for-action multifarious. When acting strictly on behaviors that worked in the past (the essence of modern science), past meanings-for-action are assumed to be relevant to the present; hence, new inquiries into meaning are out of the equation. The mathematical metaphor for this sort of compliant positivism, absent a search for *meaning*, becomes reduced to: ACTION = BEHAVIOR.[16]

Far from embracing the inevitable paradoxes and ambiguities of military intervention, systemic or analytical (a.k.a. ORSA) reasoning processes, associated with rationalism, seek to remove them. In modern military institutions, the doctrinaires provide a menu of standardized meanings for action. In contrast, the relative values, times, and spaces of postinstitutional Military Design call for critical inquiry about the relevance of those preconceived meanings. Relationalism is a belief that paradox and its partner, ambiguity, cannot be removed and ethically proclaims it *should* not be removed; hence, mindfulness of the presence of competing meanings-for-action is essential to institutional reflexivity.

One proposed meta-method of inquiry, then, is to take "inter-paradigmatic journeys"—explorations in search of paradox and ambiguity from four paradigmatic points of view.

Interparadigmatic journeys

In their remarkable book, *Sociological Paradigms and Organizational Analysis*, Gibson Burrell and Gareth Morgan (1979) induced a quadigenous (my neologism) way to conceptualize human organization—that is, describing alternative sociological views of reality (or in Kuhnian terms, paradigms): *functionalist, radical humanist, radical structuralist,* and *interpretivist.*[17] What these scholars demonstrate is that it is possible to conceive of reality based on four sets of ontological, epistemological, and methodological assumptions—the authors call these conflicting inquiries *interparadigmatic journeys* (p. 24). We will examine how each paradigm would treat Military Design efforts, keeping in mind that the interparadigmatic Military Design journeyman learns to oscillate among them.

Functionalist Military Design. Modernist military institutions should be familiar and quite comfortable with the functionalist paradigm.[18] This worldview is based on objectivist ontology and behaviorism.[19] Charles W. Ackley (1972), writing during the US involvement in the Vietnam War, criticizes the "tendency to structure" as a modernistic, dehumanizing US military sociological phenomenon:

> The pursuit of perfection, the refinement of every part, the drive to unify all parts into the superbly functioning whole which covers every option and is designed to meet every possibility is the machine mentality which in the end is self-defeating. It gets in its own way and grinds to a halt because it ignores the realities of time and man's finiteness and the necessity of daily choice and action based upon risk and imponderables of the continuous quest for Good. The Good is foreshortened to the means, the smooth functioning of the system, delight in the absolutely calculated, always encouraged efficiency of a creation become autonomous, able, we proudly say, "to run by itself. . . . A visitor to Vietnam reports in the *Marine Corps Gazette* a certain amazement that in joining an airstrike against the Viet Cong, "I felt not a twinge of guilt." Yet he had, upon arrival, then shocked at the briefing: "'You gotta work over the area good and proper.' . . . The man talked as if it were a question of ploughing [sic] a field rather than dropping napalm." But afterward, as he watched for hours how "with clockwork precision, an and the stream of fighting machines word into the shimmering air on missions of death and destruction," it was not of what was happening to human beings in the rice patties below that he thought (p. 236).

To the functionalist in the pursuit of meaning, the physical world is all that matters and even if our five senses and the plethora of existing and potential technologies that accentuate our senses cannot yet detect (or *make* "sense" of) environmental phenomena. To the functionalist, all nonteleological explanations of observable social phenomena are nonsense and fall into the category of science fiction. To the functionalist, ignorance is but a temporary state of mind until the appropriate positive, causal science is discovered, operationalized, tested, and standardized. The attractiveness of behaviorism is fostered by the science of known stimulus and response relationships called positive reinforcement (rewarding desired behaviors), negative reinforcement (threatening punishment), and punishment (delivering penalties for undesirable behaviors).

The most pervasive epistemology associated with functionalism is based on general systems theory (Bertalanffy 1968)—containing the logic, grammar, and rhetoric about all things interdependent, to include human social groups, framed as systems and subsystems, each level complete with attributions of degrees of behavioral controllability at various levels and process stages: inputs, transformation, outputs, and feedback loops. The more complicated these attributions in modeling how the system behaves, the more elaborate the system's causality is understood. The more differentiated the stratification and functionality, the more differentiated levels and specialties of military organizations and staffs have to be designed. Equipment, materiel, and positions within organizations and staffs are the systematic technology for military action. People (often called "human resources") are recruited to fill the positions receive specialized education and training in order to fill the technology of the positions by design. Hence, modern militaries functionalize work and design various specialties of intelligence, subfields of military logistics, and so forth in order to match the organization's specializations to those detailed, elaborated functional behaviors designed into the positions which make up the whole system and its stratified subsets. Military design to the functionalist is essentially a theory of stratified systematic control (both for internal control of the military organization as a technology and the controlled use of it to control other targeted systems for a desired behavioral change).

The logic structure for this paradigm is based on a teleological view—that is, all actions in the natural world have a purposeful function, often oriented on the adaptability and stability of the sociotechnical system within a definable environment or niche; hence, the purpose of knowledge construction is to operationalize that view.[20] Functional knowledge, then, is a collection of facts about causal relations in the system or subsystem behaviors in question. Once causality is made understandable and linked in larger chains to a larger, *synoptic* forms of reasoning, one can utilize that knowledge methodically to plan smaller behavioral interventions (located in local environmental niches) into bigger ones (located in the larger system).[21]

The belief is that detailed, analytical planning processes can produce lists of behavioral controls that can be synchronized to function together at the subsystem levels to change the larger system toward a desirable envisioned behavior.

In the case of Military Design, a functionalist will draw military interventions as part of larger systemic workings of national security (Figure 4.4).[22]

This diagram presents a large-scale picture of the inputs, process, and outputs of a US national security subsystem interacting with other subsystems within a larger, global system. Military interventions are, thus, *functionally designed* to achieve behavioral control of some niche aspect of the external system while assuring the protection and stability of its own national security subsystems. There is no room for paradox here.

There are, of course, rhetorical considerations of various *stratification* of functionality in an ecology of systems; therefore, communicating through what modern military institutions deem tactical, operational, and strategic levels of systems analyses. Since modern military doctrine is foundationally based on the behavioral control of additive subsystems at various levels, there is a correspondent belief that synoptic planning (the successful combination of functional stimuli and responses—i.e. planned "military operations" and their "effects"—nested at each level of the environment) is the *only* viable methodology that largely contributes to the claim to

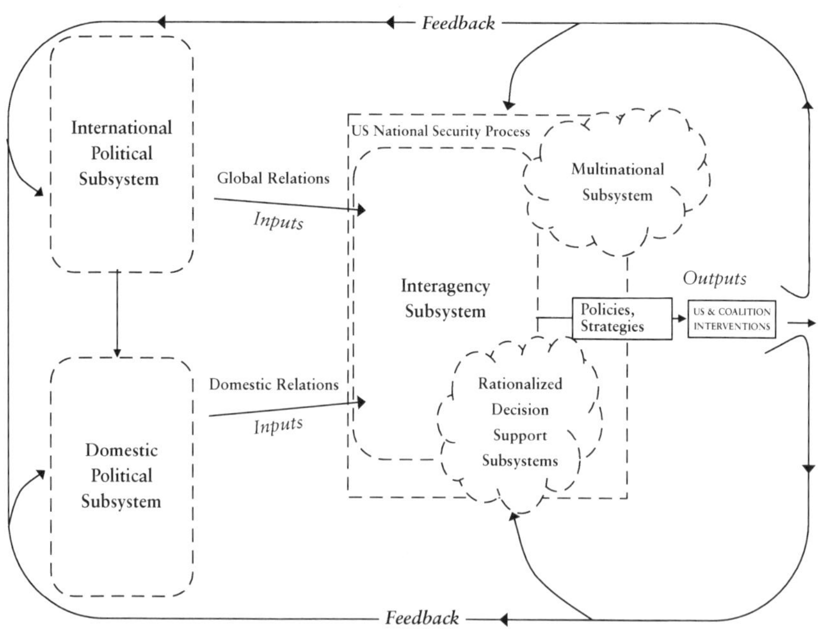

FIGURE 4.4 *View of the Functionalist: Systemic Military Design.*

"professional" knowledge. There is also the foundationalist assumption that this knowledge of how these stimuli-responses function systemically (in military terms, *intelligence*) is *progressive*—that science accumulates toward better and better holistic control of human systems (i.e. the "science of everything" is possible).

Note the functional rhetoric in this excerpt from US operational-level doctrine that is based on the design of military interventions that contribute to an interorganizational effort toward systematic behavioral control (Department of Defense 2011c):

> Joint operation planning produces multiple options to employ the US military and to integrate US military *actions* with other instruments of US national power in time, space, and purpose to achieve national strategic *end states*. Achieving operational military victory may be only a step toward achieving the overall national strategic goals and objectives. . . (emphasis added, pp. I-1 to I-2).

By "actions" and "end states," this functionalist doctrine is espousing the logic of behaviorism (i.e. stimulus-response). Geared specifically to the US military forces, doctrine further *functionalizes* the "operational level" of systemized behavioral control:

> *Joint functions* are related capabilities and activities grouped together to help JFCs integrate, synchronize, and direct joint operations. *Functions* that are common to joint operations at all levels of war fall into six basic groups—C2 [command and control], intelligence, fires, movement and maneuver, protection, and sustainment. Some functions, such as C2 and intelligence, apply to all operations. Others, such as fires, apply as the JFC's mission requires. A number of subordinate tasks, missions, and related capabilities help define each function, and some could apply to more than one joint function (emphasis added, p. III-1).

To a functionalist, the taxonomy of knowledge, education, organization, and tasks have to be correlated. The logic of management by objectives in a hierarchy of systems and subsystems is the way to taxonomically manage implementation of such additive stimuli designed for behavioral control. *Functionalist Military Design* assumes that those military individuals and units operating ("tactically") in the smaller subsystems cannot readily sense how the larger subsystems and overall systems are responding behaviorally to the stimuli planned and executed at higher or "joint" operational levels and strategic levels of a suprasystem. Hence, the positional role of the "strategic leader" is to nest subordinate missions (stimuli) into additive higher-order missions (ultimately to a grander aggregation called "national security policy"—also called grand strategy). The sample graphic artifacts depicted in Figure 4.5 (below) were taken from US military planning doctrine (Department of Defense 2011c, p. III-21 and p. III-15) that illustrate the epistemic dominance of military functionalism.

There is no room for paradox here. The taxonomy of objectives, effects, tasks, missions, and correspondent doctrines fuel a proclivity to reduce these proposed stimuli and responses to mathematical equations, providing quantitative feedback of the contributing levels (in the contemporary vernacular, "measures of performance"—MOP) as they relate to how the whole system is functioning (called, "measures of effectiveness"—MOE). MOP and MOE are officially defined as

> A MOP is a criterion used to assess friendly actions that is tied to measuring task accomplishment. A MOE is a criterion used to *assess changes in system behavior*, capability, or operational environment that is tied to measuring the attainment of an end state, an objective, or the creation of an effect. It measures the relevance of actions being performed (emphasis added, p. III-45).

The logics of systematic behavioral control and knowledge taxonomies are encased in the modern military institution; hence, also serve as *epistemic scripts* as to how the military organizes (smaller units comprise bigger formations and so forth).[23] It should be no surprise that the functionalist military institution also stratifies its knowledge and correspondent educational systems in taxonomic fashion.[24] From the radical humanist perspective (discussed in the next section), this functionalist paradigm has a dark side—functionalism also justifies existing institutionalized hierarchical

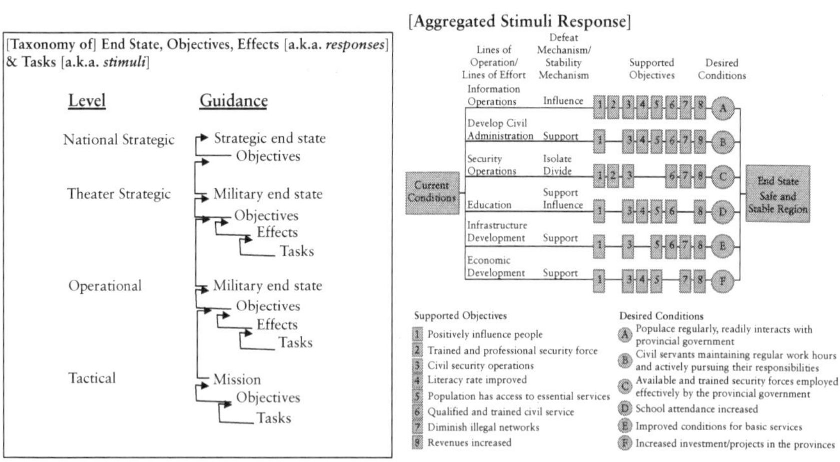

FIGURE 4.5 *Artifacts of Functionalist Military Design [with my comments in brackets].*

power structures designed for *internal* behavioral control (i.e. the commander-in-chief directs military four-star commanders who command three-starred commanders and so forth down the line). The commander-centricity of the functionalist paradigm manifests in behavioral-control epistemic scripts (that feed a larger metanarrative[25]) such as

> *The commander is the central figure in operational design*, due not only to education and experience, but also because the commander's judgment and decisions are required to guide the staff through the process. Generally, the more complex a situation, the more critical is the role of the commander early in planning (emphasis in original, Department of Defense 2011c, p. III-2).
>
> . . .
>
> *The operational approach is a commander's description of the broad actions the force must take to achieve the desired military end state.* It is the commander's visualization of how the operation should transform current conditions into the desired conditions at end state—the way the commander wants the operational environment to look at the conclusion of operations (emphasis in original, p. III-6).

The internal taxonomies of the institutionalized structures become so pervasive that members can conceive of no other way to structure—the epistemic script becomes sedimentary.

Finally, from the functionalist institution's perspective, the systematizing of interorganizational and intraorganizational military actions is highly vested in securing forms of unification of stimuli (doctrinally called *tasks* and *missions*); hence, the model makes adaptive-autonomous work at the lower, subsystem levels problematic (the paradox of higher-order control with respect to lower-order and external organizational compliance). Hence, the search for better systemic control extends beyond the organizational boundaries in that the functional designer also wants external organizations to be systematically incorporated as part of an enterprise-wide approach (Department of Defense 2011b) to intervention into others' systems:

> A systems perspective facilitates *operational design* and joint operation planning by providing the joint force commander (JFC) and staff with a *common frame of reference* for collaboration with interorganizational and multinational partners to determine and coordinate actions that are beyond the JFC's command authority (emphases added, p. IV-5).

In summary, the narrow philosophy of *functionalist Military Design* and its derivatives, general systems theory and behaviorism, includes assumptions that the world may be studied systematically. The correspondent values of disambiguation, repetition, behavioral control, and a continuity of knowledge dominate this perspective. Modern military doctrine is primarily an artifact of functionalism—it is a taxonomic categorization of stimuli and responses stratified against "levels of war." The functionalist paradigm obscures or seeks to eliminate the paradoxes of meaning in the design of military interventions, particularly at lower system levels, by reducing action of subordinate systems to that approaching its purist form of mindless behavioral control and compliance (both from internal and external perspectives).[26] The radical humanist perspective, discussed next, is quite different.

Radical Humanist Military Design. In its ideal form, the opposing paradigm of radical humanism is characterized through a subjective ontology—social worlds are constructed and can, therefore, be deconstructed. The radical humanist is always suspicious of hidden meanings and power agendas in the human milieu.[27] The logic of this paradigm includes the continuous struggle of the oppressed against the established ruling elite and its control of what constitutes acceptable knowledge (hence, the paradigm is usually tied to a Marxian theory of social revolution). Meanings-for-action are temporary and represent the domination by an ideology of manipulation that sustains those in power positions. Social unrest is just a matter of time as the oppressed groups will eventually react to realizations that their quieted voices have been deviously alienated.[28]

In the context of Military Design, the radical humanistic grammar and rhetoric is illustrated by the following quotes, the first attributed to novelist C. S. Lewis; the second to musician-poet, Bob Dylan, in his song, *Masters of War*:

> The greatest evils in the world will not be carried out by men with guns, but by men in suits sitting behind desks.[29]

> You fasten all the triggers
> For the others to fire
> Then you set back and watch
> When the death count gets higher
> You hide in your mansion'
> As young people's blood
> Flows out of their bodies
> And is buried in the mud.

From the perspective of this paradigm, what is vaunted as esoteric military knowledge, such as "authoritative doctrine," may be interpreted as manipulations by the few who control the epistemic script or metanarrative. Hence, any claim to professional (exclusive or esoteric) knowledge is viewed as an oligarchic, manipulative "conspiracy against laity" (Shaw 2008/1911, p. 29). Levels of war, for example, are construed not as the espoused tools of the trade but as assurances that those who occupy powerful positions are increasingly justified by the authoritative doctrinal frameworks that they approve.

The social invention of "strategy" (vaunted by all US war colleges) signifies an institutionalized ethic that those in the highest positions of authority in institutions of government or industry should both determine the permissible language of military science and decide on the functionalized set of behavioral stimuli and desired responses that are designed around it. The hidden meaning is that those who aspire to "strategic leadership" will be embellished with taxpayer-provided perquisites (even in so-called combat zones), chauffeurs, access to helicopters and global-reaching jets, personal cooks, aide-de-camps, entertainment allowances, spacious mansions, office suites with executive washrooms, and so forth, are the ones who demand that the masses of the enlisted are indoctrinated with "values" such as "selfless service." One soldier writes to me from his perch in Afghanistan:

> Don't even get me started on our "Rock Star Generals" and their battlefield tourism . . . it is ridiculous, and worthless. They wander around, searching for adventure and glory, only to return to their "Bat Caves" and not even inform their staffs on what they did, what they saw, what they understand now. The staff sits on the forward operating base, grinding out products and work, often to affect locations and sites they have never seen themselves; yet, their commanders have often. Their commanders are too busy to be action officers themselves, so a positive feedback loop forms of greater and greater lack of communication and confusion—the staffs spin and produce more briefings, more orders, and develop more processes—only to be frustrated by Rock Star Generals that return from their whirlwind tours with just enough time to sit in a brief and tell the staff how wrong they have it. I may sound a little bitter here, but I am sick of generals visiting sites to shoot weapons, "visit their men", or "assess the situation" which constitutes staying in VIP billets, giving a handful of coins out, having their public affairs officers snap photos of them presenting awards, and then dining on far better fare of food than their men ever get to see (anonymous soldier, personal correspondence with author).

The definition and use of the concept of military "leadership" itself is unmasked by the radical humanist as being a euphemism for the purposeful instilling of mindless dependencies on hierarchical, primarily paternalistic, authority. Likewise, being "a leader" to a radical feminist is another ploy for men's dominance, control, and hidden ignorance, as this author indicates:

> The Bush administration often co-opted women's rights empowerment as justification for the U.S. mission in Afghanistan. President Barack Obama's December 2009 speech at the U.S. Military Academy at

> West Point articulating U.S. strategy in Afghanistan moving forward emphasized national security as the primary driver for the U.S. presence and military action. There was very little mention of human rights and no mention of women and women's rights (Ginsburg 2010, p. 51).

Furthermore, the use of military science across other fields of practice and day-to-day life is part of a metanarrative designed to militarize our culture:

> As political scientists, we need to put popular culture on the table. Frequently, it is the militarization of popular culture that provides the nurturing soil for elite and institutional militarization, though the flow of causality should be constantly questioned. Imagine, therefore, these questions being placed on the research agenda of serious political science: Do civilian football matches start with a bomber fly-over? Are those graduating seniors going from secondary school directly into the military given special mention at their public school commencements? When suburban homeowners plant patriotic flags and "support our troops" signs on their lawns, are they admired by their neighbors? Do wives of male soldiers who support their husbands' missions garner more familial and public support than the soldiers' wives who voice reservations about those missions? The questions multiply: What proportion of the society's civilian teenagers think wearing camouflage pants and t-shirts make them look fashionable? Do commercial institutions—beer brewers, telephone companies—craft popular advertisements showing their products in close proximity to uniformed soldiers (Enloe 2010, p. 1109)?

A serious radical humanist scholar investigating the sociology of military science would include the perspective afforded by critical feminist theory and investigate the "dark side" potentially masked by functionalism.

Indeed, the legalistic narratives of subordination and the coercive properties of insubordination are rooted to control those who may feel alienated and would otherwise rebel. From the point of view of this paradigm, for example, the radical attempt to "overthrow" an approved military doctrine would include exposing the functionalist frames for Military Design as nothing more than alienating social myths—dark-sided, manipulative forms of knowledge that signify elitist minority control over the majority who ideally slavishly follow, as would mindless automatons (Gemmill and Oakley 1992).

Suspiciously viewed from this paradigm, functionalist formulations of Military Design are exposed not to be the outcome of an objective science, but a conspiratorial mind control over those who have lesser or no power. For example, dominant functionalist narratives, relating to commander-centricity or importance of the chain-of-command, remove any room for talk of military members forming labor unions to collectively bargain as contrary to the "good order and discipline" required for national security. Under the guise of functionalism, a shadow, "blue-collar" parallel military hierarchy (modern militaries label the "noncommissioned officer chain") is legitimized over time by the elite officer corps to create a relief valve for potential unrest and a suppression of those enlisted people who may realize their alienation and attempt to organize a rebellion or mutiny. Some excerpts from various formalized "noncommissioned officer (NCO) creeds" that I obtained from official websites help reveal these behavioral manipulations [I provide sample hidden deconstructed radical-humanist meanings in brackets]:

- US Army: "I will be loyal to those with whom I serve; seniors, peers, and subordinates alike." [Potential hidden meaning: we, the seniors, give you, the NCOs, some of our power in trade for following our orders and keeping the enlisted in line, providing the illusion that you represent their welfare.][30]
- US Navy: "I will fully support all Navy Regulations and Articles of the Uniform Code of Military Justice." [Potential hidden meaning: I will be punished for not following the rules legally sanctioned by my superiors.]
- US Marine Corps: "I will never forget that I am responsible to my Commanding Officer for the morale, discipline, and efficiency of my men." [Potential hidden meaning: make sure you keep order among the enlisted and follow the commander's orders.]
- US Air Force: "I will carry out the orders of my superiors to the best of ability and will always obey the decisions of my superiors." [Potential hidden meaning: obey or else be subjugated to prosecution under the Uniformed Code of Military Justice! By the way, we'll keep UCMJ infractions ambiguous enough to punish you as we please.]

The antidoctrine of the radical humanist sees these sorts of institutional grammars as "grand narratives" (Hatch 1997, p. 44) or metanarratives and attempt to reveal the hidden power manipulations in such speech acts. Those emancipationists who challenge these elitist narratives do so at great social risk as those who control these institutional constructions will not easily admit that this sort of Machiavellian dark side even exists. Yet, the festering goal of the radical-humanist "insurgent" is always to overthrow them, even if it takes generations.

The radical humanist sees functionalist rhetoric (such as the texts of official military doctrine) as a façade of institutional consensus about what constitutes a singular legitimate point of view for Military Design.

Meanings-for-action are indoctrinated into new members and the institution suppresses any attempt toward a redistribution of power with the powerful elite. Suppression includes Machiavellian tactics to assure frame-consensus in Military Design efforts (that I adapt from Wilkof 1989):

- Frame-consensus through *exhaustion* is a tactic for generating consensus used when a military doctrinal issue has been hashed and rehashed over a period of time and one party finally gets so tired or decides they have better things to do that they do not want to spend any more time and just shut up about the issue at hand.
- Frame-consensus through *pruning* consists of cutting down the list of influential people among whom Military Design consensus by agreement is attempted. This is a tactic to avoid getting many people involved in doctrine writing or war plans by not telling many there is a project under way; thus, those who do not know will not or cannot object. This tactic is risky because people finally find out they may upset the façade of consensus. The goal is to have enough influential people on board that when others find out they go along with the project.
- Frame-consensus through *destruction of credibility* consists of rendering others noninfluential by calling their credibility into question so that they will shut up or so that others will stop listening to them. The two major ways of calling others' credibility into question are by bringing up Military Design mistakes made on past projects or by demonstrating in front of many others that they are wrong on a set of doctrinal issues.
- Frame-consensus through *ignoring others* is when one does not listen to someone else or some other group. The hope is that the people or group in question are not influential and/or will tire of fighting over the doctrinal or planning issue and give up.
- Frame-consensus through *exchange* is generated when at least two parties agree that neither party will create problems for the other's design project.
- Frame-consensus through *sidetracking* is accomplished by getting a party who has been critical of a certain design project interested in other projects, thus eliminating him/her from the design team.
- Frame-consensus through *flattery* is implemented by elevating others' influence so that s/he is no longer critical of a design project. This is accomplished by diverting their attention to a small, insignificant doctrinal or planning issue, elevating their influence vis-à-vis that issue and thus increasing his/her positive visibility in the institution.

Their gratitude for getting positive exposure prevents them from being overly critical of the design project or other issues.

- Frame-consensus through *co-opting* consists of making others who have been critical of a design project a member of the team. The purpose is to change their criticism from a destructive to a constructive, doctrinally sensible form. Because they are now members of the project team, they feel more ownership for the problem and feels that their criticism applies to the work they are doing as well as the work that other team members are doing.
- Frame-consensus through *threat*, when it works at all, only works in a superior-subordinate relationship. This form of consensus building usually operates implicitly and infrequently in professional organizations (which calls into question whether modern military institutions can make a claim that they represent a "profession"). In essence, it is agreement obtained through fear of a poor performance review or loss of job and pension. This "commander-centric" tactic does not work well because talented people can usually find a job somewhere else and/or that it is difficult to fire people especially in government bureaucracies (pp. 194–5).

There are still at least two more dark-sided manipulations:

- Frame-consensus through the *use of ambiguity* is when one successfully uses unclear terms of reference that means something different to each group involved in a Military Design project so that each thinks they have the correct definition; hence, agree to the frame without really having a true consensus of (shared) meaning. Here, doctrines or plans are written to be purposefully ambiguous (I adapt from Stone 1997, pp. 156–62).
- Frame-consensus through *misinforming* is when a participant purposely uses made-up facts to support getting to consensus. This is the dark side of agreement and expertise, so the others believe this to be a morally clean tactic (personal correspondence with Mr. Karl W. Speights, US Joint Forces Command on October 27, 2010).

Inquiry methods by radical humanists include attempts to deconstruct approved doctrinal narratives or official statements to reveal that they create distortion in communications (Habermas 1976, p. xiii). In other words, the functional rationalist's narrative is "primarily a political concept used to legitimate the exertion of power" (Rutgers 1999, p. 27). If these power-motivated distortions are neither admitted nor confronted by the institution, the possibility of the Habermasian ideal of *communicative action* for Military Design is reduced (Habermas 1971). An otherwise participatory process of gaining frame consensus is distorted if the "approved" functionalists' metanarrative is the only source of derivative meanings. Hence, communicative rationality can only exist in terms that will seem radical to the powerful who rule the functionalist institution—fueled by democratic values, particularly to the fair representation of others' ideas, to include the minority voices of those who have weak power. Therefore, attempts to prestructure the process of Military Design (the essence of the functionalist approach to published doctrine or planning) may or may not satisfy a diverse constituency or potentially affected participants in the design process.

To the likely cringing disgust and even anger of the functionalist, there may even be protestant arguments over how to start a fair conversation (over who sets the agenda) and even about the shape of "the table" and where to sit at "the table" for design efforts. These arguments are commonly squelched with a claim to superior functionalist doctrine vaunting objectivity and the removal of such irrational, "political" squabbles. The functionalist is especially rewarded as s/he has an easier time justifying budgets (e.g. the illusion of value-free "science" that functionalism provides makes for justifiable programmatic appropriations from Congress).

An ideal participative Military Design process based on the radical humanist paradigm, then, implies universal-subscribed *pluralistic ethics* for overcoming hidden meanings by voicing and listening to differing meanings without fear of retribution, such as collaboration, openness to dialogue, self-subjection to fair negotiation, and sensitivities to affected participants and potential coalitions. Frame consensus, in its most democratic and morally ethical form, conveys Military Design "that is open to creative, new possibilities in a climate that is created to ensure all people and views are heard, where unanimity is desirable but not required" (Jacobs 2002, p. 119). Conditions for this ethical consensus would have to remove systemic hierarchical forms of power to prevent unilateral control; hence, an ideal communicative action is more possible and distorted communication is lessened. The morally clean tactics for frame-consensus would, then, include a definitions of *agreement* where everyone eventually shares (or at least tolerates) the same meaning-for-action in a certain situation (Harmon and Mayer 1986, p. 312).

Appropriate frames for military action are geared to whether frame-consensus has been reached among the participants in the Military Design project; therefore, the process tends to involve the messiness of capturing and exploring ambiguities of meaning, engaging in critical dialogue, and participating in fair negotiations and bargaining sessions. Finding meaning for action is about establishing a highly participatory, mutual relationship among other collaborators who together intend to make real changes that reflect their mutual purposes. Here, statesmanship would involve taking a more integrative view of judgment rather than a systemic behavioral control or self-interested view.

Willing participants are driven by a need for evolving a group consensus. Hence, they may incorporate collegiality, collaboration, and an attitude of "we are all in this together." As already mentioned, participants may also encounter Machiavellian values involving such things as manipulation, deception, and use of coercive participation and equivocation. Evocative rhetoric ("from the gut") may be more valued than rationalistic argumentation. Therefore, time for building relationships is critical to establishing mutual trust or at least a condition of "trust but verify." "Going to the balcony" or "socializing" at a cocktail party may contribute more toward communicative rationality than a formal engagement at the planning table.

Military Design, acknowledging the radical humanist paradigm, embraces the political messiness of consensus (to include wariness of the Machiavellian tactics that contribute to distorted communications), the presence of paradoxical values, and the ideal, yet institutionally radical, form of pluralistically based communicative rationality. Whereas radical humanism is based on the subjectivist ontology, the radical structuralist paradigm (addressed in the next section) assumes objectivity and serves to explain why radical systems change with correspondent advances in technology.[31]

Radical Structuralism: The Antidesign. From this objectivist worldview, the entire ecological system is uncontrollably transformed and not just the incremental component parts of it as with the purely functionalist point of view. The logics of change include those vested in chaoplexic systems (Horgan 1996; Bousquet 2009), punctuated equilibrium theory (e.g. True et al. 1999), long-wave economics (Kiel and Elliott 1999), and other such theories of "disruptive" technological changes (e.g. Tushman and Anderson 1986; Christensen 1997).

The logic of Military Design, conveyed by this *transformationalist* paradigm, would be not to confirm or conform to existing military doctrine or other technologies, but to reveal "leap over" knowledge and methods never before conceived.[32] From chaos comes a new order. Reported examples would include those punctuations or disruptions brought on by World War I and subsequently experienced by the US Navy and German Army during the interwar period (Murray 1996, p. 317). Military Design would be about emancipated meanings-for-action from the "baggage" of routinized technologies illustrated by the rise of the US aircraft carrier—displacing the battleship—and the German's relatively radical concept of *Auftragstaktik*—use of purposefully ambiguous "mission orders" to permit more decentralized initiative. The method is to act in contrast with the normal techniques of acting, resulting in a state of liberation from the old meanings imbedded in the legacy techniques for action. The radical structuralist rhetoric is revealed in a kind of antidesign slogan: "if it's not broken, break it!" It is more important to innovate even if breakthrough weaponry (like precision-guided munitions and instruments of cyber warfare) or peacemaking technology (like nuclear weapons) would mean radical changes to otherwise institutional momentum.

Such radical technologies burst forth in unexpected ways from the complexities of a competitive environment and those that work can afford radical, asymmetrical advantages to those who adopt them.[33] If the functionalist frames military situations as problems of adaptation *to* the environment, the radical structuralist sees the system-changing, disruptive, or revolutionary effects of technological shifts *on* changing the whole social system to include altering civilization itself (Mumford 1934). L. Douglas Kiel and Euel Elliott (1999), for example, claim that radical changes to governing systems in American society can be traced to revolutionary economic and technical advancements (seen as 50 to 65-year cycles) (p. 636). Economic downturns during periods of technological transition create demands for transformations. The first technoeconomic wave the authors frame as harnessing "wood, water, and wind" for industrial development (p. 627). Eastern industrial growth instigated beliefs that the elitist-based central and local governments were not helpful to the structure of the working and growing middle classes; hence, populist-era demands for the American colonists to revolt against British rule.

The second technoeconomic wave, followed by the US Civil War, was "coal, rail, and steam" (p. 629). Calls for elimination of the spoils system and for the establishment of the merit system in American government civil service were logically based on the technoeconomic efficiencies and bureaucratic designs of the day. With the depression of 1870, the need for an even hand between labor and big business and a merit-based, efficient government bureaucracy altered how society functions. The success of maneuver by train was a Prussian technological breakthrough that fundamentally changed the efficiency of systematic warfare forever (Howard 1961). By the late 1880s and early 1890s, this wave recognition was translated into major reform legislation. Punctuated by results of the Spanish-American War, by 1899, the US military was playing catchup to the transformative age of coal, rail, and steam through lagging bureaucratization of military staffs (Hittle 1961).

The third wave was based on the "oil, auto, and internal combustion engine" technologies (Kiel and Elliott 1999, p. 630). As this wave hit, so did the predictable economic transitional downturn that spurred radical change. The Great Depression was arguably the result of a technoeconomic provocation for governmental reform; hence, the New Deal or American "welfare state" was formed followed by an unprecedented "military state" propelled by the discontinuity of nuclear power.

The fourth technoeconomic wave, "microelectronics," is now on the rise, and it is characterized by a shift to the "hollow state" where government is more and more by proxy (p. 631). Third-party services, which were traditionally provided by government structures, are being increasingly farmed out to nonprofit and profit organizations. This is commensurate with present-day proclivities for governments to contract with commercial firms for what were considered proprietary tasks of the military (Singer 2008). The use of unmanned drones to find and attack targets is an electronic form of outsourcing.

After the Cold War, radical structuralists argued passionately that such a punctuating crisis was upon us. For example, listen to these, now decade-old, narratives from Robert H. Scales (2001):

> The nature of war is changing and the rate of change is more rapid than any similar period of modern history. Evidence of how profoundly contemporary events have affected America's style of war is clearly documented within the historical record of American conflict since the end of the Second World War. For almost forty years we planned for a return to a total war with the Soviets—a war that never came—while we evolved, through bloody practical experience, a new style of limited liability wars fought for ends not necessarily vital to our national interests at the time (p. 3).
>
> . . .
>
> The corollary to Newton's fundamental law of physics echoes with a sense of urgency: every successful technical or tactical innovation that provides a dominant military advantage eventually yields to a countervailing response that shifts the advantage to the opposing force. America's military dominance in firepower and attrition warfare has been on display for almost five decades. We must anticipate a future military challenge that will attempt to defeat our preoccupation with precision strike. We must use the time we have in the decade ahead to restore balance in our future method of war. Our future arsenal of military capabilities must include a 21st Century sword with two equally compelling edges: precision maneuver as well as precision firepower (p. 43).

For the United States in particular, one could argue that the "competency-destroying technologies" (Tushman and Anderson 1986) of radical Islamic networks have radically altered the international social system and challenged the ability of the highly institutionalized US military and its Westphalian-systematized military coalitions to compete with them. Hence, the radical structuralist military designer (or better described as the antidesigner) is not centered on continuity of knowledge (as the functionalist's doctrine would argue); rather, the intervention is framed around crises[34] and the "new normals" that repunctuate meaning in unpredictable ways (well, at least for the time being). The institution, hence, should be oriented on becoming an "un-learning organization" (or become forever "postinstitutional" in an anarchical way) rather than a learning one. The chains of discovery and inquiry are unpredictably interactive.

To a radical structuralist, institutions are nothing but "competency traps."[35] Continuing to design military interventions through the lens of a functionalist is to experience the frustration that ". . . problems are never solved . . . at best they are only re-solved – over and over again" (Rittel and Webber 1973, p. 160), at least until a radical technological shift occurs. I reinterpret Horst Rittel's and Melvin Webber's distinguishing properties of wicked situations, revealing the frustrating view of die-hard, functionalist military designer's quest for disambiguated clarity:

- *There can be no functionalized problem formulation for military intervention.* This includes the recognition that wicked situations defy the use of taxonomic-categorical definitions and that more information does not make the meaning-for-action less ambiguous. "Understanding," from a functionalist point of view, is an illusion.
- *There is no stopping rule for military intervention.* That is, past technologies or "best practices" for military intervention may continue to be used even if conditions change (i.e. they become competency traps). Conditions morph more rapidly than a planned, programmed, or budgeted change could keep up; hence, the initial plan for action becomes disconnected from the current situation. Finally, turnover and fluidity of participants in the affected organizations or institutions further confounds the search for stable meanings-for-action.
- *When designing military interventions, there are no true or false solutions, but bad to good solutions.* Military interventions are politically, culturally, and psychologically charged, that is, they are infused with the sometimes hidden values of those in power or with influence; hence, unseen value judgments, emotion, and intuition—seldom rational-economic reasoning—can and will dominate.
- *There are no immediate or ultimate tests for side effects for military interventions.* Because the situation is so complex, with variables that exhibit the dynamics of mutual causality, no one or no group can predict what will happen when we militarily intervene. Planning for future years to functionally structure military forces will likely be fraught with *type III error*—solving the wrong problem with precision (Mitroff and Kilmann 1981). And we will never know it until it is too late (i.e. ironically, functionalists plan their own surprise).
- *We may have one shot as we undertake a military intervention as there will be irreversible consequences.* Even if the military acts in committing resources to a single course of action, the dynamics of taking action itself will radically change the system and the previous conditions will be irretrievable. The linear stimulus and response mindset of the functionalist is a fallacy.

- *Military doctrine and other available technologies will fail as there can be no enumerable or exhaustive set of functional, preset solutions.* Meanings-for-action can seem like "bad or worse," or the lesser of two evils, or may even be incomprehensible—functionalist military planners metaphorically call this phenomenon the "solving world hunger"—a kind of impossible challenge, not unlike the intractable messes associated with prosecuting the next military intervention with old solutions. Trapped in functionalism, past solutions define the problem.
- *Every military intervention is unique (what the radical structuralist would see as randomly infused with anarchic knowledge).* Restated, crises, by definition, are not solved by capabilities the functionalist has developed for past crises. That is what makes them a crisis.
- *When the functionalist thinks we've isolated and defined "the" military problem, it is probably a symptom of nonmilitary problems.* To the radical structuralist, there is no single problem but a systemic network of interactive and interdependent problems that is too complex to unravel. The functionalist use of "root causal analysis" does not and cannot work.
- *ORSA-based "gap analysis" does not work.* The functionalist quest to find gaps between ideal end and where military interventionists perceive things are can be explained in too many ways and there is no foreseeable systematic procedure or a set of metrics to get to the "right" answer. No one can tell the future. While this fact makes functionalist solutions appear fruitless, if conditions sour, it does give political actors opportunity for framing a façade of alternative (unproven) functional solutions to convince voters to elect them (or promote them).
- *The functionalist designer has no right to be wrong.* Trapped in the functionalist's expectation to effect deliberate, additive system-wide behavioral changes with stratified means, the on-the-scene commander and the institution s/he represents are still held responsible for the outcomes even if there is no way to know whether or not things will work out as planned (interpreting Rittel and Webber 1973, pp. 161–6).

Martin van Creveld (1991) takes a radical structuralist, frame-breaking, futuristic point of view about the discontinuities of warfare:

> We are entering an era, not of peaceful economic competition between trading blocks, but of warfare between ethnic and religious groups. Even as familiar forms of armed conflict are sinking into the dustbin of the past, radically new ones are raising their heads ready to take their place. . . . Unless the societies in question are willing to adjust to the rapidly changing

> new realities, they are likely to reach the point where they will no longer be capable of employing organized violence at all. Once this situation comes about, their continued survival as cohesive political entities will also be put in doubt (p. ix).

True-blue radical structuralists would reject the whole idea of planned Military Design. Any sense of the past as lessons learned would serve only to blind the radical shifts that may be already underway.[36] Radical shifts in applied knowledge conceivably disrupt total societies and even the entire global human system. Military futurist (in the sheep's clothing of the radical structuralist) think the trick is to try and step outside the current technological wave to see the next one coming—something Thomas S. Kuhn (1996) claimed was impossible in his trace of *The Structure of Scientific Revolutions*:

> Just because [the paradigm shift] is a transition between incommensurables, the transition between competing paradigms cannot be made a step at a time, forced by logic and neutral experience. Like the gestalt switch, it must occur all at once (though not necessarily in an instant) or not at all (p. 150).

Military futurists, then, are hardly more than Shaman rain dancers and their proposed strategies their rain dance. The interpretivist (discussed next) may well disagree with Kuhn and claim it is possible to critically reflect in- and on-action and artfully reconstruct present meanings as things unfold in smaller steps.

Interpretivist Military Design. Instead of the functionalist's question, "What is the structure of strategic reality?" the interpretivist asks, "How is strategic reality socially constructed?" (*à* la Brown 1977, p. 19). Like the radical humanist, the interpretivist claims ontological subjectivity (in philosophical terms, this paradigm is antipositivist or at least postpositivist). Interpretive anthropologist Clifford Geertz (1973) makes this assertion:

> Believing . . . that man is an animal suspended in webs of significance he himself has spun, I take culture to be those webs, and the analysis of it to be therefore not an experiential science in search of law but an interpretive one in search of meaning (p. 5).

The methods of the interpretivist may involve "thick description:"

> What the ethnographer is in fact faced with . . . is a multiplicity of complex conceptual structures, many of them superimposed upon or knotted into one another, which are at once strange, irregular, and inexplicit, and

> which he must contrive somehow first to grasp and then to render. And this is true at the most down-to-earth, jungle field work levels of his activity: interviewing informants, observing rituals, eliciting kin terms, tracing property lines, censusing households . . . writing his journal. Doing ethnography is like trying to read (in the sense of "construct a reading of") a manuscript – foreign faded, full of ellipses, incoherencies, suspicious emendations, and tendentious commentaries, but written not in conventionalized graphs of sound but in transient examples of shaped behavior (p. 10).

An interpretive approach to Military Design values the necessity of relatively conservative, evolutionary changes to past *cultural constructions* of reality that occur in "muddling through" (successive limited comparisons—continuously asking for updated meaning: "are we doing better now than we were before we took this action?") (Lindblom 1959) while extending and eventually displacing older metaphors (Schön 1963; Ricœur 1976; Helman 1988). A steadfast interpretivist would argue:

> Hierarchy produces decisions conforming to preestablished problem definitions and categories of problem solution. The proper ends of action are presupposed, and . . . action is seen as an instrument for their attainment. . . . [I]nterpretivists . . . stress that the personal projects that orient action are marked by a far more fluid relationship between ends and means, between deciding and doing. Although ends and goals may orient action, action itself may also reveal new and unanticipated meaning . . . (Harmon and Mayer 1986, p. 315).

So, it goes then that interpretations are a linguistic art form; hence, over time they are manifested as cultural artifacts (or human-created meanings). The most important aspect of human action is meaning; certainly not behavior. Cultural meanings are retrospective and extended from past interpretations in improvisational ways; therefore, there can be never be radical sensemakings for Military Design (Williams 2010, p. 41). In that regard, all patterns of cultural meanings that attempt to frame what is happening are retrospective to past sensemakings (Weick 1995, pp. 24–30). Mark Turner (1988) writes:

> A culture's common conceptual categories and their relations, which I will call its category structures, highlight certain connections between concepts, and mask possible alternative connections. *Analogies exist to unmask, capture, or invent connections absent from or upstaged by one's category structures.* For us to recognize a statement as an analogy, we must recognize that it is some way putting pressure on our category structures (emphasis in original, p. 3).

For example, in the interpretive paradigm, a variety of detailed writings of military history would be profoundly beneficial to the interpretation of ongoing events and benefit the active designing or reframing of present or planned military interventions as a *hermeneutic project* (Williamson 1996, p. 320; see also Neustadt and May 1986).[37] Exploring historically the social psychology of what has led to surprise and institutional failure—for example, a *collapse of sensemaking* (Weick 1993)—may be quite beneficial to the prospects for interpretive Military Design, especially as surprise pertains to wicked situations (Rittel and Webber 1973).[38]

Whereas the functionalist uses the term "art" as a catchphrase to encapsulate knowledge not yet available for design purposes, the interpretivist sees art as a mainstay of Military Design.[39] "Art is the performance of a unique act" (Dewey 1934, p. 285), whereas the functionalist sees military action as mainly pre-engineered or routinized work. John Dewey argues:

> Rigid classifications are inept (if they are taken seriously) because they distract attention from that which is aesthetically basic – the qualitatively unique and integral character of experience of an art product (p. 226).

The orientation of the interpretivist is on the aesthetics of uniqueness and that of the functionalist on the science of sameness (another example of the paradoxical condition of the postinstitutional Military Design project). Dewey continues his description of art as

> . . . a group of activities that are, respectively, recording, constructive, logical and communicative. There is nothing aesthetic about art itself. The products of these arts become esthetic [to the beholder]. . . . [D]irect sensuous qualities like those of color and tone are irrelevant. The demand for shapes is satisfied when our motor imagery reenacts the *relations* embodied in an object—as, for example, "the fan-like arrangement of sharply convergent lines and exquisitely phrased skyline of hills, picked up at intervals into sharp crests and dropping down merely to rush up again in long rapid concave curves" (emphasis in original, p. 106).

The interpretivist relies more on intuition—a source of tacit meaning, beyond functionalist rationality:

> "Intuition" is that meeting of the old and new in which the readjustment involved in every form of consciousness is effected suddenly by means of a quick and unexpected harmony which in its bright abruptness is like a flash of revelation; although in fact is prepared for by long and slow incubation. Oftentimes the union of old and new, of the foreground and background, is accomplished only by effort, prolonged perhaps to the point of pain. In any case, the background of organized meanings

> can alone convert the new situation from the obscure into the clear and luminous. When the old and new jump together, like sparks from the poles are adjusted, there is intuition. This latter is thus neither an act of pure intellect in apprehending rational truth nor a Crocean grasp by spirit of its own images and states (p. 277).

With regard to the internal paradoxes of this paradigm, Dewey's is what a functionalist would see as an incongruous description of artful design. Military Design is construed as an interpretive art that includes the "metaphysical dualism" of the purposeful deconventionalization of language and emotional feelings therein:

> Works of art, like words, are literally pregnant with meaning. Meanings, having their source in past experience, are means by which the particular organization that marks a given picture is effected. They are not added on by "association" but are either, and equally, the soul of which colors are the body or the body of which colors are the soul – according as we happen to be concerned with the picture . . . not only are intellectual meanings carried over from past experience to add expressiveness, but so are qualities that add emotional excitation, whether the excitation be of serenity or poignancy (p. 123).

The interpretivist engaged in Military Design would not reject the functionalist view except to point out that the paradigm's ontological assumption of objectivity is ridiculous. Functionalism and the technical rationality of stratified systems theory and behaviorism are cultural inventions and should be used when it seems to work on the basis of more intuitive judgments about the situation at hand and critically discarded when not.[40] Artfulness would be associated with blending old contemplations into new ones (encapsulated by the French word *bricolage*, as used by anthropologist Claude Lévi-Strauss 1966, p. 30). A good example of this could be seen during the 1994 US military intervention into Haiti, when the US military artfully created an Army helicopter-borne, troop assault concept from the deck of a Navy aircraft carrier—representing improvisation from old concepts into jazz-like extensions. Another such example was the US Army's 9th Infantry Division operations from Navy ships and lighterage in the Mekong Delta during the Vietnam War.

An interpretivist would also argue that the problems with objectified cultural ways of interpreting situations are that they tend to predict only that surprises will occur because of the expectations they foster. Eliot Cohen and John Gooch (1990), in an unusual book, interpret military failures, like the Japanese raid on Pearl Harbor, much differently than the military historian who typically attributes surprise to systemically poor intelligence or to romanticized senior leadership that should have paid more attention to the obvious signals in unfolding events. Cohen and Gooch instead interpret military failures from layering organizational perspectives, to include those associated with cultural interpretations and institutionalized assumptions. In lieu of homogenizing a "lessons learned" science of success, these authors attempt to take interpretive approaches to military organizational failures that include accounting for unique culturally or institutionally fostered collapses of sensemaking.

The interpretive paradigm for Military Design, hence, involves mindfulness of attentions to our "enactments" (Weick 1995, pp. 36–7). Those realities we give attention and meaning to in certain institutionalized ways assure that our actions also affect meanings we assign to them; hence, we cannot find meaningful action strictly in terms of predesigned categories and behaviors. As such, a military organization, then, is "a network of intersubjectively shared meanings that are sustained through the development and use of a common language and everyday social interaction" (p. 39, quoting Walsh and Ungson 1991).

Functional rationality is a culturally driven template to indoctrinate institutional members as uncritical (worse case mindless) followers. Documenting language in official military doctrine may be interpreted as an attempt to institutionally remove the "everydayness" from that development and make any reification to be "common sense." *Mindfulness* would include challenging the commonness of institutionalized sensemakings and hence heeding pronouncements of meanings-before-action as potentially *mindless* (Weick and Sutcliffe 2001, p. 42). Social meaning comes from interrelating while being mindful in- and reflecting on- action, not prior.

Karl E. Weick and Karlene H. Roberts (1993) studied interrelational aspects of sailors operating on an American aircraft carrier as a kind of antithesis to meaning-before-action mindlessness. The crux of the investigation was to find out why there were not more accidents when such an organization is an accident waiting to happen. Framing the highly reliable organization that an aircraft carrier is includes the concepts of individual and collective (group) mind, which is stunningly insightful. Possibilities emerge to describe why accidents or the absence of accidents are "normal" based on combinations of individual and group "mind." The authors conclude:

> Despite their high potential for normal accidents, carriers are relatively safe. Our analysis suggests that one of the reasons carriers are safe is because of, not in spite of, tight coupling. Our analysis raises the possibility that technological tight coupling [e.g. mindless following of detailed procedures] is dangerous in the presence of interactive complexity, unless it is mediated by a mutually shared field that is well developed. This mutually shared field, built from heedful interrelating, is itself tightly coupled, but this tight coupling is social rather than technical (my brackets, pp. 377–8).

Similarly, Scott A. Snook (2000) takes an interpretive stance on the accidental shooting down of two US Army Blackhawk helicopters by US Air Force friendly fire as a matter of *practical drift* toward an eventual collapse of sensemaking. During long-term military operations (as was the case in enforcing the no-fly zone over northern Iraq in the 90s), heedful interpretations of what had to be accomplished were documented in a rather sophisticated operations order. As time progressed and military units rotated in and out of theater, the sense that was made in the original order (intended to tie smaller-scale activities together) drifted into other ways that were oriented on more recent experiences and practices that seemed to fit individual or smaller group minds.

The rules to coordinate air traffic in a combat zone (for prevention of fratricide) that were clear in the original order, over time became irrelevant as the dozens of actions based on "fragmentary orders" issued over the months that followed, collective mind drifted away. The assumptions that the technically tightly coupled organization should otherwise succeed, were literally shot down for lack of a sustained, collective mindfulness. The original reason for meaningful rules-for-action in a lengthy military intervention, with participants constantly coming and going, had shifted beyond reason for heedfulness. The "social construction of the campaign" changed so incrementally that, with grave results, important actors who rotated in did not notice why rules were made in the first place.

The interpretive paradigm would require a radical departure from the *exdigenous* perspective (assuming an objective outside view based on deductive learning) invested in the functionalist paradigm. The interpretivist view requires situational immersion (an *indigenous* view of inductive learning).[41] In her 2010 monograph, anthropologist Anna Simons deftly critiques those who seek functionalists solutions (she coins the terms, *genericize* and the [T.E.] *Lawrence Paradox* to signify these solutions as learning mythologies).[42] Simons exposes the institutional failure to appreciate the depth of experiential learning and intuitive forms of knowing needed to prosecute complex military interventions:

> The Lawrence paradox refers to our propensity to turn unduplicable lessons into generic principles as if anyone should be able to apply them (p. vi). . . . [It involves] the penchant to genericize in and of itself teaches the wrong lesson. It implies that once the right lessons have been taught and trained, anyone should be able to apply them. Yet, history suggests this is hardly the case. More to the point, those who orchestrated successful campaigns in the past invariably broke new ground. That is *why* their campaigns succeeded. This was usually in the wake of something old and tried, which means such individuals came to the situation able to read and analyze it differently than their predecessors, or they saw different possibilities, or both (pp. 21–2).

Simons remains critical about the functionalist approach to doctrine in "... that it requires too much updating. As it is, [the Department of Defense] is forever changing terms, which then requires that training be realigned with whatever are the new terms' points of reference" (p. 22). In a related article (Simons 1999), she points to other issues pertaining to the interpretive study of military interventions. She alludes in her conclusion that military interventions may be fueled by ignorant interpretations of these complex social phenomena:

> Perhaps the vantage point from which we view war today is really a precipice, and in trying to pierce the fog of others' wars, we have lost sight of the edge on which we ourselves teeter. It seems almost too apropos to point out that most who read this article have been lucky; we have escaped war's tornado-like fury. Not so those who cannot read this or anything else because their lives have already been dominated, disrupted, shattered, or ended by armed conflict. Tellingly, this is exactly the distinction—and the information-scarcity-injustice divide—that many military analysts believe will feed future war. If they are correct, we will not have to worry about a [Huntingtonian] clash between "civilizations." Instead, those on the attack will be illiterate, hungry, amoral barbarians (p. 96).

From the interpretive paradigm, then, Military Design should focus more on how interpretations are going and less on planned objective (or better stated, objectified) effects. Consider changing the name "military objective" (a functionalist view) to "military subjective" (an interpretivist view).

Summary

I can now employ a quad-chart of Military Design, similar to the Burrell and Morgan rendition (1979, p. 29), with these four paradigms relationally in mind (Figure 4.6).[43] Note that the intent of the model is to permit a "fly's eyes" look primarily at the meaning-for-action constructions for Military Design—toward relational prospects discovered during interparadigmatic journeys and the paradoxes these transits enable us to see. The relationalist, who energetically seeks to find paradox and ambiguity, sees the world as "mutualistic, heterogenic, symbiotic, interactionist, qualitative . . . and contextual. . ." (Cameron and Quinn 1988, p. 2, quoting Maruyama 1976). In lieu of dialectical (two ends of a continua) reasoning, perhaps the idea of *quadrilectical reasoning* (four ways of seeing) has merit to describe the simultaneous considerations of logics, grammars, and rhetoric each contribute. I employ them relationally as *ideal types* because there may be, in reality, no purist in each of them (represented by the dotted lines shown on this graphic).[44]

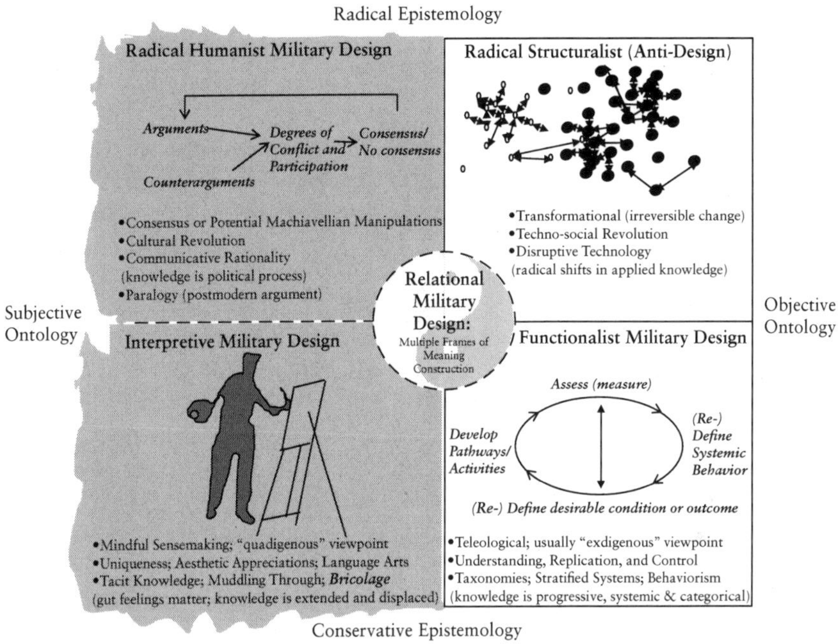

FIGURE 4.6 *A Relationalist View of Military Design.*

In that regard, one might analogize these paradigms as political parties. Members of political parties are seldom, if ever, ideological purists and they may take positions on specific issues that may differ from others in the same party. Just as there are paradoxes and ambiguities associated with Stone's (1997) competing values (equity, liberty, efficiency, and security) that make for political complexity, so are there in and among these sociological paradigms.

The narratives and epistemic scripts associated with each paradigm may be difficult to discern in the pursuit of Military Design, yet it may be helpful to treat them as one would examine political positions: Does objectivity (a functionalist or a radical structuralist position) or subjectivity (an interpretivist or a radical humanist position) seem to characterize the search for frames of reference? Does the situation seem to demand radical points of view (a radical humanist or structuralist position) or more conservative meanings (a functionalist or interpretivist position)? Whereas a rationalist-functionalist may see ways to address these either-or questions as unidirectional and classificational, a relationalist would seek to replace the "or" in these questions with "with respect to"—treating subjective::objective and radical::conservative as continua while finding patterns among them.

A burgeoning military designer or design team, then, involved with reframing a military intervention, has to be open to multimeanings of mind (Greek philosophers called this *epoché*—the temporary suspension of disbelief in another viewpoint), much like anthropologists who attempt to study an alien culture (e.g. through "thick description" and from multiple points of view) (Geertz 1973 p. 6). The paradigms described above provide a means for revealing the paradoxes of meaning for action. The idea is not to find the one that works (this would reflect the seductive utilitarianism of the functionalist paradigm), but to remain heedful that they, relationally (enabled by interparadigmatic explorations), offer ways to sense the ambiguity and paradoxes of meanings that emerge.

For relational Military Design philosophy to take hold, rationalist-modernists would have to acquiesce. If such acquiescence is intellectually feasible, institutional attempts toward paralogical acculturation must include providing emancipatory opportunities to practitioners (and I am quite pessimistic about this prospect because of the radical shift in power arrangements this would require). Modernist military institutions have created a high degree of functionality and the belief seems to extend to the idea that the synthesis of functions constitutes an act of a unified *profession of arms*. A critical inquiry into this belief is the subject of the next chapter.

Notes

1 Sociologist Max Weber (1994) actually defined the entire field of sociology in terms of social action: "In 'action' is included all human behavior when and insofar as the acting individual attaches a subjective meaning to it. Action in this sense may be either overt or purely inward or subjective; it may consist of positive intervention in a situation, or of deliberately refraining from such intervention or passively acquiescing in the situation. *Action is social insofar as, by virtue of the subjective meaning attached to it by the acting individual (or individuals)*, it takes account of the behavior of others and is thereby oriented in its course" (emphasis added, p. 228). Weber continues with this important idea: "The line between meaningful action and merely reactive behavior to which no subjective meaning is attached, cannot be sharply drawn empirically" (p. 229) (i.e. the equation above is confirmed as a concept, not as an empirical fact).

2 As I am referring to socially induced (meaningful) action, this is short hand for a "plurality of *inter* acting actors" (emphasis in original, Parsons 1954, p. 228).

3 Jean-François Lyotard (1984) describes *paralogy* as a "model of legitimation" that rejects "grand narratives" of modernism (which supports powerful elites) and places more validation in the "postmodern scientific discourse" of the "little narrative (*petit récit*)" that "disturbs the order of reason," generates "blind spots" and, contrary to the Habermasian ideal of consensus, "defers consensus" (pp. 60–1). This form of discursive inquiry and temporary meaning (i.e. there will be no permanent meaning) is similar to *abductive reasoning* proposed by Atocha Aliseda (2006)—"a reasoning process invoked to [temporarily] explain a puzzling observation" (p. 28). One could argue

that paralogy would acknowledge sensemaking methods similar to the phenomenologist and the limitations of metaphoric reasoning (I attempted to describe in Chapter 2).

4 Peter L. Berger and Thomas Luckmann (1967) interpret Karl Manheim's view of relationalism (Mannheim used the term *relationism*) as: "To denote the epistemological perspective of his sociology of knowledge – not a capitulation of thought before the socio-historical relativities, but a sober recognition that knowledge must always be knowledge from a certain position" (p. 10). Furthermore, Berger and Luckmann stab deeply into institutionalization process in their definition of *knowledge*: "objectivated meanings of institutional activity" (p. 70), hence indicating that the meaning portion of the equation is already decided by the institution, arguably making institutionalized meaning-for-action a mindless form of behaviorism. According to Hayden White (1978), paradigms "become interpretive strategies when we realize we are stuck on one and see the value in using others" (p. 65).

5 "Indigenous" refers to both positions of emic-internal/external.

6 "Exdigenous" refers to both positions of etic-internal/external.

7 One exception is what S. L. A. Marshall (1947) (and other social science investigators that followed) claimed as to what really happens in small units in combat where soldiers seem to take action on behalf of the emotional meanings they draw from fear and from each other. A later study (Wong et al. 2003) also suggests that soldiers take action because of the meaningfulness they draw from the institution, in large part from the indoctrination and conditioned training they receive before being sent into intervention situations.

8 Authors US Army Lieutenant General Julian J. Ewell and Major General Ira A. Hunt, Jr, writing in the early 70s, before the end of the American war effort in Vietnam, say: "The analytic approach when tried on the battlefield seemed to help produce sizable increases in both overall performance and efficiency. Whether these improvements were due more to good basic concepts or to good execution or both is difficult to determine" (1974, p. v). One of Ewell's and Hunt's more interesting findings was openly critical of the use of operations research and systems analysis techniques in Vietnam: "In Vietnam, with all its ambiguities, one was dealing with a highly repetitive operation. It was somewhat comparable to an assembly line-whereas one could visualize a 'western war' as an episodic or climactic affair with periods of intense decisive activity followed by longer periods of low activity. It would appear that this type of conflict might require a different approach [than] an analytical point of view" (p. 236).

9 The history of the 9th Infantry Division reveals no lack of ingenuity in the American conduct of military operations during the war (e.g. mixing riverine-based and air mobile actions). These missions were conducted with amazing imagination and improvisational use of existing technologies (like barge-based artillery and using Navy ships as brigade headquarters). So, the use of rationality in the Military Design is certainly compatible with creativity in the micro-behaviors and their micro-ends that are assumed to add up to the accomplishment of the macro policy and end-state. I propose that the problematization issue is with simplifying complex social milieu into smaller,

assumed more manageable "root problems"—forming the taxonomies of problem sets and techniques to solve them. This reflects what I would call the *ideology of technical rationalism*—synonymous with the modernist's approach to Military Design.

10 The word paradox has an ironic Greek etymology. "Para" is a prefix meaning "beyond." The suffix "-dox" comes from *doxa* that translates to "belief." From a relational perspective, then, the word paradox *is* a paradox as the relationalist believes paradox is a normal state of human social construction; therefore, paradox is *not* beyond belief. Perhaps the best way to portray the relational view is to describe paradox as when two ideas contradict each other, yet both are considered to be "true." Relational forms of creativity would include finding ways to accept "truth" in opposites. For example, the story from the Vietnam War where a US soldier participating in the strategic hamlet program said, "We have to destroy the village in order to save it." A commanding officer's logical contradiction (or irony?) of having to send soldiers into offensive battle while trying to protect them from harm. Recruits join the military to defend freedom while giving up their own. From a relationalist view, a "paradox" is not synonymous with a "dilemma" in that a situational dilemma is presumed to have an eventual disambiguation (Cameron and Quinn 1988, p. 2).

11 I use the word *dramatic* in that the commander-centric military institution invests in the wisdom of a single being—the commander. *Paralogy* recognizes that the military commander is just as prone to confirmational and conformational biases as anyone else. To the rationalist, commander-centric institution, this idea is radical as it detracts from the necessary power of the commander as the ultimate decision-maker in Military Design.

12 These authors limit relationalism as between two entities. Others have referred to four-way relational perspectives, described from a psychological level as *Janusian thinking* named for the Roman god, Janus (Rothenberg 1979). For example, according to Louise A. Holland (1961), in addition to perceiving the Christian God as four-faced, Janus was also believed by Romans to be a *quadrifronic* (or four-faced). Janus was believed to be ". . . the bright sky, he is the special aspect of the sun at the beginning of his half-yearly cycle; he is chaos, he is time, he is the father of time itself and the creator of all things; he is the spirit of the house door, and hence the guardian of the city gates and of the boundaries and the transitions; he represents a '*rite de passage* . . . [he is] a complex enigma. . . . The four faces [that Janus] sometimes wore were hardly enough for a god who looked so many ways' " (emphasis added, p. 3). Psychiatric-theorist Albert Rothenberg's (1979) definition of Janusian thinking is: "conceiving two or more opposite or antithetical ideas, images or concepts simultaneously" (1979, p. 55). It is highly related to Rothenberg's psychiatric concept of *homospatial thinking*—associated with paradox and transformational thinking (p. 66) —that "consists of actively conceiving two or more discrete entities occupying the same space, a conception leading to the articulation of new identities" (p. 69). I see the institutional-level *relational perspective* described by Ming-Jer Chen and Danny Miller (2011) as analogous to Rothenberg's individual-psychiatric view of Janusian thinking. (For *Janusian thinking* in a military context, see Paparone and Crupi 2002).

13 My extended description of Lyotardian *paralogy* is: the study of countering modernism by purposefully exposing contradictions in the logics of "normal" science.

14 One view of the wisdom of democracy as a form of governance (dealing with complex social situations) is not geared to rationality (end-states) but to a never-ending process of balancing values with respect to a plurality of judgments over time (Harmon and Mayer 1986, p. 313–14).

15 Capitalizing on the medical metaphor, I referred to these unpredictable side effects as *iatrogenic* in a previous chapter. Borrowing from literary circles, *irony* would arguably also be a near-synonym. I have heard officers returning from Iraq and Afghanistan refer to this phenomenon as *the whack-a-mole syndrome*, where one line of military operation paradoxically contributes to the worsening of another condition. For example, the killing of an insurgent may contribute to a vengeful generation of future insurgents. The good intentions of building of a school with a monetary grant from outside sources of capital may create social dependencies that cannot be sustained with a local economy. And so forth . . .

16 The positivist separates fact from meaning; hence, who needs to explore meanings when you can rely on higher authority and objective facts (that speak for themselves) to govern action (Lincoln and Guba 1985, p. 29)? A relational way to criticize the idea that facts represent fundamental truth are John R. Searle's (1995) revelations about the ambiguity of "social" and "institutional" facts. For example, "War is always a form of intentionality; hence it is a war only if people think it is a war" (p. 89). To label the US-Korean War a 'war' is 'unconstitutional;' so it was labeled a 'United Nations police action'. . . . War as a social fact can exist no matter how it came about, but under the US Constitution, war as an institutional fact exists only if it created by an act of Congress, a type of speech act I call Declaration. Perhaps after the Vietnam War and Persian Gulf War, we are evolving an institution of common law war, like common law marriage (p. 89). In my view, it is better to seek the subjective meanings (plausible social and institutional facts) for why military interventions occur than to seek causes. Causal relationships are merely objective chains of behavior (Nash 1969, p. 234).

17 The contributions of Gibson Burrell and Gareth Morgan (1979) were very influential in the way I created the Multi-Frame Typology of Metaphors in Chapter 2.

18 It is also called *structural-functionalism* (e.g. Parsons 1954, p. 226).

19 I agree with Michael M. Harmon and Richard T. Mayer (1986) that behaviorism "is not a school of thought, as such; rather, it is an intellectual orientation to a methodology that defines observable and generalizable human behavior as the only legitimate subject for study in the social sciences" (p. 125).

20 In many ways, these ideas stem from a nineteenth-century view of social Darwinism and Auguste Comte's *positivism* which, as a precursor of behaviorism, includes "laws of human development" and elaborate hierarchical classification systems (see Martineau 1853).

21 Nancy Roberts (2000) describes synoptic planning as "integrated comprehensiveness . . . a conscious effort launched by top management to integrate decisions that compose the overall strategy to ensure that plans are consciously developed, mutually reinforcing, and integrated into a whole" (p. 299).

22 This is my adaptation of the systems model of national security decision-making developed at the US Naval War College (Alvi-Aziz and Gvosdev 2010).

23 The idea of *epistemic script* is a dramaturgical concept which means societies, institutions, and groups "capture shared assumptions about the production of new knowledge" (Boxenbaum and Rouleau 2011, p. 279). If knowledge of military interventions is objectified to be taxonomic, for example, so will be military knowledge about organizing, educating, and training militaries, and so forth. Psychologists have called this the "dominant narrative" (Bruner 1991). These scripts serve as the logic grammar, and rhetoric of a paradigm.

24 In fact, one of the purveying psychology scholars, Elliott Jaques, spent time in the 80s until his death in 2003 assisting the US Army build its officer development and assessment program around his *stratified system theory* (SST) (Jaques 1976)—the theory behind the *management-by-objectives* movement. The conceptual essence of SST is that bureaucratic hierarchy is the best way to organize for accountability and control; so, if you find out what makes present leaders at the top end of the hierarchy successful, you can train, educate, and select successors with those same qualities (Jaques 1986). The US Army's officer evaluation system, for example, has been based on SST for over three decades.

25 *Metanarrative* is a phrase borrowed from critical theory and particularly the postmodern views of philosopher, Jean-François Lyotard (1984). For Lyotard, modern science is a metanarrative or "grand" narrative. A metanarrative is both a belief (an "ism") for those who are in naïve acceptance and a manipulation for the powerful. His method is to deconstruct metanarratives and present them as mythical stories of progress espoused by modernists. He defines *postmodern* as "incredulity toward metanarratives" (p. xxiv).

26 Perhaps this view helps critique the functionalist desire to make warfare more and more human-free with the use of remotely piloted drones, robots, and so forth.

27 According to Peter L. Berger and Thomas Luckmann (1966), "When a particular definition of reality comes to be attached to a concrete power interest, it may be called on ideology" (p. 123). So, in our equation, ACTION = BEHAVIOR + MEANING is primarily derived from the ideology of power.

28 A dramatic military historic case in point is associated with *chateau generalship* and the French Army "indiscipline" of 1917 following the meaningless casualties of the Nivelle Offensive during World War I (Keegan 1999, p. 329). French civilian protests against "the big industrialists" occurred near-simultaneously (p. 330).

29 According to my personal correspondence with the CS Lewis Foundation, Clara Sarrocco stated this quote is attributed to Lewis in a speech President Ronald Reagan gave to the National Association of Evangelicals in 1983. Yet, it appears to be a condensed interpretation in Walter Hooper's Preface in the 1961 edition of CS Lewis's *Screwtape Letters*: "I live in the Managerial Age, in a world of 'Admin.' The greatest evil is not done in those sordid 'dens of crime'

that Dickens loved to paint. It is not done even in concentration camps and labour camps. In those we see its final result. But it is conceived and ordered (moved, seconded, carried and minuted) in clean, carpeted, warmed and well-lighted offices, by quiet men with white collars and cut fingernails and smooth-shaved cheeks who do not need to raise their voice. Hence my symbol of Hell is something like the bureaucracy of a police state or the offices of a thoroughly nasty business concern" (p. 10).

30 It is not unusual in the school where I work to pass by a classroom of Army students reciting the NCO Creed in chorus, with the right hand up, and while standing.

31 *Technology*, according to Rupert F. Chisholm (1988), is a rather encompassing concept that includes "all the knowledge, information, material resources, techniques, and procedures that a work unit uses to convert system inputs into outputs—that is to conduct work" (p. 39). So, by this definition, military science is a technology as it seeks, for example, to transform a nation's resources (inputs) into an instrumental military force (output).

32 Continuing with our equation, ACTION = BEHAVIOR + MEANING, meaning in this paradigm is derived from the objectification of breakthroughs in technology. Peter L. Berger and Thomas Luckmann (1966) put it this way: "Reification implies that man is capable of forgetting his own authorship of the human world, and further, that the dialectic between man, the producer, and his products is lost to consciousness [in my view, this is a pretty fair sociological definition of 'technology' that complements the one in the previous footnote]. The reified world is, by definition, a dehumanized world. It is experienced by man as a strange facticity, an *opus alienum* over which he has no control rather than as the *opus proprium* of his own productive activity" (p. 89).

33 The epistemic script of the radical structuralist would include such constructs as "asymmetric warfare" and "irregular warfare" to make their case.

34 I define *crises* as those situations that cannot be addressed by existing technologies or through relatively easy, incremental modifications to them.

35 I like the way James G. March (1994) defines a *competency trap* as, "the ways in which improving capabilities with one rule, technology, strategy, or practice interferes with changing that rule, technology, strategy or practice to another that is potentially superior" (pp. 96–7).

36 Today, the radical-structuralist-based "future-war" arguments, including warnings of the end of warfare as we know it, are plentiful and quite popular. Just a few contemporary examples among dozens include: Alvin and Heidi Toffler (1993); Samuel P. Huntington (1996), and Frank G. Hoffman (2006). The "purist" radical structuralist might deny that such forecasts are possible. If radical change is predicable, then it is hardly radical. Also, one could argue that those who argued for a scientific way of warfare (like J. F. C. Fuller 1925) were the radical-structural futurists of *their* time.

37 *Hermeneutic* methods are normally reserved for the humanities and literary arts. The word "derives from the Greek god, Hermes, who interpreted the words of gods for humans . . . its meaning [of late] is 'the study of the relationship between reason, language, and knowledge' " (Harmon and Mayer 1986, p. 323).

38 Karl E. Weick allegorizes the *collapse of sensemaking* in the story of some firefighters who did not "drop their tools" when faced with a surrounding fire and hence could not run fast enough as to escape as others who dropped their tools did. The moral of the story is that we carry meanings and use them to sense-make in emergent events (we fail to drop the old meanings) (Weick 1993).

39 For example, in the US Defense Department's official Dictionary (2011a), *operational art* has a distinctly functionalistic definition: "The cognitive approach by commanders and staffs—supported by their SKILL, KNOWLEDGE, EXPERIENCE, CREATIVITY, and JUDGMENT – to develop strategies, campaign, and operations to organize and employ military forces by employing ends, ways, and means" (emphasis added). I read this as ART = S + K + E + C + J, synoptically intertwined in the individual's (frontal-lobe-of-the-brain) cognition. To the interpretivist, this would seem to be an overly concrete, positivistic view of art (like an artist given only five colors to work with to interpret a fall landscape). They may also complain that this definition seems to lead one to believe that creativity can be taught programmatically as would other military technical competencies (for a critique of this competency-based approach to education and training in modern militaries, see Reed et al. 2004).

40 W. Graham Astley (1983) calls such cultural inventions, "intentional fictionalization of the reality under examination" (p. 113).

41 *Etic* (outsider) and *emic* (insider) are terms normally found in the field of interpretive anthropology. No wonder that the methods of interpretive inquiry are like those of the in-the-field approaches to anthropology (ethnography, case studies, etc.).

42 *Genericizing* denotes a fallacy of thinking that what one learns from experiencing one successful set of solutions can be applied generally to other situations. Simons seemingly draws on the analogy from the statistical sciences term, "generalizability" of findings. This concept is similar to the "competency trap" metaphor spoken earlier in this chapter.

43 In constructing this graphic with Gibson Burrell and Gareth Morgan (1979) in mind, I was also heavily influenced by the quad-chart developed by Andrew H. Van de Ven and Kangyong Sun (2011, p. 60).

44 Max Weber (1994) uses *ideal types* (or "pure type") in his descriptive theories of sociology as, more or less, relational heuristics. "In no case does it refer to an objectively 'correct' meaning or one which is 'true' in some metaphysical sense. It is this which distinguishes the empirical sciences of action, such as sociology and history, from the dogmatic disciplines in that area, such as jurisprudence, logic, ethics, and esthetics, which seek to ascertain the 'true' and 'valid' meanings associated with objects of investigation" (p. 228). Weber employs ideal types as substitutes of one's own paradigm to prevent the investigator's own institutionalized value-biases that would make them interpret others' behavior as "irrational"; hence, rendering the investigator incapable of discerning the logic, grammar, and rhetoric behind that particular meaning for action for someone else or their institution. Use of the purity of the type enables the inquiry to see others' action as better interpreted as deviations or extensions from that ideal. The use of the Weberian "ideal type" is essential to a relationalist approach to a postinstitutional Military Design education (more on this assertion in the next chapter).

5

The Reconstruction of Military PROFESSION

It is important to keep in mind that the objectivity of the institutional world, however massive it may appear to the individual, is a humanly produced, constructed objectivity.

PETER L. BERGER and THOMAS LUCKMANN,
The Social Construction of Reality

To use a simple analogy, what happens is that in our empirical investigations to become aware of the fact that we are observing the world from a moving staircase, from a dynamic platform, and, therefore, the image of the world changes with the changing frames of reference which various cultures create. On the other hand, [traditional] epistemology still only knows a static platform where one doesn't become aware of the possibility of various perspectives and, from this angle, it tries to deny the existence and the right of such dynamic thinking.... Instead of perspectivism, the out of date epistemology must set up a veto against the emerging new insights, according to which man can only see the world in perspective, and there is no view which is absolute in the sense that it represents the thing in itself beyond perspective.

KARL MANNHEIM in his personal correspondence April 15, 1946 with KURT H. WOLFF published in
The Sociology of Knowledge and Sociological Theory (1959)

Social construction theory postulates that there is a human-interactive process behind the creation of institutional knowledge structures; in other words, the theory suggests how knowledge is socially constructed to form institutions. Indoctrinations are ways for institutional members to think and act together with the "certainty that phenomena are real and that they possess certain characteristics" (Berger and Luckmann 1967, p. 1). Constructionists ontologically assume that institutions see no difference between the world "out there" (externality) and the institutional epistemology (internality) that makes-believe that world.[1] Knowledge, therefore, consists of habituated meanings-for-action, manifested from the indoctrination of rules and values that subscribers play out in context. Context is the socially interactive, internalization of the meanings about the world. Here are some important postulates of social construction theory as developed by Peter Berger and Thomas Luckmann (1967):

- Man's consciousness is determined by his social being;
- Man has a false consciousness based on deception, self-deception, and illusion as a necessary condition of social life;
- Man's view of the world is relative or relational;
- The focus of inquiry is on the phenomenon of *commonsense knowledge*;
- Institutional man considers social facts (*commonsense*) as things; and
- Commonsense knowledge is the constructed reality we share symbolically with others in the normal, self-evident routines (e.g. roles and rules) of everyday life (emphasis added, pp. 5–23).

In this chapter, I will employ this theory in an attempt to describe the modernist social construction of military PROFESSION[2] and to hopefully increase the chance of institutional reflexivity about that construction.

Modernist-oriented sociologists (e.g. Parsons 1954; Janowitz 1960; Huntington 1965)[3] have written extensively to construct the ideal of PROFESSION. Lately, there seems to be a growing consensus among modernists that the military has become too bureaucratized.[4] Snider et al. (2002, 2005) describe PROFESSION based principally on a social-Darwinian ecosystems view, vested in the work of sociologist, Andrew Abbott (1988).[5] The essence of Abbott's functionalist theory is that the role of a professionalized institution would be to control and protect its knowledge "jurisdiction"—preventing competing external groups from impinging on that proprietorship. The way of the PROFESSION, then, is to generate expert knowledge as a competitive means to preserve professional "jurisdiction" that separates the professional from the laity. Abbott explains:

> Each profession is bound to a set of tasks by ties to jurisdiction, the strength and weaknesses of these ties being established in the process of actual professional work. Since none of these links is absolute or permanent, the professions make up an interacting system, an ecology (p. 33).

I interpret this modernist's declaration of the primacy of expert knowledge as an implicit claim to *foreknowledge*.[6] I restate the claim as, "Professionals predict, laypeople can't." This interest in certainty appears spurred by the logic of establishing a science of ways and means toward an end (Weberian *Zweckrationalität*, which translates to "ends-base rationality"). Ways and means are manifested as specialized "bureaus" (e.g. equivalents to military service departments and functionalized staff sections in military headquarters) that rationalize the organized division of labor—a corollary to what modernists today refer to as *competency mapping* (Reed et al. 2004).[7]

According to Max Weber's theory of bureaucracy, the modernist demand for esoteric competencies as the key way to *avoid* becoming bureaucratic is oxymoronic. Correspondent to the Weberian descriptions of occidental, modern, legalistic societies are the demands of industrial capitalism, specialization of occupational roles, and demand for maximized efficiency in work (i.e. bureaucracy). Bureaucracy is a type of institution that "promotes a 'rationalist' way of life. . . ." (Weber 1946, p. 240). . . that is, "rules, means, ends, and matter-of-factness dominate its bearing" (p. 244). Weber also links the qualities of bureaucracy to the "needs arising from the creation of standing armies" (p. 212). Take note of Weber's descriptive theory of bureaucracy that replicates Abbott's modernist construction of PROFESSION:

- Defined jurisdictional areas are governed legalistically, by "rational codification of law" (p. 217) and the design of the organization is focused on official positions (not individuals). Individuals hold office; the office survives individuals—the hallmark of long-lasting civilizations—and individuals are granted pensions from the state. The office requires government financing (through taxation) through a systematic budget in order to stabilize salary and office functions. Lower offices are stratified under higher offices and there is a hierarchy and correspondent rank or grades in order to fill those offices. Officials are appointed to rank and position by a superior authority on the basis of merit (not politics) and are granted legal authority to give commands to subordinates.
- Governance of work is based on written rules and set techniques; hence, offices are filled by "trained experts" (Weber calls these experts "professionals") (p. 211).[8] "Expert knowledge" (p. 235) of rules and techniques requires special learning, stimulating the need for modern schools. Performance of official and specialized duties are sanctioned by virtue of technical qualification. A key example is the rise of modern "mechanized warfare" as a vocational calling for leaders as "technicians" (p. 222).[9] Armies are seen in the context of the bureaucratic state as the "means of warfare in the hands of the state" (p. 223). "Every bureaucracy seeks to increase the superiority of the professionally informed by keeping their knowledge and intentions

secret . . . it hides its knowledge and actions from criticism" (p. 233) [I interpret this as self-disciplining—policing its own].

- Functional purpose of the office is clear as are its expected ethical values (that include "objective indispensability and 'impersonal' character," i.e. removal of all personal favoritism) (p. 229). At the same time, the higher the office, the more the social esteem and the greater the legal sanctions against those lower who disrespect the higher office.
- Performance of the office is managed through quantitative measures of habitual task performance ("calculable rules" of technique and economics) (p. 215). Work is administered only through means of modern communications [originally by virtue of railroads and telegraph; of course today with the speed of electronic mail, cell phones, and video teleconferencing].

The words PROFESSION, "bureaucracy," and correspondent standardized knowledge (or doctrine) are derived from the Weber's sociological ideal type and essentially describe the same phenomenon. Hence, for Snider, et al. to argue that the military PROFESSION has become too bureaucratized would be a tautological fallacy through the eyes of Max Weber.

Weber's ideal type of bureaucracy, with its accompanying teleology, *Zweckrationalität*, should sound familiar as it seems to coincide so well with the Abbott's (and his followers) functionalist view of PROFESSION. Functionalism (and its correspondent general systems theory), rationalism, behaviorism, and bureaucracy are ontologically, epistemologically, and methodologically of the same modernist breed. Competency mapping would seem quite logical to a functionalist's prescriptive view of expert knowledge (perhaps only an etic observer could detect the tautology). A modernist view of military PROFESSION as equated with application of esoteric knowledge exists inseparably within the epistemology of a Weberian modern military bureaucracy (i.e. MILITARY SCIENCE = MILITARY BUREAUCRACY).

For modern military institutions and their correspondent functionalist approach to Military Design, the dominant theory of professional effectiveness is centered on the ideal of competency mapping, where standardized knowledge is not only vaunted but also stratified according to organizational ranks and positions. In other words, competency mapping involves distribution of taxonomic military knowledge to complement the bureaucratic levels of officer rank that, in turn, correspond to hierarchical organization and specialized positions, pay scales, and so forth.[10] For example, what the US military calls "professional military education" (PME) is a functionalist attempt to map rationalized (ways and means) knowledge structures onto a coexisting design of organization so that they are essentially one and the same. It should be no surprise, then, that the design of PME is a matter of determinate practice based on foreknowledge.

The following are examples of how modernist militaries (in these cases the US Air Force, Navy, and Marine Corps) can frame education around competency mapping (note the production line logic as well):

> Each of the three leadership levels within the Air Force is distinct from but related to the levels of warfare and requires a different mix of competencies and experience. Leadership at the tactical level is predominantly direct and face-to-face. As leaders ascend the organizational ladder to the operational level, leadership tasks become more complex and sophisticated. Strategic leaders have responsibility for large organizations or systems (United States Air Force 2006, p. 9).
>
> . . .
>
> Developing Airmen best happens through a deliberate process, one that aims to produce the right capabilities to meet the Air Force's operational needs (p. 13). . . . Force development is a series of experiences and challenges, combined with education and training opportunities that are directed at producing Airmen who possess the requisite skills, knowledge, experience, and motivation to lead and execute the full spectrum of Air Force missions (p. 14).

The Navy Leadership Competency Model says this:

> As applied to the Navy, the competency model applies to every level and position of Leadership. A competency is defined as a behavior or set of behaviors that describes excellent performance in a particular work context (Job Role, Position, or Function). These characteristics are applied to provide clarification of standards and expectations. In other words, a competency is what Superior performers do more often, with better on the job results (Department of the Navy 2012).

The following is from a symposium report on Small Unit Decision-Making (SUDM) conducted by the United States Marine Corps (2011b):

> The SUDM initiative's goal is to accelerate the acquisition of expertise at the small unit level by systematically emphasizing the five core competencies
>
> [adaptability, sensemaking, problem-solving, meta-cognition, attention-control], integrating more deliberate practice with them, and employing research-supported instructional techniques to better facilitate development of them (p. 5).

As these extracts illustrate, if the US military educational institutions were a person, I fear the psychiatric diagnosis would be along the lines of "obsessive-compulsive" tendencies toward competency mapping. Our inquiry, then, should be considered as an effort, as would a psychotherapist, to "emancipate" the "patient" from this psychic prison. The "therapy" I propose is a reflexive position afforded by the social constructionist perspective. The modernist institution offers too narrow a worldview—an ideology—that disfavors alternative knowledge structuration and stifles a more open military knowledge-construction philosophy. The dominant epistemic assumption of *foreknowledge of practice* as a condition of *professional determinacy* should be replaced with *indeterminate meaning for practice* under constant conditions of *professional doubt*.

Artifacts suggest the former dominates PME. Competency mapping thoroughly dominates the US Defense community of colleges and universities. A striking artifact is the *Officer Professional Military Education Policy* (OPMEP) (Department of Defense 2009b). Mimicking the synopticism that dominates military planning, modernist PME reflects a systemic stratification (mapping) of learning objectives that presumably integrate toward higher and higher levels associated with rank and position. These are intended to govern US Defense Department courses and colleges that seek to develop competent officers—from cadets ("precommissioned") to senior officers (i.e. up to and including three-star "general/flag" ranks).[11] Note this stratification scheme invested from the following OPMEP text:

> a. PME Levels. The continuum relates five military educational levels to five significant phases in an officer's career. The PME Continuum posits the production of the largest possible body of fully qualified and inherently joint officers suitable for joint command and staff responsibilities. (1) Precommissioning. Military education received at institutions and through programs *producing*[12] commissioned officers upon graduation. (2) Primary. Education typically received at grades O-1 through O-3. (3) Intermediate. Education typically received at grade O-4. (4) Senior. Education typically received at grades O-5 or O-6. (5) General/Flag Officer (G/FO). Education received as a G/FO.[13]
>
> b. Levels of War. The continuum portrays the focus of each educational level in relation to the tactical, operational, and strategic levels of war as outlined in joint doctrine, especially as described in Capstone and Keystone Joint Doctrine (particularly JP [Joint Publication] 1, 2-0, 3-0, 4-0, 5-0, and 6-0). It recognizes that PME and [Joint] JPME curricula educate across all levels of war (Department of Defense 2009b, p. A-A-2).

The functionalist should comfortably claim nirvana to the extent where these stratified mappings of competencies correspond well to the hierarchy. Those at the "Precommissioning" level (cadets) are expected to learn at the lower "knowledge" and "comprehension" levels in the knowledge taxonomy (Bloom 1956). A precommissioning example follows [my comments in brackets]:

> *Know the fundamentals of a* [joint task force] *JTF organization* (Department of Defense 2009b, p. E-B-3). [Note the foundationalist ("fundamentals") tone of the modernist epistemology present in this objective. The organization scheme for a military intervention revolves around the "joint task force" which is an uncritical given—the use of a JTF is just "is."]

Only the more senior officers are expected to achieve the higher cognition levels of learning—toward higher "analysis," "synthesis," and "evaluation" levels.[14] For example,

> *Analyze the appropriate mix of joint functions to develop joint operation plans* (p. E-J-2). [Note the explicit functionalism incorporated in this objective leaving no room to critically question whether it is appropriate to synoptically plan military interventions. The whole idea of functional-synoptic planning can and should be criticized (e.g. see Henry Mintzberg's treatise 1994).]

It should be no surprise, as indicated in Figure 5.1, that the modernist institution reserves these higher levels of learning to the progressive officer grades. The figure shows the percentage of OPMEP learning objectives plotted across officer grades according to Bloom's Taxonomy.

The institutional danger is akin to the *self-fulfilling prophecy* (Merton 1968) (a concept similar to institutional reification discussed in Chapter 1 and *single-loop learning* discussed below).[15] Unfortunately, the structured functionality of the OPMEP assures that only those who fill higher authority positions are afforded higher-level learning challenges and the educational

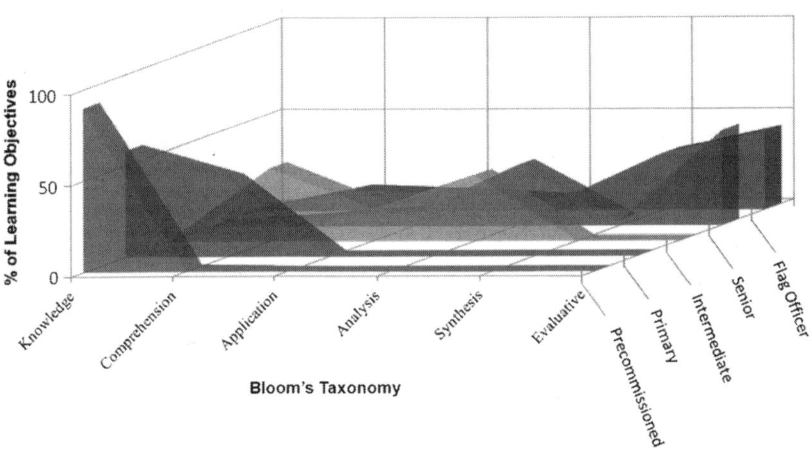

FIGURE 5.1 *Dumbing Down.*

opportunities to be reflexive (involving the correspondent authority to act creatively and critically deviant).

What should be more disturbing to the etic observer is that out of the 246 OPMEP learning objectives, I found that even when those learning objectives that profess to actually address critical and creative aspects of flag officer practice restrict students to theories, frames, and concepts derived exclusively from the functionalist paradigm. Even those learning objectives that require *evaluation* (Bloom's highest form of learning) tend to rely on existing, rationalistic episteme. For example, here is one required for war colleges [my comments in brackets]:

> *Evaluate the DOD and intergovernmental systems and processes by which national ends, ways, and means are reconciled, integrated, and applied* (Department of Defense 2009b, p. E-D-1). [Note the requirement to evaluate is restricted to using the bureaucratic (Weber's *Zweckrationalität*) frame of *ends*, *ways*, and *means*. The stratified systems mapping of Weberian commonsense (institutionalized) knowledge also limits the students to systemic designs.]

Even when some forms of *art*, *creativity*, or *criticism* are directed by the OPMEP, their meaning is wrapped and trapped in functionalism. The following excerpts illustrate this point:

> *Comprehend the art and science of developing, deploying, employing, and sustaining the military resources of the Nation, in conjunction with other instruments of national power, to attain national security objectives* (p. E-D-10). [The writer of this objective assumes one can comprehend art as one can science. In other words, there is an assumption that art and science are of the same ilk, epistemologically. Note also the reference to "instruments of national power"—a sure sign of the unitary functionalist paradigm.]
>
> *Evaluate critical, creative, and complex thinking and decision making by strategic leaders* (p. E-G-4). [This is the only objective (mapped to the Industrial College of the Armed Forces) in the OPMEP that uses the word *creative*. And note that this sole objective is hardly focused on the learner's quality of feeling (affection is the essence of the artistic and aesthetic domain), but instead focused on the rationalism of "strategic leaders" with the "mapping" assumption that one can learn critical, creative, and complex thinking by evaluating others' who have made it to the top. Who gets to pick who exemplifies a "strategic leader?" Case studies used here include stereotypical failures (e.g. General William Westmoreland's role in Vietnam and the McNamarian attrition strategy) as well as stereotypical heroic characters (as is the case at the US Army War College is the romantic image of General George C. Marshall). This

> approach ignores opportunities for the learner to collaborate and criticize the notion of "complex thinking" (is there such a thing?), be creative in doing so, and investigate what "complexity" means to them (the latter inquiry presents a dilemma to the functionalist as, even by modernist definition, complexity cannot be disambiguated). The stratified systems' view is explicit and can be critically deconstructed: how can competency mapping toward "strategic leadership" (whatever that means) work under conditions of complexity? There is no room in this learning objective for this sort of critical inquiry about the words expressed in the learning objective itself.]
>
> *Analyze the strategic art to include developing, applying and coordinating diplomatic, informational, military, and economic (DIME) elements of national power.* [While I have a sense that "art" can be criticized, uniquely appreciated, and described in aesthetic terms, I do not think the author of this objective had that sense of what "art" interpretation means. Art analysis implied here is the process of developing, applying, and coordinating "elements" of operational art (again, a functionalist term mimicking the technical competence prescribed in "lower level" joint doctrine publications)].

I could find no OPMEP learning objective that explicitly or implicitly required counternarrative forms of inquiry (e.g. idiographic, cognitive-linguistic, hermeneutic, phenomenological, literary, dramaturgical, and affective forms of finding ulterior meanings in texts or in context). In the OPMEP, subjective, relational judgments appear to "whisper" softly, if at all, while objectivity and technical rationalism "shout" loudly.

Again, competency mapping is inexorably linked to the modernist episteme of military PROFESSION. In 2012, the US Chairman of the Joint Chiefs of Staff confirms that: "It is a profession of experts in the use of military power to defend America" (Dempsey 2012, p. 9). Here is a similar confirmation from a US Army flag officer:

> We have learned that we possess expert knowledge that is unique to the Army profession and that we have an obligation to continue to expand on that body of expert knowledge for the benefit of the profession. As Army professionals, our expertise is the ethical and effective application of expert knowledge by certified professionals (Cone 2011, p. 73).

Note the technical rationality imbedded in these assertions, particularly laying claim to effective application of expert knowledge and the certification of the practitioner to apply it. Surprisingly missing from the extant literature on military sociology has been a critique of this modernist claim to "expert knowledge" which I argue is better characterized as cybernetic, single-loop learning (Argyris and Schön 1980).

I describe single-loop learning (or its other social-psychological variants I listed in Chapter 3) as a characteristic of the sedimentation[16] in the functionalist paradigm (particularly cybernetic-systems theory). Learning is restricted in the context of the self-referencing language system—the Lyotardian metanarrative (or grand narrative) of the modernist military institution. I will illustrate through modernist typifications—artifacts reflecting single-loop learning associated with military science, such as

> *Defining the problem* is essential to solving the problem. It involves *understanding* and isolating the root causes of the issue at hand—*defining* the essence of a complex, ill-defined problem. Defining the problem begins with a review of the tendencies and potentials of all the concerned actors and identifying tensions among the existing conditions and the desired end state. Operational design employs various elements [termination, military end state, objectives, effects, center of gravity, decisive points, lines of operation, lines of effort, direct- or indirect- approach, anticipation, operational reach, culmination, arranging operations, forces and functions, and assessment] to develop and refine the commander's operational approach. These conceptual tools help commanders and their staffs think through the challenges of understanding the operational environment, *defining the problem*, and developing this approach, which guides planning and shapes the concept of operations (emphasis added, Department of Defense 2011c, pp. xx–xxi) .

The message here is that professionalizing officers is a matter of building competency to disambiguate conditions, define "the problem," and then solve it through the employment of "conceptual tools" for design (I refer back to the "science project" in the Preface). To the instrumentalist, there will then be two sorts of *lessons learned* about the employment of tools of the trade.[17] If military interventions appear to be unsuccessful, the lessons are attributed to (1) *designer incompetency*—not applying tools correctly; and/or (2) *tool inadequacy*—that doctrinaires must return to their drawing boards to retool (i.e. modify or replace the concepts and then remap them). If we look at the historical constructions of US military doctrine, we see evidence of both instrumental approaches to learning. The following report provided by a contributing author to the US *Joint Center for Operational Analysis (JCOA) Journal* illustrates the *designer incompetency* explanation:

> The principle of *unity of command* for example was articulated as a "Combat Principle" as early as 1914 in US Field Service Regulations and should be fully internalized by now. It can hardly be considered a lesson learned from contemporary complex operations. It is more appropriate to consider it a lesson learned long ago that has been affirmed by our

> experience in contemporary complex operations. This of course begs the question, "If the lesson was learned, why has it not been applied?" (emphasis added, Miklaucic 2011, p. 34).

Here, learning involved posthoc explanations of ignoring or misapplying the tool (neither recognizing nor challenging the underlying utilitarian ethic or functionalist paradigm associated with *unity of command*). The institution resorts to the single-loop program of a retraining or removing of the incompetent actor.

Next, we examine the *inadequacy of tools* explanation, garnered through changes to doctrinal publications. Reading past issues of Joint Publication 3-0, *Doctrine for Joint Operations*, we see conceptual tools that were formulated on how to form integrated operations through "functional commands"—*land, maritime, air, and special*—with respect to Service-pure, Army, Navy, Air Force, and special operations commands (Department of Defense 2001, p. II-6). Two revisions later (Department of Defense 2011b, p. III-1), the "joint functions" are redesigned to be more "precise" and include: *command and control, intelligence, fires, movement and maneuver, protection, protection, and sustainment.* Over the decade between publications, the original integrating functionality (land, maritime, sea, and special) was somehow deemed insufficient to properly design joint operations; hence, additional tools were identified for more detailed integration. The same article from the *JCOA Journal* illustrates this single-loop reasoning:

> We cannot afford to rely on processes that are random, coincidental, or episodic to learn lessons in complex operations. A methodical process should be established which can identify prospective areas for examination, effectively articulate proposed lessons in the appropriate syntax, validate lessons distinguishing true lessons from individual experiences, and disseminate them. Once a pattern is observed, additional collection and analysis is required to articulate, validate, corroborate, or refute the potential lesson. This is not a simple process. It requires time and precision. Yet this is the core of the lessons learned process – the core of the scientific approach and of discovery. . . . Lessons not disseminated to those who might benefit from them are lessons lost – and as Santayana said, "Those who cannot learn from history are doomed to repeat it" (p. 38).[18]

There are a couple of issues with this sort of learning. First, the conclusions are highly suspect as those reporting on (historic) meanings on action have likely internalized a lot of "tacit," experiential knowledge ("indigenous" knowledge that cannot be told—like the indescribable experience of knowing-in-action as if riding a bike) (Schön 1995, p. 243; Polyani 1966). As every situation will be a unique challenge, even if one could report meaning-on-action unambiguously, it does not mean that knowledge is generalizable to other situations. Such meaning is developed uniquely *in* action and hence is ephemeral. Schön insists

> . . . most knowledge is tacit knowing, knowing-in-action. Situations arise, however, where our knowing in action doesn't work and we get surprised. And sometimes, in these circumstances, we have the ability to think about what we are doing while we are doing it, to turn our thought back on itself in the surprising situation. To restructure our thought and to conduct what I call an on-the-spot experiment (p. 244).
>
> . . .
>
> reflection in action and reflection on it . . . are, I think, a major part of what counts as artistry in practice (p. 247).

Second, how can such "learning" remain unchallenged—that one can map competence or incompetence and develop coping skills in terms of "conceptual tools." In other words, why should the "environment" conform to the functionalist military science? Why should a military intervention in complex (i.e. ambiguous, uncertain, unpredictable, and so forth) social milieu be subject to utilitarianism that is tied to reductionist-, predictive-, and systemic- "tools" for Military Design? The idea of scientificizing lessons from recent history (such as proposed by the *JCOA Journal* writer above) epitomizes the modernist aspirations of nominal and nomothetic progressivism and the reduction education to a subsystem that exists only to promote the *performativity* of the larger system (Lyotard 1984, p. 48).[19]

Indeed, mapping competencies into "professional" layers of schooling are better described as performativity efforts—to reduce dysfunction in the larger system and capture cybernetic (single-feedback loop) learning to know when to progressively correct performance and improve knowledge. Knowledge is legitimated toward manipulation of the functioning of "the environment" projected as a stratified system (in our present discussion, design of militaries and military interventions to match that hierarchical scheme). "Lessons learned" (a.k.a. "best practices") are afforded attention as systemic proof of functionality (signifying competence) or demonstrate dysfunctionality (signifying incompetence or the need to refunctionalize). Exercising the emancipatory inquiry (deconstructing the prevalent ones and finding e.g. counternarratives) is unthinkable in the modernist view of PROFESSION (except by those placed in the highest positional authorities).

There are other ways to construct ideals of PROFESSION. In the next section, I will focus on a relational philosophy of PROFESSION suggested by others, such as Donald A. Schön (1983, 1987), who reframe the professionals as *those who design meaning beyond those common to the institution*, through reflexive processes, particularly when faced with *indeterminate zones of practice*.

Indeterminate zones and reflective practice

What is hopefully clear by now is that the modernist sees the military PROFESSION as a systematically structured, technical-application-based role that serves on behalf of a larger social system. The functionalist envisions the PROFESSION as tied to an institution that is dedicated to standardization linked to the "pursuit of science . . . and its practical application. . . ." (Parsons 1954, p. 48). A social constructionist, such as Donald A. Schön, can reframe the ideal of PROFESSION quite differently; more as a *reflective practice* with the associated role being that of a *bricoleur*, socially accustomed to the artful, improvisational, and fluid formations of knowledge.

Rather than the belief in supremacy of "expert" foreknowledge that anticipates action, Schön proposes that professional education and practice should be recast as a matter of crafty divergence—reflexive inquiry and theory-making *in* action, coupled with critical retrospection about the quality of that inquiry and theorizing *on* action.[20] Ambiguity is an ethic (socially normalized), particularly in recognition of the indeterminate zones of practice of military professionals. Schön (1971, pp. 6–7) quotes Tolstoy's *War and Peace* (I took the liberty of substituting in "military designer" for "commander-in-chief" to make the point in the present context):

> The [military designer] is always in the midst of a series of shifting events and so he never can at any moment consider the whole import of an event that is occurring. Moment by moment the event is imperceptibly shaping itself, and at every moment of this continuous, uninterrupted shaping of events the [military designer] is in the midst of a most complex play of intrigues, worries, contingencies, authorities, projects, counsels, threats and deceptions, and is continually obliged to reply to innumerable questions addressed to him, which constantly conflict with one another (p. 211).

That is not to say that past reported inquiries and theories that do not work now should be ignored; rather, that they may serve as heuristics or improvisational frames that are extended and displaced in- and on- action:

> The nonroutine situations of practice are at least partly indeterminate and must somehow be made coherent. Skillful practitioners learn to conduct *frame experiments* in which they impose a kind of coherence on messy situations and thereby discover consequences and implications of their chosen frames. From time to time, their efforts to give order to a situation provoke unexpected outcomes – "back talk" that gives the situation a new meaning. They listen and reframe the problem. It is this . . . that constitutes a reflective conversation with the materials of a situation – the *designlike artistry* of professional practice (emphasis added, 1987, pp. 157–8).

Knowledge is epistemologically "a horse of a different color" here:

> . . . if you are dealing with a unique situation, then by definition you cannot apply to it standard categories of analysis and action. Because if it's unique, just that about it which is unique does not fit those categories. And therefore, you have to do something on the spot in such a situation, something that involves invention, which involves reconfiguring the problem, which may involve *redesigning categories* so that they fit it (Schön 1995, p. 239).

The focus of the educator (better described as a facilitator), then, would be to coach and participate in the practitioners' reflective conversation with the confusing situation at hand (signifying wicked situations in-the-now) and with situations past (implying relational reframing of history and new knowledge-makings about recent experience). As such, the facilitator coaches the practitioners to articulate conversations in practicum and to interpret critically past history texts and others' reported experiences. Attendance in traditional courses and classrooms is insufficient to promote deep excursions into history and others' experiential learning; hence, "a reflective practicum demands intensity and duration for beyond the normal requirements of a course" (p. 311). Employing cherry-picked case studies (with the lessons learned preprogrammed based on competency mapping) and homogenizing curricula (so that each PME student receives the same education) continues institutional overlearning (hypostatization of single-loop learning) and limits designers to categorical solutions that serve as the only way to define "the" problem (Cohen et al. 1972).

Design-as-reflective practice involves bringing the confusing world into heterogeneous *thought trials* (Weick 1989) (or in Schön's terms, *frame experiments* or *on-the-spot experiments*). Practitioners enact in real time or reflect on experiences with that confusing world, coached by relationalist educators. Conversations in the midst of confusion should not be strictly governed by modern, rationalist theories that may dangerously provide the illusion of situational understanding; rather, as Weick (1995b) suggests, being engaged in a more fluid ontology and epistemology—theoriz*ing* processes of "abstract*ing*, generaliz*ing*, relat*ing*, select*ing*, explain*ing*, synthesiz*ing*, and idealiz*ing*" (emphasis added, p. 389).

In lieu of applying *Zweckrationalität* (ends-based rationality) or other bureaucratic prescriptions to design, postinstitutional Military Design would be reframed as "interim struggles" (Weick, p. 389) where practitioners become actively and collectively immersed, imaginative, and mindful in sensemaking-while-acting. The purpose of theorizing, then, is not always to generalize meaning-for-action to some future situation (object learning) but to inquire and gain incremental insights into confusing situations at hand or into reexamining those from the past with altered frames (subject learning). When accustomed to befuddlement as normal when faced with indeterminate zones of practice, designers expect situations that are "complex, defamiliarizing, rich in paradox" and hence clear "away conventional notions to make way for artful and exciting insights" (DiMaggio 1995, p. 391).[21] The postinstitutional military PROFESSION, then, largely reflects these searches for meaning-in-context and much less for pre-engineered, specialized meanings that the modernist refers to as "expert knowledge."

The *petit récit* and professional ethics of the *bricoleur*

Social philosopher Alfred Schütz (1964) defined rationalization as the "transformation of an uncontrollable and unintelligible world into an organization which we can understand and therefore master, and in the framework of which prediction becomes possible" (p. 71). This bears a striking resemblance to what mission analysis (mentioned as a military planning step in Chapter 3) and other methods of synoptic planning are believed to promise. For example, while US military doctrinaires assume that there are such things as "ill-structured problems"; from postinstitutional frames of reference, this presents an unreflexive tautology.[22] Situations cannot be conceived as problems without a useable intellectual structure to frame them; hence, the construct, "ill-structured problems," is repetitious. When faced with indeterminate zones of practice, they are the institutional shibboleths and typifications that are ill-structured, not some external phenomenon labeled "problems" and defined by them. A contemporary of Schütz, Herbert Blumer (1969) puts it this way: "objects, events, and situations do not convey their own meanings, [rather] we confer meaning on them" (p. 134). Faced with the unknowability of military intervention, *bricolage* becomes a reflective, improvisational process of designing meanings in- and on- action.

Armed with a broadened philosophical array of one's institutional situatedness, metaphors (see Chapter 2), reconstructions of the familiar (see Chapter 3), and paradigms (see Chapter 4), the reflective military designer is ideally positioned in the role of *bricoleur*.[23] Ideally, she is socially comfortable criticizing the way the community of competency-trained planners traditionally conceives of militaries and their interventions and notices that "new" doctrinal functions are not much more than intraparadigmatic (self-referential) frames. She argues to her design team that the assumption of systemic analyses and other functionalized approaches to operations are not serving the effort at hand very well. To enable alternative views and arguments, the postinstitutional military designer may suggest bringing in outsiders to help view the situation from alternative perspectives. Through

FIGURE 5.2 *"Joint Combat Patrol" in Afghanistan.*

(US Air Force photo by Tech. Sgt. Efren Lopez taken 18 Jan 2010. Released to the public domain by DOD and available online at Defense Imagery Distribution System.)

critical dialogue, they together confront very different forms of meanings-for-action (or inaction) uniquely formed around the novelty of the situation at hand. Some of those others have been educated in nonfunctionalists' ways and/or are indigenous to local situations as to have developed tacit forms of knowing that make shared meaning problematic if not impossible. However, appreciating that the situation is complex and not understandable may encourage a sense of humility for both those exdigenous and indigenous to the situation.

Ideally, the participants discover that categorical functions and the myth of competencies are parts of a procrustean metanarrative and serve to distort communicating what has happened or is happening. Forms of nominal and nomothetic reasoning cannot explain the process of researching-in-action and deeper meanings brought forth by reflections on action. One (perhaps a non-Occidental participant) participating may reveal to others that indoctrinated competencies promote categorical thinking and categorical thinking promotes categorical acting (e.g. examine the photo above, Figure 5.2, indicates the Military Design "frame" seems to be the functional competency of *troop protection*).

Paradoxically, the reflective military designer is both defiantly provocative and deftly collaborative. These become two important relational ethics of the designer's bricoleur role (Gergen et al. 2004, p. 17). She provokes *interparadigmatic journeys* and facilitates Schönian *conversations with the situation* by bringing others, from outside the institution (who distinctly perceive the world in very different ways), to design. Consensus is not the objective; in fact, finding paradoxes (e.g. irreconcilable values) in the situation is important. Participants do not seek scientific logic (this is not a science project); they inquire *paralogically*.

Jean-François Lyotard (1984) presents his postmodernist idea of "paralogy" that encouraging deviance may assist in designing small narratives (*petit récit*) as the most legitimate way to deconstruct and challenge the modernist metanarrative and its derivative theories for action. Here, design participants are aware of "language games"—mindful that one should (at least temporarily) divorce from- and circumscribe- the logic of the institution (where the winner of the "language game" has already been decided by those in power). Lyotard suggests that the *petit récit* is a countering, paralogical language game designed to "disturb the order of 'reason'" (violating the institutional rules for the game), and purposefully generate "blind spots," and "defer consensus" indefinitely (p. 61).

In many ways, the *petit récit* is an antidoctrine, or perhaps expressed better as an antidote to doctrine. Reducing complex situations to categories (such as doctrinal naming conventions or competency mappings) reflects oversimplification and an illusive sense of understanding. Institutional framings are, by definition, based on actions believed to have worked in the past. Single-loop learning is related to *deductive reasoning* (e.g. application of existing frameworks, such as systems theory). In modernist Military Design, this would involve sizing up the situation using doctrinal terms (such as offense, defense, stability, and so on), institutionalized mnemonics (such as METT-TC, PMESII, and DIME[24]), MOEs/MOPs, standardized map symbols, system-of-systems analysis, and so forth.

Lyotard (1984) is careful to emphasize that when one starts playing the language game, one may have to face harmful social risks (p. 60). First, playing the language game challenges those in power whose "'arrogance' means . . . that they identify themselves with the social system conceived as a totality in quest of its most performative unity possible" (p. 63). Consideration of a countervailing small narrative may result in loss of power; hence, the "'move' ignored or repressed . . . because it too abruptly destabilized the accepted positions . . . ." (p. 63). Facilitating alternative, paralogical norms may be the most important advice when faced with indeterminate zones of practice and yet the modernist institution will insist on scientific norms. For example, US Army doctrinaires published *The Operations Process* (Department of the Army 2011b), a manual that reduces the philosophy of design to just another teleology, a methodological tool of synoptic planning, particularly for decisions imposed by those in the upper hierarchy. Here, commander-centricism calls for "decisive leadership" (a value that is arguably antithetical to engaging in open dialogue) and that the commander develop "a thorough understanding" in order to formulate effective solutions to complex, ill-structured problems" (p. 3–1). Quests for scientific-like understanding all but ignore the possibility of indeterminate zones of practice.

Synoptic planning routines demanded by modernist doctrine serve to "deliberate" paralogy. The rational-analytic schemes obstruct opportunities for constructing the *petit récit*. Synoptic planning-as-design cannot be "right" because design of indeterminate practice requires dynamic ontology (e.g. subjectivity with respect to objectivity), a discontinuity of epistemology (e.g. employing categorical nouns with respect to verbs), and divergent methodologies (e.g. nomothetic with respect to ideographic methods). While modernist military doctrinaires continue to describe design as a parallelism to synoptic planning regimens, the *petit récit*, inherent to postinstitutional Military Design, serves as the antimodel. In advocating postinstitutional Military Design, I postulate that there can be no concept for military intervention in general (as modernist doctrinaires would insist); rather, military interventions are historically situated and interpreted uniquely in- and on- action. The designer-as-bricoleur, hence, becomes intimate with various accounts of that historicity and wary of institutionalized preconceptions.

A *petit récit* would involve constructing rich or thick descriptions—prose often employed by cultural anthropologists (e.g. Geertz 1973), linked to *inductive thinking* (theory building from an indigenously reasoned position) and *abductive reasoning* (creating *tentative* stories or guesses about the surprises that are going on) (Aliseda 2006, p. 28; Peirce 1878). Communicating richly is the ability to bricolate meaning from the situation at hand without being hampered by a single paradigm or set of theories. For example, Karl E. Weick (2007) describes a technique called *E-Prime* (he attributes to scholar E. W. Kellogg) that strives for communications that do not use any derivative of the verb *to be* (pp. 14–19). Weick explains that when. . . :

> I'm forced to forego the verb to be, I pay more attention to particulars, context, and the situation. I also tend to see more clearly what I am not in a position to say. . . . When people perceive flowing experience, those undifferentiated sensations gradually take on explicit meaning when they are named, systematized, and formalized. When people name and formalize, they move farther away from their initial impressions (p. 18).

Another challenge of the bricoleur is to try and communicate *relationally* (see Chapter 4), for example, along continua rather than in categories (more common phrases are "thinking outside the box" and "patterned thinking"). For example, the modernist indoctrinated mindset frames the idea of "critical thinking" around scientific values, deemed "universal intellectual standards" of *clarity, accuracy, precision, relevance, depth, breadth, logic, significance,*

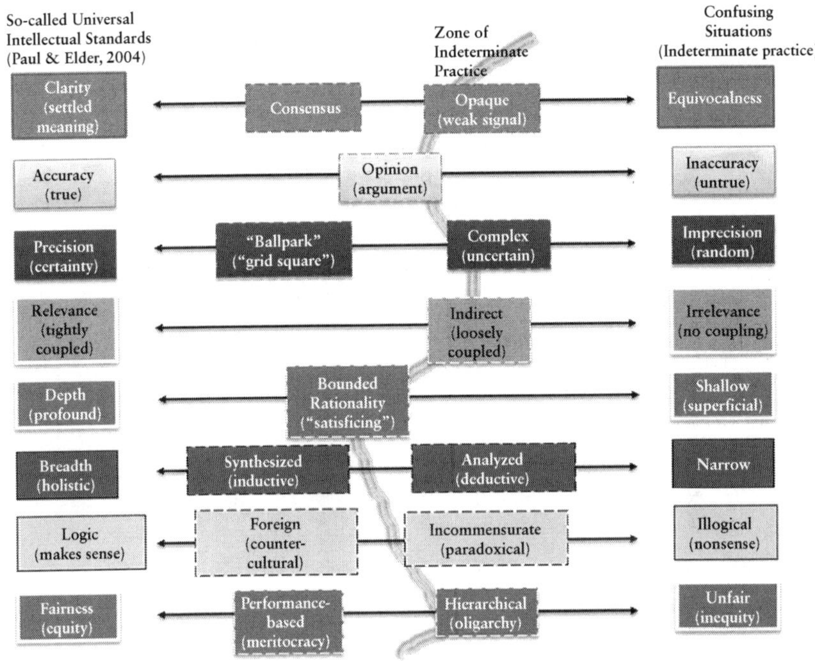

FIGURE 5.3 *Plotting the Zone of Indeterminate Practice.*

and *fairness* (Paul and Elder 2004, pp. 7–9).[25] From the modernist point of view, all critical thinking is oriented on making a difficult situation into an understandable situation (with the belief that more information will lessen the ambiguity of the situation). A bricoleur may redesign these modernist (scientific) values and develop relational continua, listing the in-betweens and opposites of these so-called universal intellectual standards (as I have tried to arrange in Figure 5.3):

Rather than expending energy disambiguating "the situation" in order to arrive at the ideal values shown on the left side of the chart, the bricoleur realizes that plotting the zone of indeterminate practice better represents appreciation of the wickedness of the situation at hand.[26] There are many more examples of employment of relationalism rather than categories. Deborah Stone (1997), for example, refers to the relational episteme this way:

> Categories are human mental constructs in a world that has only continua. They are the intellectual boundaries we put on the world in order to help us apprehend it and live in an orderly way . . . [but] nature doesn't have categories; people do. Given a world of continua, there is infinite choice about how to classify . . . [hence] science cannot settle questions of meaning (pp. 375–6). In a world of continua, boundaries are inherently unstable (p. 379).

Again, accepting the postinstitutional view of discontinuity in military science, the bricoleur may choose to reframe, relationally, along continua rather than in the illusory clarity of categories. For example, a Military Design effort could bricolate from the modernist's *principles of war*; signifying paradoxical patterns of operations as to afford different appreciations of which polarities should dominate in a particular context (Paparone and Crupi 2005): offense::defense; simplicity::complexity; economy of force::mass, and so forth.

The context matters and effective dialogue is "historically and culturally situated" (Gergen et al. 2004, p. 9). A "broad church of approaches" can prevent epistemic fallacy (i.e. "confusing what is with what we take it to be") (Archer 1998, p. 195). Exploring a diversity of senses, feelings, aesthetics, and spirituality can create emancipatory opportunities for the bricoleur. Seeking an inconsistent ethos (divergent sets of historic accounts and cultural – and psychological – value preferences) is quite a departure from the consistent normative values (such as getting the US military staffs to singularly, if not mindlessly, follow the commander's "guidance" in a planning process). We cannot rely on a "science of selection" for who should participate in design sessions. What constitutes "talent" is itself prone to an institutional value bias. Postinstitutional Military Design signals opportunities for indigenous and exdigenous voices in the endeavor.[27]

The less powerful may offer important counternarratives; their minority *petit récits* must have a voice. Hierarchical values are detrimental to paralogy and the accompanying quest for conflicting *petit récits*.[28] Design participants must somehow leave rank and positional authority "at the door" and not confuse passionate argument with insubordination or disrespect. Active or reflective listening practices are important ("I heard you say . . . [rephrasing] . . . , is that about right?"). Chris Argyris (1985) suggests these additional norms:

- Advocate positions as forthrightly as possible, but do so in a way that encourages others to question them.
- Ask for a better-supported argument whenever someone states a disagreeable position, or help the arguer better assess the position.
- Use illustrative data (storytelling) and make lucid, cogent arguments when evaluating another person's argument.
- Apologize if, in the process of dialogue, you act in ways that appear to upset others. Assure them that this was not the intention (provided that is genuinely the case) and state the intent and the reasoning behind it.
- Ask for the reasoning behind actions that you find upsetting, in order to appreciate the other's intentions (pp. 258–9).[29]

While being sensitive that humor is a cultural manifestation, the bricoleur may be influential while participating in critical dialogue demonstrating that they can laugh at themselves when realizing what they originally thought to be true is not. Although difficult to translate across cultures and languages, jokes, puns, and other forms of humor jab at established rules, norms, and even values (the latter often being "taboo"). To be deviant is to be irreverent and to be irreverent is to be creative—essential to the process of critical dialogue and creativity. As Michael D. Cohen and James G. March (1986) assert, it is hypocrisy that transforms thinking, not conformance:

> Playfulness is the deliberate, temporary relaxation of rules in order to explore the possibility of alternative rules . . . [that is], a little heresy can go a long way . . . [and] humor, play, and silliness can reduce tension and encourage irreverence. [Those involved in design should] . . . [s]upplement the technology of reasoning with a *technology of foolishness* (emphasis added, p. 223).

Sociological explorations may be as helpful as psychological ones. The US Defense colleges' and universities' contemporary mantra of teaching *individual* students *how to think* in lieu of teaching them *what to think* exemplifies a sort of arrogance toward the hope of unbiased rationality given the emancipatory forms of dialogue proposed here.[30] Military schools could provide practitioners more opportunities for forms of critical dialogue and coaching toward improvisational "conversations with the situation" (Schön 1987, p. 42) where "communities of practitioners are *continually* engaged in . . . worldmaking" (p. 36). We cannot presuppose what or how bricoleurs might think while engaged in localized, smaller-language games (in fact, one should hope for being surprised). If *being surprised* is not considered a paramount value in educating for design, then military education is not providing overt opportunities for the role of a bricoleur of new meanings in- and on- action. The community of practice should stress that acting may be required before "finding" meaning for subsequent action (e.g. as with the deeply immersed Military Design teams operating in-the-flow of unique local situations exploring improvisational approaches to craftwork and the emergent tasks discussed in Chapter 3). There is no substitute for opportunities to bricolate meaning, both *in*-practice and *on*-practice.

Summary

In this chapter, I have tried to reconstruct the ideal of military PROFESSION away from the modernist's competency-mapping methods that are well encapsulated by the Weberian ideal-type of bureaucracy. To the modernist institution, the professional's role is that of a scientist, and his rationalized organization and military interventions are but "science projects." Confronted with indeterminate zones of practice, the institutional metanarrative (couched in modern military science) is exposed as an ideology: a habituated construction of reality.

Philosophical Underpinnings	Modernist Military Institution	Postinstitutional
Ontology	Objectivist (Realism)	Objectivist and Subjectivist (Indeterminate Zones of Practice)
Epistemology	Foundational (Eventual science of everything). Characteristics –Positive; Legitimacy of knowledge is through measurement; Genericize-ability; Context-free; Emotion-free; Nominal; &, Nomothetic (taxonomic categorical, cause-and-effect). Perspective: Beforeintervention: etic. During: etic and emic. Progressive Doctrine: Lessons learned; Best practices.	Relational (multi-framing and paradox). Characteristics –Ambiguous and paradoxical; Legitimacy of language is an historic, socio-political interactive & adaptive process; Knowledge is Ephemeral and indigenous-to-the-situation. Perspective: Quadigenous. Discovery of meaning in-and on-action; Paralogical constructions of *petit récit.*
Methodologies	"Science Projects:" (1) Define Problem; (2) State desired end; (3) Develop tasks from doctrinal theory-for-action (e.g. hierarchical levels of war; "lines of effort" as operationalized independent variables; standardize language); (4) Perform tasks within doctrinated capabilities; (5) Measure effects (operationalized dependent variables) & adjust method; & (6) Feedback to prove theory efficacy.	Affirmative postmodern approach; Metaphoric reasoning; Deconstruction of metanarratives and reconstructions of meaning; Inter-paradigmatic journeys; "Conversations with the situation"); Hermeneutics/Exegesis; Causal-loop diagrams; Ethnography; &, Idiography.
Ethics	Bureaucratic; Conformism; Technical rationalism; Reductionism; Functionalism; Behaviorism; &, Operationalism.	Deviance; Reflexivism; Relationalism
Exemplar Theories	Operations Research, Stratified Systems, Architectural sciences, Mathematical Supersets (e.g. Task-& Functional-Mission Analysis), & Synoptic Planning (systemic and teleological ideology)	Institutional theory; Sensemaking; Critical theory; Heuristics/Cognitive linguistics; Chaos and complexity ("chaoplexity"); &, Social construction theory.
Professional Role of Military Designer	*Scientist-planner (e.g. apply esoteric, technical knowledge in the design of the military and military interventions)*	*Bricoleur (e.g. artistic improvisationalist of meaning; historian of knowledge; interpretive sociologist; crafty scientist)*

FIGURE 5.4 *Comparative Views of Profession.*

What I propose here is a prospective role of the military designer—as a bricoleur—based on Lyotardian paralogy. Here, the postinstitutional PROFESSIONAL attempts to incorporate patterns of uncertain, unique, and paradoxical meanings explored in the *petit récits* of Military Design endeavors that can be at least temporarily emancipated from the modernist's metanarrative. I constructed Figure 5.4 in an attempt to summarize and illustrate the philosophical shift I have tried to incorporate in the book to this point.

One way of exemplifying an ongoing *petit récit* is for me to ask the reader to immerse into a "conversation" between two bricoleurs who have struggled in their practice under the social restraints of the modernist metanarrative. They seem to walk loyally and dutifully with one step in the institutional world and with extraordinary sidesteps into a postinstitutional world.

Notes

1 Perhaps this duality of reality (internal and external) helps explain why sociologists do not speak of "ex-stitutions" but "in-stitutions."

2 PROFESSION is what I consider yet another "usual suspect" to add to the three (strategy, leadership, and planning) described in Chapter 3.

3 Kurt Lang (1972) provides a comprehensive review of the modernist literature on the sociology of the military complete with an annotated bibliography.

4 In their first edition (2002), Don M. Snider, Gayle L. Watkins, and Lloyd J. Mathews attempt to segregate bureaucracy from profession and write: "The Army is neither a public-sector bureaucracy manned by civil servants nor is it a business with employees. It has been and continues to be a profession, one which military professionals serve with deep pride and immense personal satisfaction (p. 3)." In the 2007 edition, Snider creates the same (imaginary?) tension between modern profession and bureaucracy: "And herein is the basis for the natural tensions within the Amy's dual character. Predominantly, the Army is a profession focused on developing and adapting the four clusters of expert knowledge mentioned earlier. In other situations . . . the Army is a hierarchical bureaucracy . . ." (p. 14). This is a fallacious duality.

5 Strangely, Andrew Abbott (1988) argues that his eco-systems view is an alternative to functionalism (p. 316), whereas the systems view is cut from the functionalist paradigmatic "cloth." He also argues that bureaucracy is antithetical to professionalism and associates bureaucracy with organization as something conceptually separate from profession (p. 151). Again, my argument here is that Weberian bureaucracy and professionalization are sociologically tautological. In fact, he mentions Weber only once—p. 177—without citation and, without explanation, does not address Weber's seminal work on bureaucracy. Finally, he argues that only some professions socially construct their knowledge without theoretically explaining how knowledge is created for those that do not (p. 178).

6 By foreknowledge, I am referring to predictive science (the expectation of knowing what to do when presented with a problematic situation). Andrew Abbott (1988) and other modernists present the professions work as the application of knowledge; and, that application is knowledge's main purpose (p. 53). Those (e.g. Record 2003; Yarger 2010) who use the quote from Carl von Clausewitz (1984/1832), "The first, the supreme, the most far-reaching act of judgment that the statesman and commander have to make is to establish . . . the kind of war on which they are embarking" (p. 88) are, in effect, demanding that military science serve as a foreknowledge of happenstance (e.g. "diagnosing" correctly before going to war). This sort of requirement for prescience begs for the taxonomies (i.e. kinds) and other typological elaborations that modernist military doctrines provide; yet, the danger is such nominal approaches always oversimplify and serve as the basis for self-fulfilling prophecies (Merton 1968).

7 The US Office of Personnel Management operationally defines competencies—as a function of skills, knowledge, and abilities (SKAs) that are mapped to positions in the government. The US armed forces are designed around the same concept. For example, the Department of the Army (1984) states: "The objectives of standardization are as follows: a. Improvement and sustainment of proficiency and readiness among soldiers and units throughout the Army. This will be accomplished by universal application of approved practices and procedures. b. Reduction of the adverse effects of personnel turbulence (such as retraining) following reassignment of soldiers. This will be accomplished by eliminating different methods of performing the same tasks or procedures at the new assignment. c. Elimination of local modification to approved standardized practices and procedures." Furthermore, "Standardization will be attained by – (1) Standardizing the procedures used by soldiers and units to operate, maintain, and support major weapon and equipment systems. (2) Identifying those basic tasks that will be performed in the same manner and to the same standard in like units throughout the Army" (p. 1). These are behaviorist constructions (meanings for action are "mapped" into the position that is objectified—"existing" separate from individuals who fill it). Standardization is another word for competency mapping.

8 It is interesting that Weber actually attributed the professionalization of the priesthood as characterized by the bureaucratic-rationalization of knowledge—in the more original meaning of the word, *doctrine*, that is, the Catholic Church's doctrine (Ritzer 1975, p. 631).

9 Max Weber was himself a reservist in the German Army and saw active service as an officer in hospital administration during World War I.

10 United States Code, Title 10, Chapter 107 makes the stratification of PME, according to officer rank and position, a legal requirement. Stratified-systems theory (Jaques 1976, 1986) seems to be reified even to the point of being legislated.

11 A radical humanist would point out that the educational epistemology of the modernist military institution addresses only those in the upper hierarchy (i.e. commissioned officers). The word "training" applies primarily to the enlisted and noncommissioned officers. The education-training dichotomy of the

institution reveals a sense of social class and confirmation of power. Also, why are four-star flag officers not included (is there a hidden epistemic script that says, "If you make four star rank, you no longer need to learn")?

12 "Producing" is an interesting word that should not be ignored in this narrative. The underpinning logic here is that education involves manufacturing commissioned officers on an education assembly line. Products are mapped to ranks and positions that exist outside the individual officers. Like production lines of automobiles programmed by General Motors, there are the Chevy's and there are the Buicks and Cadillac's.

13 O-1 ("officer, first grade"), etc. refer to the officer rank structure in all US military service departments. For example, in the US Navy, O1 is an ensign; in the Army, it is called a second lieutenant. An O-10 is a four-star rank—the highest rank attainable since the end of World War II. In the enlisted ranks, a corollary scheme is used (E-1 through E-9).

14 The OPMEP subscribes to still another hierarchical scheme—a behavioral classification system—that lists evaluation at the highest level of cognitive behaviors. The scheme (originally developed in Bloom et al. 1956) is based on the analogy of biological taxonomies (p. 1), the "Dewey Decimal System" (p. 14), and on behaviorism (pp. 11–12) (I critiqued behaviorism as a modernist fallacy in previous chapters). The creators of the taxonomy included "thinking" as a behavior (p. 26). I am not endorsing the use of a behavioral taxonomy here but am using its logic, grammar, and rhetoric to illustrate still another stratified knowledge construction that parallels the way DOD structures its education (all part of the same, institutionalized functionalist paradigm).

15 Sociologist Robert K. Merton (1968) used a military example to explain this concept: ". . . it is believed that war between two nations is inevitable. Actuated by this conviction, representatives of the two nations become progressively alienated, apprehensively countering each 'offensive' of the other with a 'defensive' move of their own. Stockpiles of armaments, raw materials, and armed men grow larger and eventually the anticipation of war helps create the actuality" (p. 477). Michael D. Cohen et al. (1972) referred to this human phenomenon as *garbage can decision-making* where solutions look for problems. In my view, mindless acceptance of institutionally derived meanings makes action and behavior synonymous. Meaning-for-action that is institutionally hypostatized serves uncriticized as intent and purpose. Perhaps the most cited example of a war that began in this manner is World War I, where the German mobilization and maneuver plan itself (a.k.a. the Alfred von "Schlieffen Plan") dictated the decision for war (i.e. the plan was a self-fulfilling prophecy).

16 I mean sedimentation as described as the last stage of institutionalization in Chapter 1.

17 The official US DOD definition of "lesson learned" is: "Results from an evaluation or observation of an implemented corrective action that contributed to improved performance or increased capability. A lesson learned also results from an evaluation or observation of a positive finding that did not necessarily require corrective action other than sustainment" (Department of Defense 2011e, p. GL-3). The epistemic script here is clearly based on a cybernetic

(systems) model of learning and a modernist (positivist) epistemology. Jean-François Lyotard (1984) is critical of this modern science grand narrative—the utopian "self-regulating system." This belief reduces sociology to the process of eliminating dysfunction in the "system."

18 George Santayana (1998) also wrote that "history is always written wrong. . ." (p. 397). So, it is appropriate here to note that this author is guilty of using Santayana's oft "cherry-picked" aphorism that hardly represents Santayana's more complex philosophical discussions. Interestingly, Santayana wrote that war was irrational in his treatise (accordingly, how could one rationalize the history of it as this author suggests?). In that regard, he wrote that mythology and dogma have histories too (Santayana's implied quandary is how to separate these from nonfiction).

19 Jean-François Lyotard (1984) criticizes the modernist singular discourse: "The true goal of the system, the reason it programs itself like a computer, is the optimization of the global relationship between input and output – in other words, performativity" (p. 11).

20 Donald A. Schön (1987) again calls this modernist expectation of professionals to have foreknowledge, *technical rationality*—the misleading belief that "practitioners solve well-formed instrumental problems by applying theory and technique derived from systematic, preferably scientific knowledge" (pp. 3–4).

21 Paul J. DiMaggio (1995) goes on to explain the usefulness of *defamiliarization*: "I refer to the process of enabling a native – of society, an organization, or an academic discipline – to see his or her world with new eyes. . . . But this must not go too far. The conventional justification for neologisms is that the old words carry too much baggage to convey new ideas or perspectives. At the same time, too many neologisms render a theory too strange for people to grasp. . . . Arguably, all good theory has a germ of paradox" (p. 392).

22 Furthermore, the Department of the Army (2011b) asserts that design is about placing participants in "purpose-built, problem-centric" design teams "based on their expertise relative to *the problem*" (emphasis added, p. 3–6). The Army also conveys that there can be "understanding [of] Ill-structured problems" (p. 3–2). This is absurd if only from the fallacious basis of why the design team would move to a design philosophy if it could be "problem centric" or if it were just a matter of sharing information to achieve "understanding?" This distorted modernist view of design reinforces the community to see the world only through the functionalist paradigm.

23 The military designer "scripts" the situation at hand through *bricolage,* creating "new knowledge through improvisation rather than through adherence to a specific theory, method, or paradigm" (Boxenbaum and Rouleau 2011, p. 281). In Lyotardian terms, this epistemic script becomes a deviant *petit récit* (see below) that may often be in opposition to the institutional *metanarrative* (e.g. in the context of the present book, modernist military science)

24 METT-TC—mission, enemy, terrain and weather, troops available, time available, and civilian considerations; PMESII—political, military, economic, social, Infrastructure and Information; and DIME—Diplomatic, Information, Military, and Economic.

25 The booklet (Paul and Elder 2004) is used by US Army Command, General Staff College and US Army War College, and other Defense schools to teach critical thinking in terms of what the booklet calls "universal intellectual standards." These standards seem to reflect the utopian, scientific values of the modernist.

26 In the Department of the Army (2011b) Field Manual 5-0, the word *understanding* is used over 250 times. To a more reflective military designer, this may indicate a kind of institutional arrogance.

27 Insofar as situational immersion is concerned, anthropologist Anna Simons (2010) summed up her research of history's most profound military designers that, "Without any formal training in anthropology, such disparate figures as T. E. Lawrence, Douglas MacArthur, Joseph Stilwell, George Kennan, and Edward Lansdale all proved adept at turning their insights about another culture to strategic effect. More significantly, the strategies they came up with succeeded as instruments of war" (p. 5). Immersion into local situations, coupled with the ability to richly communicate, is essential to critical and emancipatory dialogue.

28 Many organization theorists have expressed written support to this thesis. The most sophisticated relationalist view is captured in the *Competing Values Framework*, concisely summarized in Kim Cameron and Robert E. Quinn (1999).

29 These ethics (more like person-to-person etiquette) are designed to loosen institutional habituation for small groups; for a wider scale, see Parson's (1954) insightful chapter on "The Problem of Controlled Institutional Change" that may generally guide a quest for institutional reflexivity (pp. 238–74) (despite his limited orientation being based on structural-functionalism). Interestingly, in the chapter, Parson speaks about postwar occupation denazification issues in the context of a strongly institutionalized German society, circa late 1940s.

30 I might add that there are a plethora of US Defense-funded studies concerning the psychological capability of the individual officer, usually in the rather romantic ideal of an informed, singularly expert "commander" who must be educated toward making rationalistic military designs (e.g. Sterling and Perala 2005; RAND 2009). Sociological research questions may be more fruitful: How does an institutional context serve to mimetically frame Military Design? How can designers reframe beyond these institutionalized collective frames of reference? Is wisdom in Military Design better described as a multiperson, multiparadigmatic, emancipatory endeavor?

6

Un Petit Récit From the Field

Grant Martin and Ben Zweibelson

Editor's note: I hope the following exchanges between two US Army majors offer the reader a petit récit and some insights about the sociology of military science and any prospects for postinstitutional Military Design. I asked them, based on their experiences in combat zones, to write generally about: "How does the institution want you to 'think' and how is that working?" They approached this topic through an exchange of emails over several months, while one was stationed in Fort Bragg, North Carolina (post-deployment from Afghanistan) and the other deployed to Afghanistan. They tried to address their experiences in their military staff planning roles with regard to several topics found in the previous chapters: issues with modernism, obstacles to a postinstitutional shift, answering questions of meaning for action, criticism of official doctrines that seem to too narrowly frame Military Design, social circumpressures that prohibit trying new ways to "reframe," taking issue with "one best way" of framing meaning-for-action, the value of applying heuristics from past interventions, finding paradoxes among unacknowledged competing organizational values, addressing assumptions that are too taboo to challenge, the tyranny of measurement (the illusion of hard science), and oligarchic systems of knowledge. [My editorial remarks are in brackets.]

Grant is a US Army Special Forces officer who has served two tours in Afghanistan and multiple deployments in support of United States Special Operations Command, South. Ben is a US Army Infantry officer from Connecticut who has over 18 years of combined enlisted and commissioned service, served two tours in Iraq, and is presently serving in Afghanistan. They have individually published articles on design-related subjects in a variety of online journals.

CHRIS PAPARONE,
March 2012

Ben: Let's start out this sharing of experiences by talking about modernism – to include its related belief systems of progressivism, logical positivism, rationalism, reductionism, and behaviorism – and whether you think it is pervasive in our military culture and may serve to keep military designers from being more creative.

Grant: I can think of numerous examples of modernism in my Army experience that may have hamstrung Military Design and presented obstacles to being creative. One great example is the Army's approach to complexity science. Instead of asking ourselves whether there are different ways with which to approach complexity, we acknowledge that there are certain instances of greater complexity, but then simply advocate more of the same reductionist approaches we have used in the past. I think the special operations community tends to do something similar: instead of developing our own unique approaches or questioning our published doctrine, systems, and processes, many times we simply try to do those things better – the Army's Military Decision Making Process comes immediately to mind and our application of that process to Unconventional Warfare (UW). That we will not question whether a rational decision making process fits with UW strikes me as coming directly from a Modernist culture.

Ben: I see that there is the dual tension between the ideals of having a universal science and the hierarchy's desire to control knowledge that both work together to prevent creative and critical thought. What I mean is that modernist military science permeates nearly all teaching, learning, and thinking as if there is context-free, universal application. If something works in a conflict, the institutional approach is to package it into doctrine that subsequently gets injected into our Professional Military Education (PME) curricula. Instead of tailoring our military science where creativity and innovation take priority over the quest for universal tenets, we do the opposite.

To address the second part of my point, this knowledge is steered by a top-down command-centric model that I refer to as the military hierarchy of command, control, and bottom-up reflection. Critical thinking at lower levels might help a company or squad of soldiers make quick and custom adaptations, but the span of transformation in thinking is still limited to the highest rank of the individual in the group. A squad leader can impact only his squad, whereas a general officer is believed to impact the larger organization. In some ways, this is good because it promotes stability and uniformity and reliable repetition is a comforting commodity in an uncertain and violent world. Reflection tends to start at the bottom where military action is experienced firsthand and slowly builds upward momentum only to be resisted, seemingly more and more as this questioning is received at higher levels in the organization. Self-organization and situation-specific innovations are hindered by this hierarchy of command, control, and bottom-up reflection.

Grant: I agree, and, as you say sometimes and in some ways that is good, but that universal application I would argue hurts us when it is not conducive to the complexity we face. It would be nice if we could adapt our meanings for action when we need to. I would even argue the institutional hierarchy stifles flag officer commanders as well. And it isn't just the individual commander, but their primary staffers and upper levels of the command that stifle lower-level initiative and sensemaking sometimes more than the commanders do.

Ben: I participated in the so-called 'Sunni Awakening Movement' during the surge phase of Operation Iraqi Freedom that provides a great example of resistance to "bottom-up" sources of innovation. US Army Corps and Division senior officers and staff refuting or rejecting the initial attempts by lower-level commanders to broker relationships with Sunni insurgents in their assigned regions. This refute or rejection broke under the momentum of success and after a reframing by the emergence of the *Sons of Iraq* shattered the dominant Coalition narrative that "my enemy must be destroyed, not negotiated with."

Grant: The overuse of the Army's regimented decision process is another example. In our Unconventional Warfare Planning Course at Fort Bragg, North Carolina, officers are put through hours of instruction on set planning processes and then practiced through exercises wherein they can apply these methods to UW and other special operations. Progressivism, for instance, permeates the entire planning processes, as we set up elaborate ways in which to measure or operationalize our "progress" so it would seem literal (i.e. objectified). UW planners are taught to set measurable progress, just like McNamara's "whiz kids" did during Vietnam. UW is about as complex a human undertaking I can think of and by seeming to reduce this complexity into quantifiable objectives, the institution seems to think we can come out measurably successful in the end.

We go through all the steps of the rational planning process, using the reductionist's Clausewitzian concept—center of gravity (COG) analysis—to identify the single point of enemy failure we must concentrate on to be successful along with its contributing critical capabilities, requirements, and vulnerabilities. We assume that if we can apply the right analytic technique to address the problem—that prescribed by modernistic military science—and ignore subjects like metaphysics and theology—we can be successful. We fail to take into account non-scientific approaches as a valid explanatory lens with which to look at the environment and to make sense, in a more holistic way of what we're facing.

Ben: COGs, as a wise mentor told me in Afghanistan while we were arguing with higher headquarters over the enemy's strategic-level COG, should actually be more about attending to the discourse than the output. Who really cares what you start with on a COG, or even where you end up? COGs are a conceptual tool and should not be these immovable objectifications that get wired into the campaign plan where there quickly accumulates thousands of orders, slides, and products that use that concept as a concrete foundation. They should reflect critical and creative thinking—the evolving, but tenuous understanding of a fluid and complex environment over time. Therefore, a COG, if one insists on using what I consider a rigid interpretation of a Clausewitzian physics metaphor, should transform over time as we and our rivals influence our meaning system through their actions and observations.

In theater, we were unable to critically question the monolith known as the "enemy strategic COG" because it was a core tenet within the entire organizational metanarrative and self-referential to all the earlier staff work. Instead of discourse and accepting fluid meanings shaped by our sensemakings of changing events, we were bound in the briar patch created by those commanders and their planners senior to us. Those COGs, once "settled," were immovable without those higher in the chain of command having reason to change them.

Grant: And I think we could change that if we allowed experimentation in our schools instead of routinized instruction during classroom exercises and in training. There is very little experimentation in our schools with different approaches; it is mainly rote memorization and application of approved doctrine. I would prefer the special operations community—if not the entire Army—to encourage its soldiers to constantly question doctrine, assume it is wrong, and attempt to come up with different frames with which to approach our missions.

Ben: Memorization and regurgitation take on new meanings when higher leadership develops their guidance. Our new US Army doctrine introduced concepts, such as "mission command" [Dempsey 2011] that espouses that lower elements of the organization should take initiative in the absence of detailed guidance; however, in practice I have found that this is rarely the case. In Afghanistan, I was involved in some extensive efforts where I originally started out in the highest level of the coalition organization with the group tasked to produce the overarching plan. Later I moved to a planning position in a lower-level headquarters, I essentially went from the "penthouse view to the lobby." From this lower echelon, I continued to plan and was able to draw from all of the higher level plans which I understood intimately from my prior assignment. However, because I had moved three levels down, there were two headquarters and staff elements between my new position and the original overarching plan.

Moving forward in the absence of guidance from the next two higher headquarters, I believed we produced a well-structured yet flexible and holistic campaign plan, overarching narrative, and other associated products that nested well within the highest organization's larger-scaled plan.

When we presented some of this extensive planning to our higher headquarters, there was an interesting mix of interest and apprehension. On one hand, the staffs were interested in absorbing some of the work because it helped establish their own planning framework to nest from the original higher organization's plan. Yet on the other hand, we were informally told on several occasions, "how can you plan ahead if the next higher commander or his commander has yet to give their guidance?" We were told to slow down, and wait for higher directive.

Grant: My peers and I have been frustrated many times by commands that publish guidance demanding subordinate initiative and innovation, but then structure our processes in such a way as to discourage us from breaking free from our cultural paradigms. For a specific example, the frame that NATO Training Mission Afghanistan (NTM-A) adopted to build the Afghan Civil Order Police (ANCOP) is noteworthy. In early 2010 we decided that we had to show progress with the ANCOP. Our conclusion was that the ANCOP suffered from terrible attrition rates and that we could fix that by paying them more, partnering or coaching with them more, and giving them breaks to recover from otherwise sustained combat. This was a problem framing done from a Western perspective (that attrition was bad and that these three efforts would help cut attrition). A year later and the ANCOP was still suffering from high attrition, even though we were paying more, partnering more, and attempting to get them more time off. We never approached the problem from a different frame of reference—was it just a problem from our point of view? Maybe all those leaving were unfit and we should have wanted them to leave anyway. Was the solution really to pay them more and to operate alongside them with more coalition partners? What unforeseen negative consequences did giving them time off and more "coaching" create? A reliance on behaviorism—that we could measure something and as long as that increased—we could show progress (we measured who got paid, how much more they got paid, and if fewer soldiers were getting money taken by their commanders, who and how many were partnered, and which units were given leave). We essentially designed a behavioral science project. Unfortunately we were unable to apply any creativity to fixing "the problem" (changes to these independent variables would spoil the objectivity of the experiment). And we were not even sure if there really was a "problem" except from our perspective, motivated by prospects for redeployment out of Afghanistan.

Ben: That reminds me of the time one of our sites that use the modernist model of military training and education lost power for a few days during bad weather. The program follows the same progression we use for our hierarchical organization—from basic training for privates all the way up to the senior officer war college experience. The Western trainers use PowerPoint slides, the instructors follow a "script" or doctrinal texts. Students receive and are expected to memorize and apply the standardized tasks and doctrinal concepts when required in order to pass the courses.

When the power went out for a few days, the instructors carried on, but were forced to change their method entirely. Instead of using PowerPoint projections, they told stories through their interpreters. The Afghans reacted favorably to this, and surprising to the instructors, a far greater number of students seemed actively involved, trading their own stories and using their own metaphors during the lessons. The students taught the teachers, and the teachers taught the students; it was a tapestry where learning was woven between cultures, language, conceptualizations, and differing perspectives. When the power was restored a few days later, the current teachers stated that they would try to keep this emergent method of teaching alive; but it was not long before they were back to the old, standard method of instruction and the Afghans fell back to being mostly passive learners and unengaged.

Grant: One of your first points about top-down-driven efforts to train everyone on the same things reminds me of efforts to measure all soldiers in a particular course and then aggregate those measurements to show some trends, and attempt to tweak our "assembly line" in order to get the aggregate numbers up. The emphasis is on standardized testing and collecting metrics that proved "progress" was being made. I often am confounded and speculate that our small units are successful in spite of most of our training. What makes them great, especially when faced with unique situations, are the diverse sets of strengths each person within the small unit brings to the situation and our writ-large American cultural propensity to be entrepreneurial.

Ben: Speaking of that sort of entrepreneurship, the standardization of doctrinal knowledge and procedures in our modernist military institution seems paradoxically to exist in part out of a sort of mass production logic. In Afghanistan, our headquarters continues to engage in some practices that support this standardization, potentially, in my mind, at the expense of being creative and critical. One such practice is known here as the *deep dive* meeting which is supposed to be a detailed and informative meeting on a particular critical topic between subject matter experts and the military decision-maker.

Depth implies a narrow exploration of a presumed critical topic to generate significant dialogue among members of the deep-dive group. Of the many such sessions I have attended, I did not experience open dialogue. Instead, the subject matter experts (primarily military staff members and representatives from outside organizations) developed the topic and delivered a well-rehearsed pitch to the decision-maker, with little freedom for deeper dialogue. I remember only a few interesting occasions where the topic directly impacted other organizational representatives in the room that had not been included in any of the deep-dive formal preparations. Their objections and dissenting views seemed to be considered a threat by the "well-prepared" attendees. So, now the practice is to pitch the concept to the decision maker *prior* to releasing it to elements outside the organization as it is much harder to change a decision after the meeting versus dealing with the differing views during and after a more open meeting.

Now deep dives have very little critical discourse, and dissenting opinions are nearly impossible to express for those residing inside the institution. When a staff officer has prepared and presents seventy or so highly detailed slides in the span of an hour, there is little room for dialogue, and the entire dynamic of the deep dive is fixated not on the entire audience, but on the lone senior decision-maker seated at the head of the room. By unconscious design, the decision maker controls the entire tempo of the meeting and, based on the norms that have developed, are usually the only ones allowed to comment on the topic (even if they turn around and announce that they want others to chime in with their insights). From my perspective, a deep dive is a deceptive metaphor as it turns out to be rather shallow. In a meeting format such as this, one could not risk being a critical or creative thinker out loud because even if dissenting views were valid, the institutional proclivity made silence safer than dissent.

Grant: Ben—I had my own experiences with deep dives. Fortunately, for the reasons you mention, I was able to miss most of them. The ones I attended, as you say, were controlled to an extreme level by the established institutional norms of having flag officers present and there were also enough peer pressures to keep any dissenting voices quiet. The attitude was that the most senior officer present (like a primitive clan chieftain) was in a better position than others to know what was best; thus, discourse was not necessary. The problem with this norm, prevalent in our institution in my opinion, was that there were no other forums that I was aware in which important decisions were made. So these sessions were the only chance to critically challenge the status quo.

Ben: In other headquarters in Afghanistan, meetings were often just as bad, with the additional tendency of the visiting senior decision maker serving the role of a local-problem solver. In a particularly disappointing meeting, I witnessed a general officer discuss at length the color of jacket being supplied to the Afghan local police in a particular region and whether the supplier understood the importance of all of the jackets being of the same color. The problem was that one purchase of jackets was a different shade or embellished with a stripe. My colleagues and I playfully refer to these instances as "bright shiny objects" that attract senior officer attention. Perhaps part of this senior officer reaction is simply human nature as we all tend to cling to the certainty of things we know and can address. After all, general officers were once company-grade or battalion-level officers that dealt almost exclusively with such details. Evidently they were successful at solving such details as they were promoted up the pyramid to general officer. Yet it seems to me that being a flag officer should require one to think "generally" and let the lower level officers address details such as uniform jackets.

Grant: I one-hundred per cent agree with you on the issue of senior officers at the macro-level getting involved with micro decisions. I tend to think that many of our headquarters formations are not value-added during certain types of operations (I have witnessed that flag officer headquarters and even lower HQs have little to do during counterinsurgency (COIN) and other unconventional types of interventions and thus they are constantly in search of something to do—and that search eventually leads them to the local realms. This illustrates a violation of what I think is a very important tenet of how to approach an uncertain situation: the ability to change one's organizational structure to fit the environment at hand. As we tend to apply our current structure—brigade, divisions, corps, combined task force headquarters, etc.—to every situation we encounter each level searches for meaning and relevance. But the logic of such operations turns the hierarchy upside down, where the lower levels have more potential "strategic" value than the higher ones.

I recently observed the phenomenon of leaders refusing to micromanage subordinates as I followed some US Special Forces students conducting an ambush patrol. There were two instructors following several students who had been through patrolling courses recently and several others who had received very little, if any, training on patrolling. At one point the designated student leader did not know where best to emplace the assault position. Instead of cutting off debate, the senior instructor encouraged all to voice opinions and then asked the leader to make a decision. Once the ambush was over, everyone discussed the different advantages and disadvantages of the alternatives that were available. The end result was not one dogmatic way to execute an ambush, but the realization that, depending on the particular circumstances present, through participative inquiry there can surface a number of ways in which to conduct the ambush.

Ben: You just provided a great example of one of my pet theories (e.g., Miller 2007)—swarm intelligence—where decision making occurs as an antithesis of the traditional military hierarchy.[1] Unlike hierarchies where the senior commander controls the discussion and often single-handedly makes critical decisions even at the expense of staff recommendations, metaphors of self-organizing and adaptive systems, such as those observed with bee- and ant- colonies, permit us to reframe how decisions are made logic. Swarm concepts encourage fluidity in Military Design open discussions. In order to truly introduce something like swarm theory into the traditional military hierarchy, our functionalist military institution would have to disenfranchise the chain of command. That would require a paradigm shift [perhaps toward the radical-structuralist one mentioned in Chapter 4] in how we organize, communicate, and fight. I remain doubtful that our military institution is ready to engage in these theories at the expense of how our organizations are historically defined through the tradition of hierarchical values.

Grant: Perhaps less so in our special operations culture; albeit, these values are still dominant. And as you probably would agree, institutional change takes either a long time with small increments or results from a radical jolt to the institution (such as the post-Vietnam War experience). Returning to our talk about our institutionalized modernist thinking, what other kinds of obstacles do you see ahead preventing paradigmatic shifts?

Ben: One civilian professor I encountered during my professional military education experience retired from active duty military service in the mid-1990s. He had spent his last decade on active duty planning within the functionalist paradigm with "effects-based operations" (EBO) doctrine of that era. Now charged with teaching Military Design to a more recent generation of military students, the professor besmirched multi-paradigmatic approaches to design and claim, "design is just EBO with new words." On the other hand, there are enough faculty members within our PME system that encourage critical and creative thinking on the level and scope that institutional reflexivity demands (otherwise I would not be writing any of this!). Yet some of those more reflexive instructors were often curbed or pressured informally to reinforce newly-published design doctrine despite its many flaws. One design faculty member, who by the way no longer works with the program, was not even permitted to meet with students except under off-duty conditions in coffee shops and a local Thai restaurant. The ironic thing was that I probably learned more from those "covert" coffeehouse meetings and dining on Thai food than I did in most of the official design lectures and practicums in class!

Grant: From my perspective we seem to have built up an institution over time that becomes more and more self-referencing, so that an unquestioned, circular logic underpins our actions. It is very difficult, based on social circumpressures, to criticize our institutional epistemology, for instance, because published doctrine, by design, provides the logic for how we are organized, how we train, equip our forces, etc. So to criticize that believed-to-be foundational knowledge automatically is seen as a threat. It would take no less than a radical re-working of organizational structures, our educational and training pedagogies, how we come up with our knowledge structures, and the disenfranchisement of tightly engineered processes of the Joint Capabilities Integration and Development System, Planning Programming and Budget Execution and like-processes—all threatened by the questioning of the functionalist paradigm. No one ever seems to ask what underlies our adaptation, just assuming it is our mechanistic management systems. A great example of this is how we went about growing, training, and structuring the Afghan National Security Forces after "the surge" that began in 2009 (modeled somewhat after our "surge" in Iraq). Almost everything we did came from what we learned in Iraq. We equipped the ANSF with modern vehicles, weapons, uniforms, rank systems, Western pay practices and so forth. We taught them to plan like we do and even attempted to get them to run military operations the way we would. To do anything else would have required us to question our own means and ways of doing things.

A specific example from Afghanistan is when someone once suggested in a planning meeting that maybe focusing on the minds of the average people, instead of the current powerbrokers, might lead to short-term instability and thus hinder efforts at stabilizing Afghanistan now and working towards our transition out of there. This suggestion was met with much opposition and the prevailing attitude that there is no ambiguity in what we are facing. Everyone seemed to know the template-for-meaning to use in Afghanistan, and that was what our US Army and Marine Corps field manual on COIN instructed us to do.

Ben: I see that there are some core beliefs about Afghanistan that our military institution cannot dare ask – the inquiries are taboo – yet are precisely the sort of out-of-paradigm inquiries that might help being more institutionally reflexive. I put in my own words what I believe our pervading assumptions are as follows:

- Providing security for the population will help the people prosper economically.
- Literacy is critical for building a functional enduring security force for Afghanistan.
- Afghanistan is a nation-state that requires a liberal form of governance.
- NATO can "win" the information campaign if we promote the truth, and demonstrate unwavering values while respecting the culture of Afghanistan's people.
- Afghanistan requires a western-model security force.
- The more enemy we kill or capture, the more progress we make in transitioning over to the legitimate government.
- The more insurgent fighters we disarm, the more stable the region will become.
- The Afghan population is the "strategic COG."

These statements serve a narrative that is woven into virtually every coalition plan, order, and press release. They are sacred to the point that anyone suggesting these concepts are potentially wrong would threaten the very foundation of most military efforts underway. The institution is not going to throw these assumptions out and start over, certainly not ten years into this intervention. Instead, we trod forward and beat any dissenting thought by categorically dismissing them as "crazy talk" or as expressions of "non-team players." Military Design practitioners that consider questioning these assumptions are not crazy, but when one employs a different perspective, they are dancing to the beat of a different drum.

The first assumption presents what is a complex issue as a linear-causal relationship, where "A leads to B". Yet the *Afghanistan Economic Update* published in October 2011 by the World Bank mapped poverty throughout the country and found no relationship between poverty and conflict in Afghanistan [see World Bank 2011].[2] So there are alternative views left largely unsaid in present company (I am stationed in Afghanistan as I write this to you). The second assumption also permeates throughout our headquarters. Literacy is a critical aspect of everything we do to develop the Afghan security forces to create an enduring and functional institution that operates in a generally "look like me" Western approach. The third assumption seems to reflect a national political position of the United States and our Coalition partners; therefore it goes far beyond a military institutional avoidance of critical or creative thinking. Yet the question remains valid, must Afghanistan be led by a central, liberal form of government?

Statement four deals with public perception, the clash of cultures and how our military organization seeks to win a propaganda war that is misplaced. Using our linear and Clausewitzian appeal to an already destruction-centric military we try to slay the *public opinion monster* here and seem to really believe that we can win that side of the war. While postinstitutional forms of Military Design may generate alternative views, will our modernist military collective mind ever step away from this *we can win the hearts and minds* dogma that is intertwined with our COIN doctrine? There will not be a day anytime soon where the majority of a perceived "occupied" population would view foreign troops; especially Western troops within a pre-nation-state society.

Grant: This reminds me of a conversation about perception in Afghanistan with someone who was advocating that "our side" always tell the "truth." My thought was – it doesn't matter that we think we do that – perception and world views in Afghanistan trump "the truth" on any day. Many – maybe most – already believe – no matter what we do or say – that we are there for mercantilist reasons and to undermine Afghan religion and culture that is counter to the growth of the world market.

We can spend years building up great examples, effort, and "strategic communications" to attempt to change the metanarrative – but it is all undermined by just a single example of what they already know to be "true": that we are infidels who don't care about Islamic traditions and don't care about the Afghan people.

So, I am with you – because we cannot discuss the negative implications of adapting a policy that goes against the grain of Afghan culture and perception, we are left with a possibly self-defeating narrative, or at least one that seems to get us nowhere.

Ben: The fifth assumption deals with whether we ought to build a massive, western-centric security force that the Afghans cannot afford to sustain, or should we deviate from our cherished military doctrine and build a security force that meets Afghan security needs while remaining commensurate with Afghan social norms?

Grant: It's interesting that you bring that up. In our own unconventional warfare predeployment training we assume that soldiers that might have never spent one day conducting UW will know more than the average guerilla that has been at it most of his life. The reality has normally been that when we deploy soldiers to a region, usually the government there wanted the money, modern equipment, ammunition, and military-to-military technical training that the Americans provide—instead of some special insight into how to defeat their insurgents. Everywhere we go we are mainly incorporating what we believe we know. That is, we believe what the other nations are inviting us in for is primarily what we know. What we do not seem to recognize are taking into account what a nation can afford, what is their propensity to adapt and sustain themselves, and what can best take advantage of their strengths—these are things unfortunately I do not see in our doctrine or in practice. I think this is a matter of a combination of us not being reflective on how we create and use knowledge and believing, analogically, that how we do things is why we've had historic success, such as in World War II.

Ben: Assumption six addresses our sense of linear causality with what many call the *whack-o-mole* mentality – that killing more bad guys equals progress toward a defined end. This positivist mindset builds over time so that, now more than ten years into the Afghanistan conflict, so that reframing is institutionally unpalatable. Furthermore, if one sees only what one wants to see, there is plenty of cherry-picked data that supports the narrative that "we only require one more fighting season to defeat the Taliban and Al Qaeda." I consider this a classic example of single-loop learning. It is an institutionalized military perspective because, as one senior officer put it sarcastically during a briefing, "we are just admiring the problem," implying what we really need to do is create more destruction-centric meanings for action. For example, we need to demonstrate "jackpots" and employ more successful night raids showing linear-causality (doctrinally, we actually call them *lines of operation*!) in defeating the enemy over time and space (Conklin 2008).[3] After ten years of conflict and the US raid to kill Osama Bin Laden, insurgent activity continues despite measurable success [see Ibrahim 2009].[4] Other critical commentary, such as 'A Knock on the Door' [see van Linschoten and Kuehn 2011], suggests our continuing causal story, that night raids are the safest and most effective tool against insurgents, is flawed.[5] However the cause-and-effect mindset continues with jackpot-seeking night raids in the pursuit of an elusive, yet operationally well-defined "victory."

Grant: Unfortunately, in a science project oriented institution, there is not a better metric than dead insurgent leaders. And thus the race for enemy body counts, reminiscent of Vietnam, spurs statistical competitions as various units began to spar for recognition and resources.

Ben: The seventh assumption has to do with a nearly decade-long causal story about disarming Afghan civilians. The Afghan Peace through Reintegration Program (APRP) is the latest evolution in weapons disarmament approaches. The APRP program presents yet another one-way-causal story espousing that increased disarmament leads to greater security.[6] In my view, attempts to disarm Afghans might lead to civilians to simply rearm themselves when conditions demand it. Stabilization of a region might not require disarmament if we explore beyond our belief that collecting up piles of weapons is a measure for progress. This assumption can be challenged, yet our modernist institutions and their established knowledge structures, power systems, and self-referencing habits are difficult if not impossible to overcome [for a provocative essay on methods to overcome institutional forms of *problematization*, see Alvesson and Sandberg 2011].[7]

Grant: And this is why I submit that our modernist institution is self-defeating for trying out alternative frames for Military Design. Current design doctrine does not advocate questioning underlying ontology, epistemology, and methodology, viewed together as a paradigm. There are too many institutional obstacles to admitting we might not be "right" across these philosophical considerations. We need ways to doubt and staying within the same paradigm is problematic in itself.

Switching gears, assuming modern military science cannot settle questions of meaning—how does this assertion strike you? Secondly, have you experienced times when you were directed to create a "science project" approach to finding meaning for action?

Ben: I understand there is an important distinction between how the scientific method is supposed to generate clarity in the physical (or natural) sciences with respect to the social (or more qualitative) sciences. Our military prefers the former as the core logic to understand the world. The underlying thinking is that we want quantifiable, repeatable, highly accurate, and consistent readings on social phenomena we are attempting to change. Therefore, "science projects" generate at least the illusion of certainty that we want in an otherwise uncertain world. However, military interventions into societies involve levels of uncertainty and ambiguity that cannot be reduced to an assumed scientific certainty or clarity.

I will use a physics metaphor to illustrate. Gravity is everywhere, and everything must obey it. We seek to find the same Newtonian-lawful meanings in complex human interactions. Once we think we have defined them, we assert we can employ them to control and influence through a targeting-like process (like we use for artillery and aerial bombing that appropriately rely on Newtonian physics). In conventional state-on-state military conflicts, this use seems to work. In complex social interventions, such as we are facing in Afghanistan, other sciences (such as complexity theory) may help us escape from the traditional shackles of Newtonian metaphors. Yet our modernist military doctrines continue to cling to Cartesian concepts (such as COG analysis that our doctrine demands) that always oversimplify causal relationships. Ironically, the only "gravity" that such analysis demonstrates is conceptual immobility. Working inside the Newtonian metaphor, changing a COG does not reflect paradigmatic reframing. Yet we are restricted to reframing what the COG is (not questioning the process of analyzing it to begin with).

Grant: As an institutional insider, I see us as positivists. We think we have a pretty tight grasp on scientific-like principles and therefore we have pre-made meanings-for-action. These pan out in the oft-used operations research and systems analysis (ORSA) mentality that seeks to measure every conceivable area in which we could detect a positive, cause-and-effect relationship. Of course, if years of US positive scientism did not yield the defeat of the Vietnamese communists, then I'm still at a loss as to why we do not question our meaning for action expressed in terms of measures of effectiveness. We seem to have the quest to find the right set of metrics that will fix our inadequate ones rather than question the very idea of measuring behavioral phenomena (effectively ignoring socially-derived meanings) to begin with.

Ben: Yes and this can be illustrated with my eighth assumption. I recall wargaming under the tutelage of a senior civilian advisor who had taught the traditional joint doctrinal approach to operational design for many years and had even published books on how to identify COGs. We inquired as to what the "enemy strategic COG" was to address a planning project for the Afghan National Security Force. The Coalition previously applied a doctrinal approach to "operational design" and identified COGs for itself and the enemy. The current command and staff continue with these original definitions. These were subsequently "nested" in subordinate campaign plans and a variety of other action-oriented products; hence, we seem to have built "castle walls" to defend these COGs – now longstanding meanings that frame "the problem."

During this design effort, a coalition planning group argued that the higher headquarters' position on the enemy strategic center of gravity was flawed. The conversation ensued where we sparred over the previously identified COG as being more of a subordinate, "critical requirement" (another doctrinal concept) of the "REAL" enemy strategic COG. We presented a more abstract statement of the enemy COG. As the lead planner, I consulted our tutor and he vigorously agreed with the team's position to change the COG.

When the planning team's results were submitted to the higher headquarters, a senior staff member noticed the difference in the stated enemy strategic COGs and demanded that we withdraw our finding. He said something like, "You are deviating from our approved COG, and you cannot make this recommendation which contradicts our analysis." When the team took great efforts to dialogue with that staff officer and his fellows, the higher staff element deleted all mention of any COGs in the final product before sending our analysis to senior decision makers. Whether my team's position was wrong or right, we could not challenge the higher staff's assertion. If we were more right than they, the entire campaign plan and subsequent written orders across the NATO forces would need major revision . . . and, after all, subordinate headquarters cannot see things at the strategic level better than the higher one. This all occurred within the COG analytic doctrine we were all using! It did not occur to the parties involved that the whole idea of finding a single point of failure (*the* "CoG") may have been flawed in the first place.

Grant: I remember being there and we usually saw the COG as "the will of the Afghan people" and we could not fail in our tenure on staff as it takes a long time to win that. But this goes beyond Afghanistan. In South America, wherein our anti-drug efforts arguably have not gotten us very far, we still hold that we can suspend black market forces and problematize the situation around supply rather than demand. Ironically, in legal markets, we preach the opposite (demand) as being as important if not more important than supply. Framing meaning-for-action in the so-called drug war should be pretty apparent to anyone who has studied economics. Yet we seem to suspend that interactive (complex, mutually causal) relationship when it comes to addressing the drug war with "supply" being the dominant causal story.

Our traditional mental models seem to distort reality. As far as the Afghans go – it was similar everywhere else I've been: the assumption was that everyone just wants to live harmoniously under a centralized liberal democracy – you know freedom and to be treated justly [e.g. see Hughes et al. 2002].[8] I was told we should apply Maslow's [1943] hierarchy-of-needs to all social groups. This ill-prepared me to make sense in situations where Maslow's form of rationality did not apply. My own experience has made me suspicious that there is a universal truth that all people want freedom and to be treated equally as some sort of human law of self-actualization. Yet, it seems taboo to question these liberal ideals.

Ben: I agree that much of what we are doing in Afghanistan reflects more of our own cultural perceptions and values than those of the Afghans (and theirs are far from socially homogenous). For instance, we originally provided the Afghan Army their own *value cards* that mimic the same value cards that the US Army attaches to soldiers' dog tags.[9] One might hope that we would encourage the Afghans to develop their own value cards (or another way to express their own values). NATO headquarters that focused on the Afghan Army training mission briefed initially that they designed the value cards themselves. So, a group of Western military idealized the espoused institutional values for the Afghans. No surprise that the Afghan values card first produced had translated exactly the same values as the US Army's value card (with the single exception of adding the word, "God"). The values card scenario is an example of how institutions "invent progress" by reflecting only through their own value lenses (in this case literally). The cards intended to echo our narrative that we were "professionalizing" the Afghan force. "Professionalize" appears to be synonymous with "make their military look, act, talk, and walk like ours" [In neo-institutional theory, this socialization toward mimicry is called *isomorphism* – see DiMaggio and Powell (1991)].

Grant: That reminds me of someone telling me that he viewed his job as being to shield his subordinates from every hair-brain idea from officers in the higher headquarters. He commented that he knew I probably had some cool ideas I wanted to apply to the unit as well, but cautioned for me to go slow in implementing a lot of change and seemingly bright ideas. I think I have run into a lot of craziness that emanated from our institution that rewards officers for "doing something" in their one—or two—years in a position [Some call this the "revolving door effect"]. Since we like and promote those guys who come in and have a lot of energy and "do something"—I'd argue the institution encourages this kind of circular meaning-for-action (where action itself becomes the meaning). Of course, if you mix that with a culture that only advocates these sorts of mimetics you get lots of changes that make no sense to the context they are made in and have side harmful side effects in the very social situation you are attempting to influence (I believe Dr. Paparone calls this "iatrogenic" intervention, using the medical term as a metaphor).

Ben: Is modern military science better defined as the institution's attempt to force a rigid template of rules and structure onto the complexity of the world. I would say this is what those trained in operations research and systems analysis techniques are doing. Do you have any experience with officers who are specialized in ORSA and try to employ that science in military interventions?

Grant: Ben, I am reminded of a cartoon I once saw that someone in the US Army Special Forces (SF) Qualification Course drew (and much of this seems like "insider-only" humor). It depicted an SF advisor talking to his guerilla counterpart. The guerilla asks the SF advisor, "okay – what does your manual say we should do today?" The SF advisor, as he thumbs through his manual says, "Well, let's see. As we discussed yesterday you are in the latent and incipient phase of your rebellion." He then gets to a page in his manual and reads, "Today you should take the animal out of his cage and wash it down after feeding time." To which the advisor then remarks, "I think I picked up the wrong "gorilla" manual." The guerilla then asks, "That's all-right, can we just go kill some government troops?" A tiny head with a Kevlar helmet on it in the corner of the last frame then pleads, "But, wait- the next page talks about forced mating!" The point was that a few of us were a little unsure of the validity of field manuals that provided the science of conducting COIN interventions. It seemed to us that "revolutionaries" probably got by with less manuals and doctrine and achieved a lot more through spontaneous and flexible actions.

Now, on the ORSA-trained officers, let me say this. I think ORSA-thinking has permeated the entire institution—to include the special operations community—as we attempt to optimize the use of resources by measuring everything from in-theater actions (such as number of enemy killed) to schoolhouse learning. I think the tell-tale sign that formalized military planning—based largely in the science of ORSA—is ineffective in complex military interventions was the amount of top-down directives and plans that were all-but ignored by subordinate commands. For example, in 2007 I observed US Army brigades effectively ignoring plans sent down from the joint task force headquarters. In 2010, I witnessed a joint task force headquarters essentially ignoring an even higher authority's orders. I think this was because the rational-analytic processes we used were developed, above all, to make the optimal application of resources (apportionments or allocations of units, supply, and so forth) as the key determinant to selecting a planned course of action. Those who were told to execute were operating based on the reality they were facing (not the fictional future scenario that was forecasted in planning for what is essentially a resource optimization scheme).

Ben: I have found that ORSA-trained staff officers seem to have defensive mechanisms when discussing designs for action. They claimed my attempts at reframing tended to be more like storytelling while ORSA logic was based in mathematics – that is, reframing is rearranging factors and weights: meaning-for-action is quantifiable. With the institutional backdrop of modern military science, any deviation from a statistical proof or factorial analyses would be rejected as anecdotal; therefore, considered inferior to any operationalized evidence for planning our actions. Perhaps my most compelling example of this "*ORSAfication* of meaning" rests in the planning for the originally planned proper size of the Afghan security forces. Computer simulations were used to create the "optimal solution" through iterations of changing weights and operational definitions.[10]

As replacement planners flowed into the headquarters in the many months after this original planning, they inevitably asked where the number came from. Although I was not part of the research group that did that analysis, I can relay from the story as I was told by others familiar with the origin of the number. They explained that the COIN mathematical formulas for population-to-security-force ratios were run in computerized simulations that considered many operationalized variables, to include insurgent-number estimates and Afghan census data early in the initial planning on designing an Afghan security force. After numerous simulation runs, remarkably, the output supposedly came to nearly the same size force conclusion that the Soviets had computed in the 1980s when they occupied Afghanistan! After additional cost-constraints were added to the model, the first solution was modified to another number – the optimal force that could accomplish the mission of securing Afghanistan at some acceptable, calculated risk. The ORSA scientists argued that the number was quantitatively supportable, dismantling any counterarguments or critical inquiries that were based in qualitative evidence. Since that phase of the plan existed long before our current crop of planners entered into the conversation, it seems to have been reified, and critically questioning the force size was all-but forbidden. This clearly stymied reflexivity and the ability to consider refinements.

Interestingly, when a new senior commander arrived in Afghanistan, he brought both his hierarchical power and a refreshingly critical perspective. He questioned this number as well as many other ORSA-modeled outputs used to make important decisions. Here is my adaptation of the *iron law of oligarchy*: flag officer decisions are immovable objects until confronted by questions of the replacement flag officer or the overriding decision of his higher authority. While it was liberating to see my headquarters begin to consider transformational ideas through the clear and more philosophically-open guidance of a new commander, it frustrated me that the same headquarters had been riddled with many other critical inquiries on the very same issue countless times. The difference is, of course, now the rank and position were coupled with these counterarguments [Cohen et al. (1972) characterize this sort of coupling as part of "Garbage Can Decision Making" (GCDM) processes].

By the way, did you ever get the feeling that you were forced to attempt to find "the one best way" (through COG analysis, etc.)? I personally thought that our espoused "best course of action" was really tied to fit our current structures and programs [This is another characteristic of GCDM – i.e. solutions that look for problems. The theory is that "rationality" is evaluated by institutionalized habits and shared typifications, not some extrainstitutional validity.]. If you did, do you think this affected our efforts when faced with potential foes that were very creative at finding new advantages against such institutionalized structures?

Grant: Yes, for example, "the one best way" was always described as winning "the will of the people." This was the panacea-like meaning-for-action that was both ambiguous enough to incorporate a diversity of organizations who had their own solutions that looked for problems and resource-constrained enough to squelch multiple sources of alternative framings that may have made different sense.

A great example of being caught in our own preset solutions when dealing with the Afghans was when we were told to plan for fielding remotely piloted vehicles (flying drones) to the Afghan security forces. After arguing that this was too sophisticated a technology for the Afghans to sustain, one staff officer asked, "Well, if they don't have RPVs, how will they gather intelligence?" I must have looked perplexed – surely the bad guys had a rather robust intelligence collection capability without RPVs! [Here is a good example of what Schön (1983, 1987) calls "technical rationality," i.e. if there is an existing technology (an already-invented solution), just learn to apply it]. Of course, there were no Afghans in the room during this conversation.

Ben: Your story inspires me to recall a recent conversation I had with some very experienced logisticians in our organization. They were trying to develop the long-range plan for how the Afghans will more independently sustain their security forces over time, especially after NATO began to withdraw combat forces. I was quite impressed that the logisticians already thought critically enough to see the Afghan "push-package" system of resupply as something the Soviets taught them during their occupation (and the idea stuck). The logistics officers accepted that they could not transplant the American military logistics ("pull" or requisition-based) model to the Afghans. This seemed appropriate thinking on their part; but as I began to find ways to reframe and critically question some core assumptions, it became clear that we were still going to provide the Afghans a logistics system that would work for us – developed in a way that we could teach them. In other words, we were only capable to teach them something that we already knew- and we know how to conduct "push" logistics within a specialized science, expressed through the use of high technology, and modern electronic communications. What we institutionally forgot was how to run a "low-tech" logistics process, for example, the way our predecessors did during World War II.

Grant: I'd like to move on to another topic. Did institutional pressures cause us to ignore the possibility that each second, minute, and day of a military intervention is different in some way from the previous? If so, can you give examples as to how our decision processes were an obstacle to addressing this fluidity?

Ben: Ah, now I can reframe around complexity science concepts. What you are talking about is the emergent state of a system or how a complex system transforms over time where our "friendly" actions (or inactions) interact with a complex social milieu. Such interactions fundamentally change system behavior with unpredictable and amplified consequences. Despite this, we seem to hold to our original plans, to include the desired end-states that are mired by generally sequential lines of operations and effort that pay scant attention to side effects. I consider our obsession with night raids, I mentioned earlier, as one example of how a successful mission conclusion (e.g., insurgents killed or captured) is believed to be additive toward a "strategic end state." We seem marvelously effective with our high-tech and precision raids with drones and special operating forces, to include well-trained Afghan special operations and SWAT-like police forces. Yet, however gratifying the completion of these short missions are, there is a mutually interactive game underway – our opponents are improvising and adapting to our short term successes. With appreciation of complexity science, one would have less proclivity to believe in one-way causality and be much more sensitive to small changes that can have unpredictable, amplified effects [These radical-structuralist concepts were characterized as *chaoplexic* by Bousquet (2009)].

Grant: I have experienced this myself. We wrote up a campaign plan in Afghanistan in 2009 and did not substantially alter it from that point on. In 2010 we revisited the plan and made minor changes. Instead of developing structure, decisions, and operations that could adapt quickly, our year-old meanings-for-action (expressed in this plan) constrained us in the ever-changing regions and provinces. Our overarching planning constructs seemed to make us less flexible and, if anything, the area security (brigade commanders acting within the confines of "this is my territory and that is yours") construct unintentionally made our brigade commanders myopic. In addition, I remain quite skeptical about "campaign plans" from higher that are supposed to unify subordinate operations when each area and population were so different. With a complexity science frame, one would have to consider bottom-up, self-organizing ways to operate, making a compelling argument that top-down orders are preventing these grass-roots actions from happening.

Ben: Grant, switching to how the military creates and adapts its knowledge, how do you interpret what went wrong for us in the Vietnam War and how reflexive do you think the institution is in the current context?

Grant: As I understand it (and what I am about to say is an oversimplification), we supported a central government that the South Vietnamese people did not identify with or had a sense of legitimacy toward. Then we concentrated on fighting both an insurgency and a conventional force from the North that were threatening the existence of that same government. We also fought the war limited to the point that local commanders were generally compelled to keep away from enemy cross-border safe havens. Then we trained the South's military in our likeness and relied on our air power, combat support, resupply, and funding. After crippling this insurgency for all intents and purposes in 1968, we lost the popular support of our own citizens. When we pulled out in the early 1970s, our Congress (based on the unpopularity of the War) stopped funding and support to the South. The South was relatively quickly defeated by the North's conventional forces. The parallels with what has happened in Afghanistan are apparent to me (perhaps less the context of a larger "cold war" and potential superpower nuclear war).

Ben: Grant, I agree with your concise assessment. Like Vietnam, in Afghanistan we are taking our post 9–11 stated goal of defeating a global terrorist threat (one that resulted in our operating on the ground in Afghanistan). We seem to have taken the idea that the root cause of terrorism is societal; hence, we must change the society that fosters it (I would call this the root-causal story). In retrospect, does our national security really rest on whether Afghanistan has a central government? Does it require Afghanistan's economic re-structuring toward global integration? Does it require a technologically-savvy military, literacy programs, enforcement of women rights, or a variety of other changes to their pre-modern institutions? We tried equally challenging societal level interventions in South Vietnam, yet we are seemingly left again without a science to do so. Perhaps there cannot be such a science [Many social scientists have also come to this conclusion, particularly those who subscribe to alternative paradigms encompassing postmodern, social constructionist, and/or chaoplexic (Bousquet 2009) theories].

Grant: The institution seems to think that if we had fought the Vietnam War correctly – that if we had been "population-centric" from the beginning and won the people's hearts and minds early through government reforms – economic development, and security activities could have "won" the war.

Ben: I return to complexity science frames. Our reliance on modernist military science creates the illusion of social control when facing uncertainty in complex, emergent systems, regardless of whether we are in South Vietnam in 1966 or Afghanistan in 2012. Our institution has a propensity to think in terms of progressive, accumulative knowledge and uses a combination of terms and relatively static concepts codified in doctrinal publications. The idea seems to be to build mechanistic-like organizations as tools for future conflict (the metaphor of "the right tool for the job" seems prevalent). For example, our present COIN field manual seems intentionally written to serve as context-free knowledge, applicable in a universal sense wherever the military institution should apply it, whether it is in Iraq, Afghanistan, etc. Modern military science (and the structures design around it) seems to serve the antithesis of the more improvisational forms of knowledge we need.

Grant: I think we have also fooled ourselves into ignoring negative consequences that run counter to our preferred narrative and we zero in on those measures of performance that support our narrative. One example of this is the way we presented progress in our security force assistance programs. We used the number of ANSF units that were partnered with coalition units as a metric for progress. Unfortunately, as we had a limited number of coalition units, when we increased partnering it came at a cost of diluting the relationship as coalition units had to double or triple their partners. But, this was the metric that we trumpeted as "progress."

Ben: One of my favorite Mark Twain quotes is, "there are lies, damn lies, and statistics." Our institutional propensity to build more metrics continues and this supports our side's metanarrative of "winning." Let us consider the ill-fated Afghan Highway Police (AHP) created in the 2005–06 timeframe. We trained, equipped, and fielded a large police force that would operate largely like a Western-style highway patrol that can clear routes, control traffic, and help stabilize the region through law enforcement. Instead, the organization became unmanageable, setting up unauthorized checkpoints and shaking down the locals in a manner more indicative of a "protection" scheme. After NATO senior officers became aware of this, they disbanded the organization, but failed to conduct disarmament, demobilization, and reintegration (what we call "DDR") process to properly dissolve that organization. Instead, the AHP members kept their uniforms, vehicles, weapons, and ammunition and converted themselves into a local militia or warlord-style system. At the same time, NATO had another disarmament program called the "DIAG" (Disbandment of Illegally Armed Groups) that acted towards disarming militia-type bands operating within Afghanistan. On the one hand we were arming a large group with modern capabilities, and on the other we spent resources to locate and disarm them. You can imagine that our measures of performance for DIAG seemed to indicate progress, when we apparently helped create the need for DIAG.

Grant: In terms of changing modernist approaches to Military Design to a more reflexive institution, I am a bit pessimistic. A great example was our attempt to affect the competing narratives in 2010. Our narrative seemed to be, "stand up the ANSF rapidly, partner with them, and fight the insurgents alongside them for a few years in order to give them time to become independent." A competing message that undercut that narrative was often deemed as inappropriate; hence, we ignored the possibility that our assumptions encased in this narrative could be wrong.

Ben: I sometimes think it is paradoxical in that on the one hand our doctrine tells us about principles that should guide us and yet it demands that one should know when not to follow the principles. Have you ever had to try and make sense in the midst of competing institutional values? I think the latest Army overarching doctrinal concept [Department of the Army 2011c] provides a telling example of how our hierarchical and highly structured Army wants standardized behaviors on one hand, while expecting improvisation on the other. ADP 3-0 states that "doctrine acts as a guide to action rather than a set of fixed rules." By itself, this sentence should seem quite liberating; however, in the very next sentence, ADP 3-0 puts the shackles back on by explaining that the doctrine establishes the Army's understanding of the nature of military operations, and that it forms the basis for decision making, and fundamentally provides the methodology by which commanders exercise control of their organization. This reminds me of Henry Ford's remark that, "You can buy a Model T in any color you want, as long as it is black."

Grant: Again, the narrative we seemed to stick to in Afghanistan was that "the insurgency would die off if we followed the will of the people." My issue with the narrative was that it was possible that support to the insurgency was, in effect, the will of the people. But I heard no one question it, and kept driving on as if we just met the "will of the people" we would defeat the insurgency.

Ben: The underlying theme that "all Taliban are bad" is also troubling, but seems prevalent in many of our officers' stance on political settlement. If we seek to defeat what we characterized as an illegitimate government, it is possible to treat the enemy in a homogenous manner. The end to these sorts of wars seem finite and symbolically represented—whether you do it in a railway car in France after World War I, on the deck of a battleship after World War II, or at a peace table on a demilitarized zone in Korea. The Taliban and the larger depiction of 'anti-Western radical Islam' is not a unified front based in a nation-state system. Who would sign a treaty ending the conflict in Afghanistan?

Grant: Ben, I want to close with the topic concerning military epistemology—our military science.

Ben: The institution's concepts seem to come primarily from the writings of Jomini (which are very geometric) and Clausewitz (e.g., his COG metaphor and remarkable trinity). The institution seems to only handle the dichotomous views these theorists, and considers them foundational while shutting out others. I have been influenced by works of others (that do not subscribe to any such foundationalist view) such as: Gilles Deleuze and Felix Guattari [1987], Anatol Rapoport [1968], and François Jullien [2004]. These writers are overlooked in the OPMEP-governed[11] military colleges.[12] I speculate that this is because these writings counter the Jomini-Clausewitz "foundational" doctrines. Don't misunderstand me;

our education should include reading and interpreting the works of Jomini and Clausewitz. But we should reject these as foundational to military science (and certainly question official doctrinal texts also tied to them). Grant, now finishing with our reflections on epistemology, what do you think?

Grant: Our institution is hierarchical—and commander—centric. Commanders at each level have so much responsibility and authority, perhaps rightly so, that what s/he says directs our meaning-for-action—that guides our behavior. Perhaps the only way to overcome this oligarchic knowledge approval (as Dr. Paparone puts it) is through a shaking up of conventional wisdom. Different and more varied educational opportunities would go a long way to promote institutional reflexivity, but I really think it will require even greater institutional reforms. Unfortunately, radical reform is not something that happens without a tremendous shock to the institution (I would argue we did not even change much after the shock of how the Spanish-American War was fought and how the Vietnam War turned out). We should be anxious to see what happens next.

Notes

1 Peter Miller (2007) cites Thomas Seely, a biologist at Cornell University, and describes how Seely runs faculty meetings. Seely uses swarm theory to justify self-organizing discussion and permits dissension in his meetings through open discourse followed by secret ballot. “It’s exactly what the swarm bees do, which gives a group time to let the best ideas emerge and win.” For a military context, see John Arquilla and David Ronfeldt (2000).

2 “The mapping of poverty throughout the country shows the striking finding that the most poverty-afflicted areas are those not in conflict” (World Bank 2011, p. 7).

3 According to Jeff Conklin (2008): “This is the pattern of thinking that everyone attempts to follow when they are faced with a problem . . . this linear pattern as being enshrined in policy manuals, textbooks, internal standards for project management, and even the most advanced tools and methods being used and taught in the organization” (pp. 4–5).

4 Azeem Ibrahim (2009) quotes the then Commander of forces in Afghanistan, General Stanley McChrystal, on how the American military had spent the last decade fighting in Afghanistan: “looking at the war in simplistic Manichaean terms—save as many good guys as possible while taking out as many bad guys as possible—was a mistake.”

5 “ISAF may continue to hold that the capture-or-kill raids are the safest and most effective tool against the insurgency, but this remains to be proven, particularly in the context of the data cited in this report” (van Linschoten and Kuehn 2011, p. 26).

6 See Peter D. Thruelsen (2006). This report references statistics about the original Disarmament, Demobilization, and Reintegration (DDR) program that disarmed approximately 63,400 combatants from 2003 to 2006 and collected 36,500 light weapons and 12,000 heavy weapons, but the DDR framework was unsuccessful in targeting other armed groups within Afghanistan (p. 16). See also United Nations (2010), where the Disbandment of Illegal Armed Groups (DIAG) reportedly has disbanded a total of 759 illegally armed groups with 54,138 weapons collected on top of the original DDR disarmament accomplishment as of October 2010 (p. 6).

7 For example, Mats Alvesson and Jorgen Sandberg (2011) ask the provocative question: "how can assumptions be challenged without upsetting dominant groups, which hold them so strongly that they ignore the critique or even prevent one's study from being published?" (p. 259).

8 Richard Hughes et al. (2002) point out that the values of "Preserving a comfortable, harmonious group environment becomes a hidden agenda that tends to suppress dissent, conflict, and critical thinking" (p. 298). Hence, using single social theories, like Maslow's, creates our own paradoxes.

9 The US Army's espoused values create an acronym—LDRSHIP: Loyalty, Duty, Respect, Selfless service, Honor, Integrity, and Personal courage.

10 [By the way, this method is used to size US forces as well—through ORSA-generated models run for the Pentagon decision-makers.]

11 [OPMEP refers to the US Officer Professional Development Policy discussed in Chapter 5.]

12 [Interestingly, both Ben and Grant are graduates of the US Army's School of Advanced Military Studies which is not governed by official PME policy. The US Naval Post Graduate School is also "free" of those policies and is permitted to introduce students to more diversified perspectives.]

Coda: Designing Meanings In- and On- Action

The existence of and the complex interrelationship between the problems of a given time and place must be viewed and understood against the background of the structure of the society in which they occur. . . . The isolated thinker may have the impression that his crucial idea occurred to him personally, independent of his social setting. . . . Sociology, however, cannot be content with understanding immediate problems and events emerging from this myopic perspective which obscures every significant relationship . . .[where] seemingly isolated and discrete facts must be comprehended in the ever-present but constantly changing configurations of experience in which they are actually lived. Only in such a context do they acquire meaning.

KARL MANNHEIM,
Ideology and Utopia

I began this book making the assertion that *there must be and always will be a disunity of military knowledge*. Among the most profound things about epistemology that I learned while researching this book were highlighted by philosopher Nicholas Rescher (1995): knowledge does not have to have a single logic, grammar, and rhetoric. So it goes for military science. Rescher steps back and suggests epistemology is a much more complex human creation that should consider competing philosophical views, to include these about knowledge:

> *Progressivism* is the (social utopian) belief that knowledge is tested and accumulates toward some final truth about all things. The Enlightenment, Copernican-Newtonian science, Comte's positivism, and so on, constitute this approach to science. In terms of war and the conduct of warfare, progressivism entails finding greater and greater understanding. Only through understanding one can respond more determined in the right way. For the US military community, particularly the Army, doctrine assumes progressive knowledge construction and that one should constitute the "professional" body of knowledge both underpinned by this worldview and that separates the professionals from laypersons.

Many of its institutional approaches to knowledge are, not surprisingly, bound to rational-analytic, decision-making strategies (collect facts, define the problem, develop alternatives/hypotheses, pick the best alternative/method, and, as a side note, include ethical evaluations).

Retrogressivism is the antithesis of progressivism and sees the need for man's best knowledge is found in moving backwards to a better place-in-time. The more original knowledge formations are better than later, liberalized versions. This may be the underlying assumptive structure of the "Green Movement" and "ecoradicals"—those who see the earth as a living being whereas man's technology has ruined the pristine essence of "Gaia." The pre-modernist Islamist who calls for a return to the seventh century context of Muhammad and its Caliphate ideal (return to the original form of *shari'a* law) is archetypal of this ethics system (e.g., Esposito and Mogahed 2007). In the military context, there are those retrogressives who call for a "return" to the military's Westphalian "core purpose" – to fight and win the nation's wars (and not side-track into peace operations or nation-building).

Stabilitarianism signifies a belief that things remain the same and epistemology is a matter of institutions restating that cultural sameness in only incrementally different ways (e.g., Lewis 2007). The French saying *plus ça change, plus c'est la même chose* (the more things change, the more they remain the same) may link to this belief. A military stabilitarian may argue that the use of principles of war have not changed since the time of Sun Tzu (sixth century BC) (e.g., Griffith 1963); hence, these serve as timeless "muddling through" backdrops for guiding the incremental design of militaries and military interventions. The study of law (and legal-analogous precedence; e.g. Levi 1949) seems to fall in this heuristic view of knowledge, as, perhaps, does metaphoric reasoning (Schönian extensions and displacements from something familiar).

Cyclicism is a view that knowledge is produced and replaced in repetitious patterns of ebbs and flows or "swings of the pendulum." The institution remembers, forgets, and relearns. In domestic politics, the "strict constitutionalists" may see cycles to and from the values of the founding fathers over generations of Americans. As a military example, forgetting the US Army's constabulary ethic in westward expansion in the 1800s had to be relearned. The shift in conceptualizing conventional interventions from *Active Defense* to *AirLand Battle* doctrine (e.g., Romjue 1984), circa 1982, had to be again cast aside for relearning constabulary tasks (how the American West was won) in "irregular" interventions in the 1990s and into the 2000s (e.g., Birtle 1998). The racial integration of the US Armed Services in 1948 reveals a social integration cycle that repeats with the integration of homosexuals sixty years later. . .and so forth.

Anarchism sees human action as "haphazard eventuations" that are "resistant to laws and regularities" (Rescher 1995, p. 95); hence, there is no knowledge. For example, this view of ethics in some ways seems more aligned with the 2009 US *Capstone Concept for Joint Operations* that sees future warfare where "clean distinctions will rarely exist in reality; however, as often in the past, future conflicts will appear as hybrids comprising diverse, dynamic, and simultaneous combinations of organizations, technologies, and techniques that defy categorization" (Department of Defense 2009a, p. 8). Shall we, then, have to acknowledge radical meanings for action?

Whereas the modernist military institution would continue to foster progressivism as the only view of a "true" epistemology and point to the incommensurability of these views, the postinstitutional sociology of military science (i.e. through the lens of Mannheim 1936) suggests that *reflexivity* can help design organizations and military interventions beyond a singular sense of reality and find value in a plurality of views. In that regard, the Military Design that I propose involves many sociological senses of reality (e.g. multiple frames, quadigenous, etc.) that requires a philosophical shift toward: (1) searching for unusual sources of framing; (2) discovering that metaphoric reasoning is an important art form; (3) exposing and criticizing our "usual suspects" (reifications such as strategy, leadership, planning, and profession); (4) accepting the ethos of "quadigenous" or relational meanings; and (5) opening minds toward a more humble and fluid role as bricoleur, where Military Design is improvising situational meanings in- and on-action that continuously remake the profession. Sixth, I hope that the *petit récit* of two practicing military designers (majors Martin and Zweibelson) demonstrates the issues, social circumpressures, communicative artfulness, and passions that will characterize the journey toward that shift.

As a result of this book, my wish is that "the community" will take greater pains to examine why it is appropriate to reason with differing interpretations (pluralized through epistemic reflexivity), some anarchic, than to continuously seek continuity in military science. By exploring the sociology of military science (rephrased as *the relationship between ontology and epistemology* [Mannheim 1936, p. 264]; and I would add *methodology*), meaningfulness can be more like an in-the-flow process of creating unique works of art than subscribing to the wider Cartesian belief in the eventual science of everything. Reflecting on the opening epigraph in the Preface, by Millay:

Of facts . . . they lie unquestioned, uncombined.
Wisdom enough to leech us of our ill
Is daily spun; but there exists no loom . . .

The invention, changing, and discarding of the institutionalized "loom" is, in my mind, the essence of fighting foundationalism and becoming post-institutional. There exists no single loom, but looms that weave the relational meanings of militaries and military interventions in which we have found or find ourselves. This, then, is my prospectus for a Military Design philosophy.

REFERENCES

Abbott, Andrew (1988). The System of Professions: An Essay on the Division of Expert Labor. Chicago, IL: University of Chicago Press.

Ackley, Charles W. (1972). The Modern Military in American Society: A Study in the Nature of Military Power. Philadelphia: Westminster.

Alexander, Ernest R. (1986). Approaches to Planning: Introducing Current Planning Theories, Concepts and Issues. Montreux: Gordon and Breach Science.

—(2000). "Rationality Revisited: Planning Paradigms in a Postmodernist Perspective." *Journal of Planning Education and Research* 19: 242–56.

Allison, Graham and Philip Zelikow (1999). Essence of Decision: Explaining the Cuban Missile Crisis (2nd edn). New York: Longman.

Alvesson, Mats and Jorgen Sandberg (2011). "Generating Research Questions through Problematization." *Academy of Management Review* 36 (2): 247–71.

Alvi-Aziz, Hayat and Nikolas K. Gvosdev (eds) (2010). Case Studies in Policy Making (12th edn). Newport: United States Naval War College.

Archer, Margaret (1998). "Realism in the Social Sciences." In Margaret Archer, Roy Bhaskar, Andrew Collier, Tony Lawson, and Alan Norrie (eds) Critical Realism: Essential Readings. London: Routledge, pp. 189–205.

Argyris, Chris (1985). Strategy, Change, and Defensive Routines. Marshfield: Pitman.

Argyris, Chris and Donald A. Schön (1980). Theory in Practice: Increasing Professional Effectiveness. San Francisco, CA: Jossey-Bass.

Arquilla, John and David Ronfeldt (2000). Swarming and the Future of Conflict. Santa Monica, CA: RAND.

Associated Press (2007). "Bush Runs White House with Sports Metaphors" July 15. Accessed August 23, 2011 at http://www.msnbc.msn.com/id/19774480/ns/politics/t/bush-runs-white-house-sports-metaphors/.

Astley, W. Graham (1983). "Socially Constructed Administrative Science Is." In Craig C. Lindberg and Cheri A. Young (eds) Foundations for Inquiry: Choices, Tradeoffs in the Organizational Sciences. Stanford: Stanford University, pp. 110–15.

Atocha Aliseda (2006). Abductive Reasoning: Logical Investigations into Discovery and Explanation. New York: Springer.

Baldor, Lolita C. (2012). "Allen Reviewing Command Climate of Bales' Unit." Accessed March 26, Associated Press at http://hosted.ap.org/dynamic/stories/U/US_ US_AFGHANISTAN?SITE = AP&SECTION = HOME& TEMPLATE = DEFAULT.

Barker, Richard A. (1997) "How Can We Train Leaders If We Do Not Know What Leadership Is?" *Human Relations* 50 (4): 343–62.

Bateson, Gregory (1979). Mind and Nature: A Necessary Unity. New York: Bantam.

Berger, Peter L. (1963). Invitation to Sociology: A Humanistic Perspective. New York: Doubleday.

Berger, Peter L. and Thomas Luckmann (1967). The Social Construction of Reality: A Treatise in the Sociology of Knowledge. New York: Anchor.

Bertalanffy, Ludwig von (1968). General Systems Theory: Foundations, Development, and Applications. New York: Braziller.

Birtle, Andrew J. (1998). US Army Counterinsurgency Operations Doctrine 1860–1941. Washington, DC: US Army Center of Military History.

Black, Max (1993). "More About Metaphor." In Andre Ortony (ed.) Metaphor and Thought. New York: Cambridge, pp. 19–41.

Bloom, Benjamin S. (ed.) (1956). Taxonomy of Educational Objectives: The Classification of Educational Goals, Handbook 1, Cognitive Domain. London: David McKay.

Blumer, Herbert (1969). Symbolic Interactionism: Perspective and Method. Berkeley, CA: University of California.

Boëne, Bernard (2003). "The Military as a Tribe Among Tribes: Postmodern Armed Forces and Civil-Military Relations." In Giuseppe Caforio (ed.) Handbook of the Sociology of the Military. New York: Kluwer Academic, pp. 167–85.

Boulding, Kenneth (1956). The Image: Knowledge in Life and Society. Ann Arbor, MI: University of Michigan.

Bousquet, Antoine (2009). The Scientific Way of Warfare: Order and Chaos on the Battlefields of Modernity. New York: Columbia University.

Boxenbaum, Eva and Linda Rouleau (2011). "New Knowledge Products as Bricolage: Metaphors and Scripts in Organization Theory." *Academy of Management Review* 36 (2): 272–96.

Bradford, Zeb B. and James R. Murphy (1969). "A New Look at the Military Profession." *Army* 2 (February issue): 58–64.

Bradshaw, Patricia (2002). "Reframing Board-Staff Relations Exploring the Governance Function Using a Storytelling Metaphor." *Nonprofit Management and Leadership* 12 (4): 471–84.

Brendler, Joseph A. (1997). Physical Metaphor in Military Theory and Doctrine: Force, Friction, or Folly? Fort Leavenworth, KS: School of Advanced Military Studies.

Brook, Tom V. (2012). Coalition Limits Details on Troops Killed by Afghans. USA Today (January 17th). Accessed February 3, 2012 at http://www.usatoday.com/news/world/afghanistan/story/2012-01-17/Troops-killed-by-Afghans/52623100/1.

Brown, Richard H. (1977). A Poetic for Sociology: Toward a Logic of Discovery for the Human Sciences. Cambridge: Cambridge University.

Bruner, Jerome S. (1991). "The Narrative Construction of Reality" (1991). *Critical Inquiry* 18 (1): 1–21.

Bunting, Josiah (1972). The Lionheads. New York: George Braziller.

Burrell, Gibson and Gareth Morgan (1979). Sociological Paradigms and Organisational Analysis: Element of the Sociology of Corporate Life. Portsmouth: Heinemann.

Cameron, Kim S. (1988). "Organizational Paradox and Transformation." In Robert E. Quinn and Kim S. Cameron (eds) Paradox and Transformation: Toward a Theory in Organization and Management. Cambridge: Ballinger, pp. 1–18.

Cameron, Kim S. and Robert E. Quinn (1999). Diagnosing and Changing Organizational Culture: Based on the Competing Values Framework. Reading, MA: Addison-Wesley.

Campbell, Joseph P. (1988). The Power of Myth (with Bill Moyers). New York: Doubleday.

Chen, Ming-Jer and Danny Miller (2011). The Relational Perspective as a Business Mindset. *Academy of Management Perspectives* 25 (3): 6–18.

Chisholm, Rupert F. (1988). "Introducing Advanced Information Technology into Public Organizations." *Public Productivity Review* 11 (4): 39–56.

Christensen, Clayton M. (1997). The Innovator's Dilemma: When New Technologies Cause Great Firms to Fail. Cambridge: Harvard Business School.

Clausewitz, Carl von (1984/1832). On War (trans. by Michael Howard and Peter Paret). Princeton, NJ: Princeton University.

Cohen, Eliot and John Gooch (1990). Military Misfortunes: The Anatomy of Failure in War. New York: Vintage.

Cohen, Michael D. and James G. March (1986). Leadership and Ambiguity: The American College President (2nd edn). Boston, MA: Harvard Business School.

Cohen, Michael D., James G. March and Johan P. Olsen (1972). "A Garbage Can Model of Organizational Choice." *Administrative Science Quarterly* 17: 1–25.

Collingswood, Robin G. (1969). "Human Nature and Human History." In Ronald H. Nash (ed.) Ideas of History, Volume 2, The Critical Philosophy of History. New York: E. P. Dutton, pp. 35–56.

Cone, Robert W. (October 2011). "Shaping the Army of 2020." Army. Arlington, TX: Association of the US Army.

Conklin, Jeff (2008). Wicked Problems and Social Complexity. CogNexus Institute. Accessed March 13, 2012 at http://cognexus.org/wpf/wickedproblems.pdf.

Cossette, Pierre (1998). "The Study of Language in Organizations: A Symbolic Interactionist Stance." *Human Relations* 51 (11): 1355–77.

DAU (2010). "Accelerating Our Second Transformation." Defense Acquisition University 2010 Annual Report. Accessed October 14, 2011 at http://www.dau.mil/pubscats/ATL%20Docs/ANNUAL_REPORT.pdf.

Davis, Paul K. (ed.) (2011). Dilemmas of Intervention Social Science for Stabilization and Reconstruction. Santa Monica, CA: RAND.

Deleuze, Gilles and Felix Guattari (1987). A Thousand Plateaus: Capitalism and Schizophrenia (trans. by Brian Massumi). Minneapolis, MN: University of Minnesota.

Dempsey, Martin (2011). "Mission Command." Army Magazine. Accessed March 11, 2012 at http://www.ausa.org/publications/armymagazine/archive/2011/1/Documents/Dempsey_0111.pdf.

Dempsey, Martin E. (2012). Chairman's Strategic Direction to the Joint Force. Accessed February 7, 2012 at http://www.jcs.mil/content/files/2012-02/020312135111_CJCS_Strategic_Direction_to_the_Joint_Force_6_Feb_2012.pdf.

Department of the Air Force (2006). Air Force Doctrine Document 1-1, Leadership and Force Development.
—(2011). US Air Force Chief of Staff Professional Reading Program. Accessed August 28, 2011 at http://www.af.mil/information/csafreading/index.asp.
Department of the Army (1984). Army Regulation 34-4, Army Standardization Policy. Washington, DC.
— (2007). Army Regulation 600-100, Army Leadership. Washington DC.
—(2009a). Field Manual 7-0, Training for Full Spectrum Operations. Washington, DC.
—(2009b). TRADOC Regulation 350-70, Systems Approach to Training Management, Processes, and Products. Fort Monroe.
—(2011a). Army Chief of Staff's Professional Reading List. Washington, DC: Center of Military History.
—(2011b). Field Manual 5-0, The Operations Process. Washington, DC.
—(2011c). Army Doctrinal Publication 3-0, Unified Land Operations. Washington, DC.
Department of Defense (2001). Joint Publication 3-0, Doctrine for Joint Operations (Obsolete). Washington, DC.
—(2002). Chairman of the Joint Chiefs of Staff Manual Number 3500.04C. Universal Joint Task List (Obsolete). Washington, DC.
—(2009a). Chairman of the Joint Chiefs of Staff Capstone Concept for Joint Operations, January 2009, Version 3.0. Washington, DC.
—(2009b). Chairman of the Joint Chiefs of Staff Instruction Number 1800.01D. Officer Professional Military Education Policy (OPMEP) (with Change 1, December 2011). Washington, DC.
—(2010). Joint Operations Environment (JOE). Norfolk, VA: United States Joint Forces Command.
—(2011a). Joint Publication 1-02, Dictionary for Military and Associated Terms. Washington, DC.
—(2011b). Joint Publication 3-0, Joint Operations. Washington, DC.
—(2011c). Joint Publication 5-0, Joint Operation Planning. Washington, DC.
—(2011d). Chairman of the Joint Chiefs of Staff Manual Number 8260.03, Volume 2, Global Force Management Data Initiative (GFM DI) Implementation: The Organizational and Force Structure Construct (OFSC). Washington, DC.
— (2011e). Chairman of the Joint Chiefs of Staff Manual 3150.25, Joint Lessons Learned Program. Washington, DC.
Department of the Navy (2011). US Navy Reading List. Accessed August 28, 2011 at http://www.navyreading.navy.mil/.
—(2012). Navy Leadership Competency Model. Accessed March 24, 2012 at https://www.netc.navy.mil/centers/cppd/News.aspx?ID = 1.
Dewey, John (1934). Art as Experience. New York: Perigee.
DiMaggio, Paul J. (1995). Comments on "What Theory is Not." *Administrative Science Quarterly* 40: 391–7.
DiMaggio, Paul J. and Walter W. Powell (1991). "The Iron Cage Revisited: Institutional Isomorphism and Collective Rationality in Organizational Fields." In Walter W. Powell and Paul J. DiMaggio (eds) The New Institutionalism in Organizational Analysis. Chicago, IL: University of Chicago Press, pp. 63–82.

Dray, William (1969). "The Historical Explanations of Actions Reconsidered." In Ronald H. Nash (ed.) Ideas of History, Volume 2, The Critical Philosophy of History. New York: E. P. Dutton, pp. 106–24.
Eisenhower, Dwight D. (1948). Crusade in Europe. Garden City, NY: Doubleday.
Enloe, Cynthia (2010). "The Risks of Scholarly Militarization: A Feminist Analysis." *Perspectives on Politics* 8 (4): 1107–11.
Esposito, John L. and Dalia Mogahed (2007). Who Speaks for Islam? What Billions of Muslims Really Think. New York: Gallup.
Evered, Roger (1983). "So What is Strategy?" *Long Range Planning* 16 (3): 57–72.
Ewell, Julian J. and Ira A. Hunt (1974). Sharpening the Combat Edge: The Use of Analysis to Reinforce Military Judgment. Washington, DC: US Army Center for Military History.
Fairhurst, Gail T. and Robert A. Sarr (1996). The Art of Framing: Managing the Language of Leadership. San Francisco, CA: Jossey-Bass.
Ferrari, Frederica (2007). "Metaphor at Work in the Analysis of Political Discourse: Investigating a 'Preventive War' Persuasion Strategy." *Discourse & Society* 18 (5): 603–25.
Festinger, Leon (1957). A Theory of Cognitive Dissonance. Stanford, CA: Stanford University.
Feuer, Lewis S. (1975). Ideology and the Ideologists. New York: Harper and Row.
FitzGerald, Frances (1972). Fire in the Lake: The Vietnamese and the Americans in Vietnam. Boston, MA: Little, Brown and Company.
Fort Leavenworth Lamp (2011). "Experienced leaders sought for brain study." Accessed October 11, 2011 at http://www.ftleavenworthlamp.com/news/around_the_force/x1158638622/Experienced-leaders-sought-for-brain-study, posted August 4, 2011.
Fuller, J. F. C. (1925). "The Lack of the Scientific Study of War." Chapter 1, Section 3, Foundations of the Science of War. Accessed September 10, 2011 at http://www.cgsc.edu/carl/resources/csi/fuller2/fuller2.asp#23.
Gaddis, John L. (1982). Strategies of Containment: A Critical Appraisal of Postwar American National Security Policy. New York: Oxford University Press.
Galula, David (1964). Counterinsurgency: Theory and Practice. New York: Praeger.
Gat, Azar (1992). The Development of Military Thought: The Nineteenth Century. Oxford: Oxford University.
Geertz, Clifford (1973). The Interpretation of Cultures. New York: BasicBooks.
Gemmill, Gary and Judith Oakley (1992). "Leadership: An Alienating Social Myth?" *Human Relations* 45 (2): 113–20.
Gergen, Mary M., Kenneth J. Gergen and Frank Barrett (2004). "Appreciative Inquiry as Dialogue: Generative and Transformative." In David L. Cooperrider and Michel Avital (eds) Constructive Discourse and Human Organization Volume 1, Advances in Appreciative Inquiry. Amsterdam: Elsevier, pp. 3–27.
Ghamari-Tabrizi, Sharon (2000). "Simulating the Unthinkable: Gaming Future War in the 1950s and 1960s." *Social Studies of Science* 30 (2): 163–223.
Giddens, Anthony. Social Theory and Modern Sociology. Stanford, CA: Stanford University, 1987.
Ginsburg, Dan (2010). "War, Militarism, and Gender: An Interview with Cynthia Enloe." *Women's Policy Journal of Harvard* 7: 51–56.

Gladwell, Malcolm (2005). Blink: The Power of Thinking Without Thinking. New York: Little, Brown.
Goffman, Erving (1959). The Presentation of Self in Everyday Life. New York: Anchor.
—(1974). Frame Analysis: An Essay on the Organization of Experience. New York: Harper Colophon.
Griffith, Samuel B. (1963). Sun Tzu: The Art of War. London: Oxford.
Grint, Keith (ed.) (1997). Leadership: Classical, Contemporary, and Critical Approaches. Oxford: Oxford Press.
Grint, Keith (2008). Leadership, Management, and Command: Rethinking D-Day. United Kingdom: Palgrave-MacMillan.
Haass, Richard N. (2001). "The Bush Administration's Response to September 11th—and Beyond," Remarks to the Council of Foreign Relations, New York, October 15, 2001. Accessed December 5, 2007 at www.state.gov/s/p/rem/5505.htm.
Habermas, Jürgen (1971). Knowledge and Human Interests (trans. by Jeremy J. Shapiro). Boston, MA: Beacon Press.
—(1976). Legitimation Crisis (trans. by Thomas McCarthy). London: Heinemann Educational Books.
Haeckel, Ernst (1900). The Riddle of the Universe at the Close of the Nineteenth Century (trans. by Joseph McCabe). New York: Harper and Brothers.
Hardy, Cynthia, Nelson Phillips, and Stewart R. Clegg (2001). "Reflexivity in Organization and Management Theory: A Study of the Production of the Research 'Subject.'" *Human Relations* 54: 531–60.
Harmon, Michael M. and Richard T, Mayer (1986). Organization Theory for Public Administration. Burke: Chatelaine.
Hatch, Mary Jo (1997). Organization Theory: Modern, Symbolic, and Postmodern Perspectives. Oxford: Oxford University.
Hatch, Mary Jo and Dvora Yanow (2008). "Methodology by Metaphor: Ways of Seeing in Painting and Research." *Organization Studies* 29 (1): 23.
Heifetz, Ronald A. (1994). Leadership Without Easy Answers. Cambridge: Belknap.
Helman, David H. (ed.) (1988). Analogical Reasoning: Perspectives of Artificial Intelligence, Cognitive Science, and Philosophy. Dordrecht: Kluwer.
Heuser, Beatrice (2010). The Evolution of Strategy: Thinking War from Antiquity to the Present. Cambridge: Cambridge University.
Hewes, James E. (1975). From Root to McNamara: Army Organization and Administration, 1900–1963. Washington, DC: U.S. Army Center of Military History.
Hittle, James D. (1961). The Military Staff. Harrisburg, PA: Stackpole.
Hock, Dee (1999). Birth of the Chaordic Age. San Francisco, CA: Berrett-Koehler.
Hoffman, Frank G. (2006). "Complex Irregular Warfare: The Next Revolution in Military Affairs." *Foreign Policy* 50 (Summer): 395–411.
Hoh, Mathew (2009). Interview with Washington Post. Accessed September 29, 2011 at http://www.washingtonpost.com/wp-dyn/content/discussion/2009/10/27/DI2009102703143.html.
Holland, Louise A. (1961). Janus and the Bridge. Rome: American Academy.
Holland, Ray (1999). "Reflexivity." *Human Relations* 52: 463–84.

Horgan, John (1996). The End of Science: Facing the Limits of Knowledge in the Twilight of the Scientific Age. Reading, MA: Addison-Wesley.

Horwath, Rich (2006). The Origin of Strategy, Strategic Thinking Institute. Accessed September 9, 2011 at http://www.strategyskills.com/Articles_samples/origin_strategy.pdf.

Howard, Michael (1961). The Franco-Prussian War: The German Invasion of France, 1870–1871. London: Metheun.

Hughes, Richard, Robert Ginnett, and Gordon Curphy (2002). Leadership; Enhancing the Lessons of Experience (4th edn). New York: McGraw-Hill Irwin.

Hunt, Sonja M. (1984). "The Role of Leadership in the Construction of Reality." In Barbara Kellerman (ed.) Leadership: Multidisciplinary Perspectives. Englewood Cliffs, NJ: Prentice-Hall, pp. 157–78.

Huntington, Samuel P. (1965). "Power, Expertise, and the Military Profession." In Kenneth S. Lynn (ed.) The Professions in America. Boston, MA: Houghton-Mifflin, pp. 785–807.

—(1996). The Clash of Civilizations and the Remaking of World Order. New York: Simon & Schuster.

Ibrahim, Azeem (2009). "Afghanistan's Way forward Must Include the Taliban." Los Angeles Times Opinion Online, December 9, 2009. Accessed March 12, 2012 at http://articles.latimes.com/2009/dec/09/opinion/la-oe-ibrahim9-2009dec09.

Iliaifar, Amir (2012) "U.S. Military Developing High-tech 'Smart' Underwear for Soldiers." Digital Trends. Accessed January 27, 2012 at http://www.digitaltrends.com/cool-tech/u-s-military-developing-high-tech-smart-underwear-for-soldiers/.

Ivie, Robert L. (1997). "Cold War and the Rhetorical Metaphor: A Framework of Criticism." In Martin J. Medhurst, Robert L. Ivie, Philip Wander, and Robert L. Scott (eds) Cold War Rhetoric: Strategy Metaphor, and Ideology (2nd edn). East Lansing, MI: Michigan State University, pp. 71–9.

Jacobs, Thomas O. (2002). Strategic Leadership: The Competitive Edge. Washington, DC: Industrial College of the Armed Forces.

Janis, Irving L. (1971). "Groupthink: The Desperate Drive for Consensus at Any Cost." *Psychology Today* 5 (November): 43–4, 46, 74–6.

Janowitz, Morris (1960). The Professional Soldier: A Social and Political Portrait. New York: Free Press.

Jaques, Elliott (1976). A General Theory of Bureaucracy. London: Heinemann.

—(1986). "The Development of Intellectual Capability: A Discussion of Stratified Systems Theory." *The Journal of Applied Behavioral Sciences* 22 (4): 361–83.

Joseph, Miriam (2002/1937). The Trivium: The Liberal Arts of Logic, Grammar, and Rhetoric. Philadelphia: Paul Dry.

Jullien, François (2004). A Treatise on Efficacy: Between Western and Chinese Thinking (trans. by Janet Lloyd). Honolulu, HI: University of Hawaii.

Jung, Carl G. (1956). Symbols of Transformation: An Analysis of the Prelude to a Case of Schizophrenia (2nd edn) (trans. by R. F. C. Hull). Princeton, NJ: Princeton University.

Kahn, David (2007). "The Prehistory of the General Staff." *The Journal of Military History* 71 (2): 499–504.

Keegan, John (1999). The First World War. New York: Alfred A. Knopf.

Khong, Yuen F. (1992). Analogies at War: Korea, Dien Bien Phu, and the Vietnam Decisions of 1965. Princeton, NJ: Princeton University.

Kiel, L. Douglas and Euel Elliott (1999). "Long-Wave Economic Cycles, Techno-Economic Paradigms, and the Pattern of Reform in American Public Administration." *Administration and Society* 30 (6): 616–39.

Kilduff, Martin and Ajay Mehra (1997). "Postmodernism and Organizational Research." *Academy of Management Review* 22 (2): 453–81.

Kilduff, Martin, Ajay Mehra and Mary Dunn (2011). "From Blue Sky Research to Problem Solving: A Philosophy of Science Theory of New Knowledge Production." *Academy of Management Review* 36 (2): 297–317.

King, Anthony, (2006). "The Post-Fordist Military." *Journal of Political and Military Sociology* 34 (2): 359–74.

Knox, MacGregor and Williamson Murray (2001). The Dynamics of Military Revolution 1300–2050. Cambridge: Cambridge University.

Krepinevich, Andrew F. (1986). The Army and Vietnam. Baltimore, MD: Johns Hopkins University.

Kuhn, Thomas S. (1996). The Structure of Scientific Revolutions (3rd edn). Chicago, IL: University of Chicago.

Ladkin, Donna (2010). Rethinking Leadership: A New Look at Old Leadership Questions. Cheltenham, UK: Edward Elgar.

Lai, David (2004). Learning from the Stones: A Go Approach to Mastering China's Strategic Concept, SHI. Carlisle, PA: US Army Strategic Studies Institute.

Lakoff, George (1991). "Metaphor and War: The Metaphor System Used to Justify War in the Gulf." Vietnam Generation Journal and Newsletter 3 (3). Accessed November 20, 2011 at http://www2.iath.virginia.edu/sixties/HTML_docs/Texts/Scholarly/Lakoff_Gulf_ Metaphor_1.html.

Lakoff, George and Mark Johnson (1980). Metaphors We Live By. Chicago, IL: University of Chicago Press.

Lang, Kurt (1972). Military Institutions and the Sociology of War: A Review of the Literature with Annotated Bibliography. Beverly Hills, CA: Sage.

Lasswell, Harold (1936). Politics: Who Gets What, When, How. New York: McGraw-Hill.

Lawson, Bryan (2006). How Designers Think: The Design Process Demystified (4th edn). Amsterdam: Elsevier.

Lerer, Zeev and Sarit Amram-Katz (2011). "The Sociology of Military Knowledge in the IDF: From Forging to Deciphering." *Israel Studies Review* 26 (2): 54–72.

Levi, Edward H. (1949). An Introduction to Legal Reasoning. Chicago, IL: University of Chicago.

Lévi-Strauss, Claude (1966). The Savage Mind. Chicago, IL: University of Chicago.

Lewin, Kurt (1958). Group Decision and Social Change. New York: Holt, Rinehart and Winston.

Lewis, Adrian R. (2007). "Culture, Genes, and War." In Adrian R. Lewis (ed.) The American Culture of War: The History of US Military Force from World War II to Operation Iraqi Freedom. New York: Routledge, pp. 1–17.

Lewis, Marianne W. (2000). "Exploring Paradox: Toward a More Comprehensive Guide." *Academy of Management Review* 25 (4): 760–76.

Lewis, Marianne W. and Andrew J. Grimes (1999). "Metatriangulation: Building Theory from Multiple Paradigms." *Academy of Management Review* 24 (4): 672–90.

Lincoln, Yvonna S. and Egon G. Guba (1985). Naturalistic Inquiry. Beverly Hills, CA: Sage.

Lindblom, Charles E. (1959). "The Science of Muddling Through." *Public Administration Review* 19: 79–88.

Lutz, Bob (2011). Car Guys vs. Bean Counters: The Battle for the Soul of American Business. New York: Penguin Group.

Lyotard, Jean-François (1984). The Postmodern Condition: A Report on Knowledge (trans. by Geoff Bennington and Brian Massumi). Minneapolis, MN: University of Minnesota.

MacIntyre, Alasdair (2007). After Virtue (3rd edn). Notre Dame: University of Notre Dame.

Mannheim, Karl (1936). Ideology and Utopia: An Introduction the Sociology of Knowledge (trans. by Louis Wirth and Edward Shils). New York: Harcourt Brace Jovanovich.

Marcella, Gabriel (ed.) (2010). Teaching Strategy: Challenge and Response. Carlisle, PA: US Army Strategic Studies Institute.

March, James G. (1994). A Primer on Decision Making, How Decisions Happen. New York: The Free Press.

March, James G. and Johan P. Olsen (1989). Rediscovering Institutions: The Organizational Basis of Politics. New York: Free Press.

Marion, Russ (1999). The Edge of Organization: Chaos and Complexity Theories of Formal Social Systems. Thousand Oaks, CA: Sage.

Marshall, Monty G. (1999). Third World War: System, Process, and Conflict Dynamics. Lanham: Rowman & Littlefield.

Marshall, S. L. A. (1947). Men Against Fire. New York: William Morrow and Company.

Martin, Grant (2011). "A Tale of Two Design Efforts (and why they both failed in Afghanistan)." Small Wars Journal, July 11. Accessed February 24, 2012 at http://www.dtic.mil/cgi-bin/GetTRDoc?AD = ADA545381&Location = U2&doc = GetTRDoc.pdf.

Martindale, Don (1959). "Sociological Theory and the Ideal Type." In Llewellyn Gross (ed.) Symposium on Sociological Theory. New York: Harper & Row, pp. 57–91.

Martineau, Harriet (1853). The Positive Philosophy of Auguste Comte. London: John Chapman.

Maruyama, Magoroh (1976). "Social and Political Interactions Among Extraterrestrial Human Communities: Contrasting Models," *Technological Forecasting and Social Change*, 9 (4): 349–60.

Maslow, Abraham H. (1943). "A Theory of Human Motivation." *Psychological Review* 50 (4): 370–96.

Mastroianni, George R. and Wiber J. Scott (2011). "Reframing Suicide in the Military." *Parameters* 41 (2): 6–19.

Maton, Karl (2003). "Reflexivity, Relationism, and Research: Pierre Bourdieu and the Epistemic Conditions of Social Scientific Knowledge." *Space and Culture* 6 (1): 52–65.

McMaster, Herbert R. (1997). Dereliction of Duty: Lyndon Johnson, Robert McNamara, the Joint Chiefs of Staff and the Lies that Led to Vietnam. New York: HarperCollins.

Meacham, John A. (1990). "The Loss of Wisdom.". In Robert J. Sternberg (ed.) Wisdom: Its Nature Origins, and Development. New York: Cambridge, pp. 181–211.

Medhurst, Martin J., Robert L. Ivie, Philip Wander, and Robert L. Scott (1997). Cold War Rhetoric: Strategy Metaphor, and Ideology (2nd edn). East Lansing, MI: Michigan State University.

Merkle, Judith A. (1980). Management and Ideology: The Legacy of the International Scientific Management Movement. Berkeley, CA: University of California.

Merton, Robert K. (1968). Social Theory and Social Structure. New York: Free Press.

Meyer, John W. and Brian Rowan (1991). "Institutionalized Organizations: Formal Structure as Myth and Ceremony." In Walter W. Powell and Paul J. DiMaggio (eds) The New Institutionalism in Organizational Analysis. Chicago, IL: University of Chicago Press, pp. 41–62.

Miklaucic, Michael (2011). Learning the Hard Way: Lessons from Complex Operations. *Joint Center for Operational Analysis Journal* 12 (3): 32–9.

Milbank, Dana (Aug 30 2004). "At GOP Convention, Echoes of Sept. 11." The Washington Post, p. A01.

Miller, Peter (2007). "The Genius of Swarms." National Geographic Magazine, July issue. Accessed March 11, 2012 at http://ngm.nationalgeographic.com/2007/07/swarms/miller-text.

Mintzberg, Henry (1973). The Nature of Managerial Work. New York: HarperCollins.

—(1987). "Five Ps for Strategy." *California Management Review* 1 (fall): 12–19.

—(1989). Mintzberg on Management: Inside Our Strange World of Organizations. New York: Free Press.

—(1994). The Rise and Fall of Strategic Planning: Reconceiving Roles for Planning, Plans, Planners. New York: Free Press.

Miser, Hugh J. (1980), "Operations Research and Systems Analysis." *Science* 209: 139–46.

Mitchell, John G. (1990). Re-Visioning Educational Leadership: A Phenomenological Approach. New York: Garland.

Mitroff, Ian and Ralph H. Kilmann (1981). The Four-Fold way of Knowing: The Varieties of Social Science Experience. *Theory and Society* 10 (2): 227–48.

Morgan, Gareth (2006). Images of Organization (Updated edn). Thousand Oaks, CA: Sage.

Morris, Van Cleve (1966). Existentialism in Education. New York: Harper & Row.

Moskos, Charles C., John Allen Williams, and David R. Segal (eds) (2000). The Postmodern Military: Armed Forces After the Cold War. New York: Oxford University.

Moyers, Bill (2012). Jonathan Haidt Explains Our Contentious Culture. February 5th interview with Jonathan Haidt. Transcript accessed February 11, 2012 at http://www.truth-out.org/jonathan-haidt-explains-our-contentious-culture/1328368654.

Mumford, Lewis (1934). Technics and Civilization. New York: Harbinger.
Murray, Williamson (1996). "Innovation: Past and Future." In Williamson Murray and Alan R. Millett (eds) Military Innovation in the Interwar Period. Cambridge: Cambridge University, pp. 300–28.
Mutch, Alistair (2006). "Organization Theory and Military Metaphor: Time for Reappraisal?" *Organization* 13 (6): 751–69.
Nash, Ronald H. (1969). "The Problem of Historical Causation." In Ronald H. Nash (ed.) Ideas of History, Volume 2, the Critical Philosophy of History. New York: E. P. Dutton, pp. 228–34.
Neustadt, Richard E. and Ernest R. May (1986). Thinking in Time: The Uses of History for Decision Makers. New York: Free Press.
Nisbett, Richard E. (2003). The Geography of Thought: How Asians and Westerners Think Differently. New York: Free Press.
OPM (2010). "A New Day for Federal Service." Office of Personnel Management Strategic Plan 2010–2015. Accessed October 24, 2011 at 20http://www.opm.gov/strategicplan/pdf/StrategicPlan_20100310.pdf.
Ortony, Andrew (ed.) (1993). Metaphor and Thought (2nd edn). Cambridge: Cambridge University.
Osinga, F. P. B. (2007). Science, Strategy and War: The Strategic Theory of John Boyd. Oxon: Routledge.
Ostrom, Elinor (1990). Governing the Commons: The Evolution of Institutions for Collective Action. Cambridge: Cambridge University.
Pace, Peter (2006). Speech at National Press Club Luncheon, Washington, DC, 17 February 2006. Accessed May 28, 2007 at www.jcs.mil/chairman/speeches/060217 NatPressClubLunch.html.
Paparone, Christopher R. and James A. Crupi (January–February 2002). "Janusian Thinking and Acting." *Military Review* 1, 38–47.
—(2005). "The Principles of War as Paradox," Proceedings, October, pp. 39–44.
Paret, Peter (Ed.) (1986), Makers of Modern Strategy: From Machiavelli to the Nuclear Age. Princeton: Princeton University.
Parsons, Talcott (1954). Essays in Sociological Theory (revised edition). New York: The Free Press.
Pasadena Sun (2012). "In Theory: Should the Military Test Spirituality?" February 16. Accessed February 21, 2012 at http://www.pasadenasun.com/news/opinion/tn-pas-0219-in-theory-should-the-military-test-spirituality,0,4689752.story.
Paul, Richard W. and Linda Elder (2004). The Miniature Guide to Critical Thinking (4th edn). Tomales, CA: Foundation for Critical Thinking.
Peirce, Charles S. (1878). "Deduction, Induction, and Hypothesis." *Popular Science Monthly* 13: 470–82.
Pepper, Stephen C. (1966). World Hypotheses: Prolegomena to Systematic Philosophy with a Complete Survey of Metaphysics. Berkeley, MA: University of California.
Perrow, Charles (1967). "The Framework for Comparative Organizational Analysis." *American Sociological Review* 32 (2): 194–208.
—(1986). Complex Organizations: A Critical Essay (3rd edn). New York: McGraw-Hill.
Petraeus, David (2010), COMISAF's Counterinsurgency Guidance (memorandum dated 10 November 2010). Accessed September 29, 2011 at http://usacac.army.mil/cac2/COIN/repository/COMISAF _COIN_Training_Guidance.pdf.

Pfeffer, Jeffrey (1981). "Management as Symbolic Action: The Creation and Maintenance of Organizational Paradigms." In Larry L. Cummings and Barry M. Staw (eds) Research in Organizational Behavior: An Annual Series of Analytical Essays and Critical Reviews, Volume. 3. Greenwich: JAI, pp. 1–52.

Phillips, Denis C. and Nicholas C. Burbules (2000). Postpositivism and Educational Research. Lanham, MD: Roman & Littlefield.

Piaget, Jean and Bärbel Inhelder (1958). The Growth of Logical Thinking from Childhood to Adolescence. New York: Basic Books.

Pierce, James G. (2010). Is the Organizational Culture of the US Army Congruent with the Professional Development of its Senior Level Officer Corps? Carlisle, PA: Letort Papers.

Polyani, Michael (1966). Tacit Dimension. Garden City, NY: Doubleday.

Pondy, Louis R. (1978). "Leadership is a Language Game." In Morgan W. McCall and Michael M. Lombardo (eds) Leadership: Where Else Can We Go? Durham, NC: Duke University, pp. 87–99.

Popper, Karl (2002/1935). The Logic of Scientific Discovery. London: Routledge.

PR Newswire (2010). "Joint DoD Task Force Releases Report on Preventing Suicide in U.S. Military." Accessed online October 11, 2011 at http://www.prnewswire.com/news-releases/joint-dod-task-force-releases-report-on-preventing-suicide-in-us-military-101313419.html.

Quinn, Robert E. and Kim S. Cameron (eds.) (1988) Paradox and Transformation: Toward a Theory in Organization and Management. Cambridge: Ballinger.

Rancière, Jacques (1991). The Ignorant Schoolmaster: Five Lessons in Intellectual Emancipation (trans. by Kirstin Ross). Stanford, CA: University of Stanford.

RAND (2009). Understanding Commanders' Information Needs for Influence Operations. Accessed February 7, 2012 at http://www.dtic.mil/dtic/tr/fulltext/u2/a510190.pdf.

—(2011). History and Mission. Accessed October 15, 2011 at http://www.rand.org/about/history.html.

Rapoport, Anatol (1968). "Introduction." In Carl Von Clausewitz (ed.) On War. New York: Penguin Books, pp. 1–80.

Record, Jeffrey (2003). Bounding the Global War on Terror. Carlisle, PA: Strategic Studies Institute.

Reed, George, Craig Bullis, Ruth Collins, and Christopher Paparone (2004). Mapping the Route of Leadership Education: Caution Ahead. *Parameters* 3 (Autumn): 46–60.

Rescher, Nicholas (1995). Luck: The Brilliant Randomness of Everyday Life. New York: Farrar, Straus and Giroux.

—(1998). Predicting the Future: An Introduction to the Theory of Forecasting. Albany, NY: State University of New York.

—(2001a). Philosophical Reasoning: A Study in the Methodology of Philosophizing. Malden, MA: Blackwell.

—(2001b). Paradoxes: Their Roots, Range, and Resolution. Chicago, IL: Open Court.

Ricœur, Paul (1976). Interpretation Theory: Discourse and the Surplus of Meaning. Fort Worth, TX: Texas Christian University.

—(1977). The Rule of Metaphor: Multi-disciplinary Studies of the Creation of Meaning in Language (trans. by Robert Czerny). Toronto: University of Toronto.

Rittel, Horst and Melvin Webber (1973). "Dilemmas in a General Theory of Planning." *Policy Sciences* 4: 161–6.

Ritzer, George (1975). "Professionalization, Bureaucratization and Rationalization: The Views of Max Weber." *Social Forces* 53 (4): 627–34.

Roberts, Andrew (2011). The Storm of War: A New History of the Second World War. New York: HarperCollins.

Roberts, Nancy (2000). The Synoptic Model of Strategic Planning and the GPRA: Lacking a Good Fit with the Political Context. *Public Productivity and Management Review* 23 (3): 297–311.

Romjue, John L. (1984). From Active Defense to AirLand Battle: The Development of Army Doctrine 1973–1982. Fort Monroe, VA: US Army Training and Doctrine Command.

Rothenberg, Albert (1979). The Emerging Goddess: The Creative Process in Art, Science and Other Fields. Chicago, IL: University of Chicago.

Rousseau, Jean-Jacques (1966). On the Origin of Language. Chicago, IL: University of Chicago.

Rutgers, Mark R. (1999). "Be Rational! But What Does it Mean? A History of the Idea of Rationality and Its Relation to Management Thought." *Journal of Management History* 5: 17–35.

Sabatier, Paul (ed.) (1999). Theories of the Policy Process: Theoretical Lenses on Public Policy. Boulder, CO: Westview.

Sanders, T. Irene and Judith A. McCabe (2003). The Use of Complexity Science: A Survey of Federal Departments and Agencies, Private Foundations, Universities and Independent Education and Research Centers. Washington, DC: Washington Center for Complexity and Public Policy.

Santa Fe Institute (2011), About SFI, accessed April 7, 2011, http://www.santafe.edu/about/.

Santayana, George (1998). The Life of Reason. New York: Prometheus.

Sassaman, Nathan and Joe Layden (2008). Warrior King: The Triumph and Betrayal of an American Commander in Iraq. New York: St. Martin's.

Scales, Robert H. (1997). Certain Victory: The US Army in the Gulf War. Dulles, VA: Brassey's.

—(2001). Future Warfare Anthology. Carlisle, PA: US Army War College Strategic Studies Institute.

Schlesinger, James R. (1963). Quantitative analysis and national security. *World Politics*, 15 (2): 295–315.

Schneider, Ann and Helen Ingram (1997). Policy Design for Democracy. Lawrence, KS: University of Kansas.

Schön, Donald A. (1963). Displacement of Concepts. London: Butler & Tanner.

—(1971). Beyond the Stable State. New York: Norton.

—(1983). The Reflective Practitioner: How Professionals Think in Action. New York: Basic Books.

—(1987). Educating the Reflective Practitioner. San Francisco, CA: Jossey-Bass.

—(1993). "Generative Metaphor and Social Policy." In Andrew Ortony (ed.) Metaphor and Thought. Cambridge: Cambridge University Press, pp. 137–63.

—(1995). "Educating the Reflective Legal Practitioner." *Clinical Law Review* 2: 231–50.
Schön, Donald A. and Martin Rein (1994). Frame Reflection: Toward the Resolution of Intractable Policy Controversies. New York: Basic Books.
Schoomaker, Peter J. (2004). Speech delivered May 4 to the Association of the United States Army conference. Accessed August 8, 2011 at http://www3.ausa.org/webpub/DeptHome.nsf/byid/CTON-6FUSYZ.
Schütz, Alfred (1962). "The Problem of Social Reality." Collected Papers Volume 1 M. A. Natanson and H. L. van Breda, (eds). The Hague: Martiners-Nijhoff.
—(1964). "Studies in Social Theory." Collected Papers Volume 2 (A. Brodersen, ed.). The Hague: Martiners-Nijhoff.
Searle, John R. (1995). The Construction of Social Reality. New York: Free Press.
Senge, Peter M. (1990). The Fifth Discipline: The Art and Practice of the Learning Organization. New York: Doubleday/Currency.
Shaw, George B. (2008/1911). The Doctor's Dilemma. Sioux Falls, SD: Nuvision.
Shrader, Charles R. (2006). The History of Operations Research in the United States Army, Volume 1: 1942–62. Washington, DC: Office of the Deputy Undersecretary of the Army for Operations Research.
Simons, Anna (1999). "War: Back to the Future." *Annual Review of Anthropology* 28: 73–108.
—(2010). Got Vision? Unity of Vision in Policy and Strategy: What It Is, and Why We Need It. Carlisle, PA: US Army Strategic Studies Institute.
Singer, Peter W. (2008). "Outsourcing the Fight." Brooking Institute. Accessed November 30, 2011 at http://www.brookings.edu/opinions/2008/0605_military_ contractors_singer.aspx.
Sjoberg, Gideon (1959). "Operationalism and Social Research." In Llewellyn Gross (ed.) Symposium on Sociological Theory. New York: Harper and Row, pp. 603–27.
Smircich, Linda and Gareth Morgan (1982). "Leadership: The Management of Meaning." *The Journal of Applied Behavioral Science* 18 (3): 257–273.
Snider, Don M. (2002, 2005), project director (Co-project director for 2nd edition is Gayle L. Watkins). The Future of the Army Profession (1st and 2nd edn). Lloyd J. Matthews (ed.). Boston, MA: McGraw-Hill.
Snook, Scott A. (2000). Friendly Fire: The Accidental Shootdown of US Blackhawks over Northern Iraq. Princeton, NJ: Princeton University.
Sookermany, Anders McD (2011). "The Embodied Soldier: Towards a New Epistemological Foundation of Soldiering Skills in the (Post) Modernized Norwegian Armed Forces." *Armed Force and Society* 37 (3): 469–93.
Spengler, Oswald (1939). The Decline of the West. New York: Oxford University.
Starkey, Ken and Sue Tempest (2009). "The Winter of Our Discontent: The Design Challenge for Business Schools." *Academy of Management Learning & Education* 8: 576–86.
Sterling, Bruce S. and Chuck H. Perala (2005). Situational Understanding, Workload, and Congruence With the Commander's Mental Model. Aberdeen Proving Ground: Army Research Laboratory. Accessed February 7, 2012 at http://www.dtic.mil/dtic/tr/fulltext/u2/a430019.pdf.
Stickle, Douglas R. (2004). Malignants in the Body Politic: Redefining War Through Metaphor. Maxwell Air Force base, AL: Air University Press.

Stone, Deborah (1989). "Causal Stories and the Formation of Policy Agendas." *Political Science Quarterly* 104: 281–300.
—(1997). Policy Paradox: The Art of political Decision Making. New York: W.W. Norton.
Stowe, Christopher S. (2005). A Philadelphia Gentleman: The Cultural, Institutional, and Political Socialization of George Gordon Meade. Unpublished doctoral dissertation, The University of Toledo.
Strange, Joseph L. and Richard Iron (autumn 2004). "Center of Gravity: What Clausewitz Really Meant." *Joint Force Quarterly* 35: 20–27.
Summers, Harry G. (1982). On Strategy: A Critical Analysis of the Vietnam War. New York: Dell.
Svechin, Alexandr A. (1992/1927) Strategy (2nd edn). Minneapolis, MN: East View.
Talbot, Philip A. (2003) "Corporate Generals: The Military Metaphor of Strategy." *Irish Journal of Management* 24: 1–10.
Taylor, Frederick W. (1913). The Principles of Scientific Management. New York: Harper & Brothers.
Thayer, Frederick C. (1972). "Productivity: Taylorism Revisited (Round Three)." *Public Administration Review* 32: 833–40.
Thompson, William I. (1971). At the Edge of History: Speculations on the Transformation of Culture. New York: Harper Colophon.
Thruelsen, Peter D. (2006). From Soldier to Civilian: Disarmament Demobilization Reintegration in Afghanistan. Danish Institute for International Studies Report 2006–7. Accessed March 11, 2012 at http://www.diis.dk/graphics/Publications/Reports2006/RP2006–7web.pdf.
Thucydides (1954). The Peloponnesian War (trans. by Rex Warner). New York: Penguin.
Toffler, Alvin and Heidi Toffler (1993). War and Anti-War: Survival at the Dawn of the 21st Century. New York: Warner.
Tolbert, Pamela S. and Lynne G. Zucker (1996). "The Institutionalization of Institutional Theory." In Stewart R. Clegg and C. Cynthia Hardy (eds) Studying Organization Theory and Method. London: Sage Publications, pp. 169–84.
True, James L., Bryan D. Jones, and Frank R. Baumgartner (1999). "Punctuated Equilibrium Theory: Explaining Stability and Change in American Policymaking." In Paul Sabatier (ed.) Theories of the Policy Process: Theoretical Lenses on Public Policy. Boulder, CO: Westview, pp. 97–115.
Tsoukas, Haridimos and Mary Jo Hatch (2001). "Complex Thinking, Complex Practice: The Case for a Narrative Approach to Organizational Complexity." *Human Relations* 54 (8): 979–1013.
Turner, Mark (1988). "Categories and Analogies." In David H. Helman (ed.) Analogical Reasoning: Perspectives if Artificial Intelligence, Cognitive Science, and Philosophy. Dordrecht: Kluwer, pp. 3–24.
Tushman, Michael L. and Anderson, P. (1986). "Technological Discontinuities and Organizational Environments." *Administrative Science Quarterly* 31: 439–65.
United Nations (1948). Universal Declaration of Human Rights. Accessed March 11, 2012 at http://www.ohchr.org/Documents/Publications/ABCannexesen.pdf.
—(2010). Disbandment of Illegal Armed Groups (DIAG). Development Programme Afghanistan, Annual Project Report 2010, project ID: 00043604;

Crisis Prevention and Recovery Component). Accessed March 11, 2012 at http://www.undp.org.af/Projects/Report2011/diag/2011-03-21-%20Annual%20 Progress%20Report%20of%20DIAG.pdf.
United States Air Force (2006). Air Force Doctrinal Document 1-1, Leadership and Force Development. Washington, DC.
United States Army Research Institute (2012). Army Design Methodology: Commander's Resource. Fort Leavenworth, KS: School of Advanced Military Studies.
United States Marine Corps (1996). Marine Corps Doctrinal Publication 6, Command and Control. Washington, DC.
—(2011a). Professional Reading Program. Accessed August 28, 2011 at http:// www.mcu.usmc.mil/LLeadership/LLI%20Documnets/LLI%20Programs %20 Catalog.pdf.
—(2011b). Small Unit Decision Making Workshop (January 12–13). Quantico: US Marine Corps Training and Education Command. Accessed March 24, 2012 at http://www.wtri.com/documents/Publications/SUDMWorkshopReportfinal.pdf.
United States War Colleges (2011). Websites accessed September 22, 2011 at:
Air War College, http://www.au.af.mil/au/awc/about.htm;
Army War College, http://www.carlisle.army.mil/usawc/about/aboutUs.cfm;
Industrial College, http://www.ndu.edu/icaf/about/;
Marine War College, http://www.mcu.usmc.mil/Pages/MCWAR%20New.aspx;
National War College, http://www.ndu.edu/nwc/History/AboutNWC.htm;
Naval War College, http://www.usnwc.edu/About/Missions.aspx.
van Creveld, Martin (1991). The Transformation of War. New York: Collier.
Van de Ven, Andrew H. and Kangyong Sun (2011). "Breakdowns in Implementing Models of Organization Change." *Academy of Management Perspectives* 25 (3): 58–74.
van Linschoten, Alex S. and Felix Kuehn (2011). A Knock on the Door: 22 Months of ISAF Press Releases. Poverty Afghanistan Analysts Network. Accessed March 6, 2012 at https://www.afghanistan-analysts.net/uploads/AAN_2011_ ISAFPressReleases.pdf.
Vickers, Geoffrey (1965). The Art of Judgment: A Study of Policymaking. New York: Basic Books.
Vico, Giambattista (1948/1744). The New Science of Giambattista Vico (trans. by Thomas G. Bergin and Max H. Fisch). New York: Cornell University.
Wakefield, Wanda E. (1997). Playing to Win: Sports and the American Military, 1898–1945. Albany, NY: State University of New York Press.
Waldrop, M. Mitchell (1992). Complexity: The Emerging Science at the Edge of Order and Chaos. New York: Touchstone.
Walsh, W. H. (1969). "Positivist and Idealist Approaches." In Ronald H. Nash (ed.) Ideas of History, Volume 2, The Critical Philosophy of History. New York: E. P. Dutton, pp. 56–71.
Walsh, James P. Gerardo Rivera Ungson (1991) "Organizational Memory," *Academy of Management Review* 16 (1): 57–91.
Weber, Max (1946). From Max Weber: Essays in Sociology (trans. and edited by H. H. Gerth and C. Wright Mills). New York: Oxford University.
—(1994). Sociological Writings. Edited by Wolf Heyderbrand. New York: Continuum.

Wedgwood, D. V. (1967). William the Silent. New York: Norton, 1967.
Weick, Karl E. (1989). "Theory Construction as Disciplined Imagination." *Academy of Management Review* 14: 516–31.
—(1993). "The Collapse of Sensemaking in Organizations: The Mann Gulch Disaster." *Administrative Science Quarterly* 12: 638–9.
—(1995a). Sensemaking in Organizations. Thousand Oaks, CA: Sage.
—(1995b). "What Theory is Not, Theorizing Is." *Administrative Science Quarterly* 40: 385–90.
—(1998). "Improvisation as a Mindset for Organizational Analysis." *Organization Science* 9: 543–55.
—(2007). "The Generative Properties of Richness." *Academy of Management Journal* 50: 14–19.
—(2009). Making Sense of the Organization: The Impermanent Organization, Volume 2. West Sussex, UK: Wiley.
Weick, Karl E. and Karlene H. Roberts (1993). "Collective Mind in Organizations: Heedful Interrelating on Flight Decks." *Administrative Science Quarterly* 38 (3): 357–81.
Weick, Karl E. and Kathleen M. Sutcliffe (2001). Managing the Unexpected: Assuring High Performance in an Age of Complexity. Ann Arbor, MI: University of Michigan.
Westmoreland, William C. (1976). A Soldier Reports. New York: Dell.
White, Hayden (1978). Tropics of Discourse: Essays in Cultural Criticism. Baltimore, MD: Johns Hopkins.
Whitehead, Alfred N. (1968/1938). Modes of Thought. New York: Free Press.
Wiebe, Robert (1967). The Search for Order, 1877–1920. Canada: HarperCollins.
Wilbraham, Antony C., Dennis D. Staley, Michael S. Matta, Edward L. Waterman (2005). Chemistry. Upper Saddle River, NJ: Prentice Hall.
Wildavsky, Aaron (1973). "If Planning is Everything, Maybe It's Nothing." *Policy Sciences* 4: 127–53.
Wilkof, Marcia V (1989). "Organizational Culture and Decision Making: A Case of Consensus Management." *R&D Management* 19 (2): 185–200.
Williams, Blair (2010). "Heuristics and Biases in Military Decision Making." *Military Review* 5: 40–52.
Winsor, Robert D. (1996). "Military Perspectives of Organizations." *Journal of Organizational Change Management* 9 (4): 34–42.
Wolff, Kurt H. (1959). "The Sociology of Knowledge and Sociological Theory." In Llewellyn Gross (ed.) Symposium on Sociological Theory. New York: Harper and Row, pp. 567–602.
—(1974). Trying Sociology. New York: John Wiley & Sons.
Wong, Leonard, Thomas A. Kolditz, Raymond A. Millen, and Terrence M. Potter (2003). "Why They Fight: Combat Motivation in the Iraq War." Carlisle, PA: Strategic Studies Institute.
Woolgar, Steve (ed.) (1988). Knowledge and Reflexivity: New Frontiers in the Sociology of Knowledge. London: Sage.
World Bank (2011) Afghanistan Economic Update. Poverty Reduction and Economic Management, South Asia Region. Accessed March 11, 2012 at www.worldbank.org.

Yarger, Harry R. (ed.) (2010). Introduction to Short of General War: Perspectives on the Use of Military Power in the 21st Century. Carlisle, PA: Strategic Studies Institute, pp 1–8.

Yingling, Paul (2007). "A Failure in Generalship," Accessed August 9, 2011 at http://www.armedforcesjournal.com/2007/05/2635198.

Zweibelson, Ben (2011). "Cartel Next: How Army Design Methodology Offers Holistic and Dissimilar Approaches to the Mexican Drug Problem," *Small Wars Journal*. Accessed September 1, 2011 at http://smallwarsjournal.com/jrnl/art/cartel-next-how-army-design-methodology-offers-holistic-and-dissimilar-approaches-to-the-me.

INDEX

Abbott, Andrew 148–50, 169n. 5, 170n. 6
abductive 140n. 3, 164
Ackley, Charles W. 114
action learning 86, 94, 97, 101n. 30
aesthetic(s) (aesthetic appreciation) 17, 57, 65–6, 82, 86, 89, 94, 102n. 34, 106, 134, 154–5, 166
affirmative postmodern (approach) critique xix, 16–18, 21
Afghanistan (Afghan) xiv, xvi, xxiin. 7, 39, 45, 70n. 24, 74, 80–1, 94, 97, 103–4n. 43, 121–2, 143n. 15, 162, 175, 178–81, 184–90, 192–7, 198n. 4, 199n. 6
Alexander, Ernest R. 90–1, 102n. 37
alienation (alienate, alienated) 2, 78, 100n. 21, 120, 122–3, 171n. 15
Aliseda, Atocha 140
Allison, Graham 9
Alvesson, Mats 187, 199n. 7
Alvi-Aziz, Hayat 144n. 22
amalgamated metaphors 64, 66
ambiguity (ambiguities, equivocation(s)) xx, 3, 25n. 24, 29, 45, 51, 66, 76, 109–14, 125–7, 138–40, 141n. 8, 143n. 16, 159, 165, 184, 188
Amram-Katz, Sarit xxin. 2
anarchism 202
Anderson, P. 127, 129
antidoctrine 123, 163
appreciative judgment (appreciate) 58, 88, 94–5, 97, 102n. 34
Archer, Margaret 166
Argyris, Chris 77, 155, 166
Arquilla, John 198n. 1
art (artistry, fine arts) 2, 34, 41, 46, 54, 57–9, 63, 65, 72, 80, 88, 90–1, 99n. 5, 101n. 22, 102nn. 34–5, 103n. 41, 106, 133–5, 146n. 39, 154–5, 158–9, 203
Auftragstaktik (mission command) 50, 127, 178
authoritative response 83–4, 86, 88–9, 95–6, 101n. 27

Baldor, Lolita C. 81
Barker, Richard A. 81
Barrett, Frank 162, 166
Bateson, Gregory 102n. 34
Baumgartner, Frank R. 127
Berger, Peter L. 4, 6, 12, 71–2, 141n. 4, 144n. 27, 145n. 32, 147–8
Bertalanffy, Ludwig von 115
Birtle, Andrew J. 202
Black, Max 29
Bloom, Benjamin S. 152–4, 171n. 14
Blumer, Herbert xxinn. 3–4, 26n. 27, 161
Boëne, Bernard 3
Boulding, Kenneth 38
Bousquet, Antoine 9, 24nn. 10, 15, 30, 34, 127, 194–5
Boxenbaum, Eva 144n. 23, 172n. 23
Bradford, Zeb B. 98n. 3
Bradshaw, Patricia 54
Brendler, Joseph A. 73

bricolage (bricoleur) 56, 70n. 25, 101n. 26, 135, 159, 161–7, 169, 172n. 23, 203
Brook, Tom V. xvi
Brown, Richard H. 28, 33, 67n. 4, 109, 132
Bruner, Jerome S. 144n. 23
Bullis, Craig 146n. 39, 149
Bunting, Josiah 50
Burbules, Nicholas C. xxiiin. 14, 16, 24n. 9, 105
bureaucracy (bureaucratic, bureaucratization) xx, 3, 7, 21, 37, 74, 88, 93, 107, 128, 144n. 24, 145n. 29, 149–50, 154, 160, 167, 169nn. 4–5, 170n. 8
Burrell, Gibson xx, 30, 33, 35, 67n. 6, 68n. 9, 71, 77, 114, 138, 143n. 17, 146n. 43

Cameron, Kim S. 8, 138, 142n. 10, 173n. 28
Campbell, Joseph P. 51
center(s) of gravity (COG/COGs) 31, 35–6, 63, 67n. 3, 74, 156, 177–8, 184, 188–9, 192, 197
chaoplexic science (chaoplexic, chaoplexity) 4, 9, 24n.10, 30, 34, 38–9, 41, 56, 64–6, 80, 127, 194–5
Chen, Ming-Jer 110, 142n. 12
Chisholm, Rupert F. 145n. 31
Christensen, Clayton M. 127
Clausewitz, Carl von 30–1, 79, 170n. 6, 197
Clegg, Stewart R. 77
Cohen, Eliot 135–6
Cohen, Michael D. xxiiin. 11, 23n. 6, 71, 160, 167, 171n. 15, 192
Cold War 44, 129, 195
Collingswood, Robin G. 46
Collins, Ruth 146n. 39, 149
commonsense 148, 154
communicative action 125–6
communicative rationality 126–7
competency mapping 85, 149–52, 155, 160, 170n. 7
competing values 4, 94, 110, 113, 139, 173n. 28
complex adaptive systems 34, 40, 79
complexification (complexity, complexify, complexified) 8, 12, 24n. 10, 30–1, 33–4, 38–40, 79–80, 85, 88, 93, 99n. 12, 110, 136, 139, 155, 166, 176–7, 188, 190, 194–5
concept extension 30
Cone, Robert W. 155
Conklin, Jeff 187, 198n. 3
Cossette, Pierre 28
counterinsurgency (COIN) 36–7, 56, 182, 184–5, 191–2, 195
craftwork 86, 93–4, 96–7, 101n. 28, 167
creative deviance 84, 86, 88–90
critical reflection 9, 20, 31–2, 67, 78
Crupi, James A. 142n. 12, 166
Curphy, Gordon 189, 199n. 8
cyclicism 26n. 30, 202

Davis, Paul K. xviii
D-Day 87
deductive 137, 163
deep dive(s) 180–1
define the problem (defining the problem, problem formulation) ix, 85, 130–1, 156, 202
Deleuze, Gilles 197
Dempsey, Martin E. 155, 178
determinism 41, 67n. 6
determinism (causal stories, causal narrative) 21, 72
Dewey, John 102n. 34, 134–5
DiMaggio, Paul J. xxiin. 5, 24n. 17, 161, 172n. 21, 190
disambiguate (disambiguated) 155–6
displacement of concepts (concept displacement, displaced concepts) 29–33, 130
disunity of military knowledge viii, 201
doctrine xv, xvii–xviii, xxiiin. 11, 1, 14, 16–18, 20–2, 23n. 5, 25n. 24, 36–7, 39, 50, 52, 54, 59, 61, 68n. 10, 84, 86, 94,

98nn. 2–3, 101nn. 28, 30, 107, 116–18, 120, 122–4, 126–7, 129, 131, 136, 138, 150, 152, 155–7, 163–4, 170n. 8, 176, 178, 183, 185–9, 191, 197, 201–2
dramaturgy (dramaturlogical) 49
Dray, William 46
Dunn, Mary 76

efficiency 8, 88, 110–12, 114, 123, 128, 139, 141n. 8, 149
Eisenhower, Dwight D. 50, 95
Elder, Linda 67n. 5, 165, 173n. 25
Elliott, Euel 127–8
emancipate (emancipation) x, 2, 29, 73, 76–7, 152
emergence (emergent, self-organizing) 13, 29, 66, 75–6, 79–80, 86, 96–7, 146n. 38, 167, 177, 180, 194–5
emic xxiin. 5, 98n. 2, 106, 141n. 5, 146n. 41
empiricism 2, 21, 90
engineering tasks 93–5, 103n. 41
Enloe, Cynthia 122
epistemic reflexivity viii, xxin. 2, xxiin. 6, 203
epistemic scripts (follow a "script" + A82) 118–19, 139
epistemological frustration 76
epistemology (epistemological) viii–x, xiii, xv, xxi, xxiii, 3–4, 17, 20, 22, 24n. 9, 26n. 30, 33–6, 38, 43, 46, 68nn. 9, 11, 76–7, 86, 101n. 25, 114–15, 139, 141n. 4, 147–8, 150, 153, 160, 164, 170n. 11, 172n. 17, 183, 187, 197–8, 201–3
equity xii, 8, 110–13, 139
Esposito, John L. 202
etic xxiin. 5, 141n. 6, 146n. 41, 150, 154
Evered, Roger 100n. 13
Ewell, Julian J. 107, 111, 141n. 8
exdigenous 106, 137, 141n. 6, 162, 166

Fairhurst, Gail T. 84
Ferrari, Frederica 73
Festinger, Leon 77
Feuer, Lewis S. 5–6, 21
FitzGerald, Frances 15, 96, 112
foreign internal defense 59
foreknowledge ix, 2, 21, 43, 69n. 19, 149–50, 152, 159, 170n. 6, 172n. 20
foundationalism (foundational) viii–ix, xviii, xxiin. 7, 18, 22, 183, 197–8, 203
frame consensus 17, 124–6
frame experiments 159–60
frame reflexivity 72, 76, 98, 98n. 1
framing (frame of reference) xiii, xx, 4, 7, 9–10, 15, 17, 21, 23n. 2, 28–9, 33, 38, 46, 49, 66, 67n. 4, 69n. 21, 72–3, 76, 83, 90, 98, 98n. 1, 101n. 21, 106, 119, 131, 136, 175, 179, 189, 203
Franco-Prussian War 10
Fuller, J. F. C. xvii–xviii, 145n. 36
fundamentalism 18

Gaddis, John L. 25n. 20
Galula, David 36
Garbage Can Decision Making (GCDM) 171, 192
Gat, Azar xxiin. 10
Geertz, Clifford 132, 140, 164
Gemmill, Gary 81, 84, 122
generative metaphors 26n. 28
genericize (genericization) xxiiin. 16, 137
Gergen, Kenneth J. 162, 166
Gergen, Mary M. 162, 166
Ghamari-Tabrizi, Sharon 13
Giddens, Anthony 104n. 43
Ginnett, Robert 189, 199n. 8
Ginsburg, Dan 122
Gladwell, Malcolm 25n. 22
Goffman, Erving 49, 69n. 21, 72
Gooch, John 135–6
grammar xx, xxin. 3, 18, 38, 73, 79, 115, 120, 144n. 23, 146n. 44, 171n. 14, 201

grand narrative (metanarrative) 54, 82, 119–20, 122, 126, 144n. 25, 156, 162–3, 167, 169, 172nn. 17, 23, 178, 186, 196
Griffith, Samuel B. 202
Grimes, Andrew J. 24n. 14
Grint, Keith 8, 83, 87–9, 102n. 33
Guattari, Felix 197
Guba, Egon G. 143n. 16
Gvosdev, Nikolas K. 144n. 22

Haass, Richard N. 40
Habermas, Jürgen 125
Haeckel, Ernst 100n. 18
Hardy, Cynthia 77
Harmon, Michael M. 126, 133, 143nn. 14, 19, 145n. 37
Hatch, Mary Jo 8, 57, 60–1, 80, 123
Heifetz, Ronald A. 83–4, 86–9, 101n. 28
Heisenberg Principle 38, 69n. 15
Helman, David H. 133
hermeneutic project 134
heuristic(s) xix, 3, 16, 34, 42, 45–6, 49, 64, 67n. 4, 75, 98, 100n. 18, 146n. 44, 159, 175, 202
Heuser, Beatrice 99n. 7, 100n. 19
Hewes, James E. 10–11
historical pseudomorphosis 77
historicity (context) 87, 164
Hittle, James D. 128
Hock, Dee 38
Hoffman, Frank G. 145n. 36
Hoh, Mathew 103n. 43
Holland, Louise A. 142n. 12
Holland, Ray 78
Horgan, John 24n. 10, 30, 34, 127
Horwath, Rich 99n. 10
Howard, Michael 128
Hughes, Richard 189, 199n. 8
humanities 34, 41, 46, 65, 80, 145n. 37
Hunt, Ira A. 107, 111, 141n. 8
Hunt, Sonja M. 84
Huntington, Samuel P. 148
hypostatization (reification, sedimentation, objectification, concretization) xix, 10–13, 16, 23n. 5, 24nn. 12–13, 33, 42, 66, 71, 77–8, 136, 145n. 32, 153, 156, 160, 171n. 16

iatrogenic 86, 88, 94, 101n. 29, 143n. 15, 190
Ibrahim, Azeem 187, 198n. 4
ideology x, xxiin. 7, 1, 6–7, 14, 19, 21, 24n. 12, 67n. 5, 120, 142n. 9, 144n. 27, 152, 167, 201
Iliaifar, Amir xi
improvisation 4, 20, 49–50, 55–6, 93, 135, 172n. 23, 197
indeterminate zones of practice (indeterminate zones of meaning, indeterminate meaning for practice) 152, 158–9, 161, 163–4, 167
indigenous 106, 137, 141n. 5, 157, 162, 166
inductive 54, 137, 164
Ingram, Helen 3
Inhelder, Bärbel 100n. 17
institutional programmed courses of action 72
institutional reflexivity viii, x, xx, 5, 24n. 17, 26n. 28, 33, 66, 72, 76–7, 79–80, 83, 113, 148, 173n. 29, 183, 198
institutionalization (pre-, semi-, full-) xix, xxin. 5, 1–22, 24n. 17, 25n. 19, 30–2, 47, 49, 69n. 18, 82, 103n. 42, 141n. 4, 171n. 16
interparadigmatic journeys xx, 114–38, 163
Iraq (Iraqi) xiv, xvi, xxiin. 7, 39, 41, 45, 48, 70n. 24, 74, 137, 143n. 15, 176–7, 184, 196
Iron, Richard 67n. 3
Ivie, Robert L. 44–5, 73

Jacobs, Thomas O. 126
Janis, Irving L. 77

Janowitz, Morris 148
Jaques, Elliott 144n. 24, 170n. 10
Johnson, Mark 27, 66, 73, 78
Jones, Bryan D. 127
Joseph, Miriam xxi
Jullien, François 79, 197
Jung, Carl G. 7

Kahn, David 10–11
Keegan, John 144n. 28
Khong, Yuen F. 44–6, 69n. 18
Kiel, Douglas L. 127–8
Kilduff, Martin 16, 76
Kilmann, Ralph H. 130
King, Anthony 23n. 5
knowing-in-action 85, 157–8
Knox, MacGregor 25nn. 21, 26
Kolditz, Thomas A. 141n. 7
Korea (Korean War) 44, 48, 53, 143n. 16, 197
Krepinevich, Andrew F. 107
Kuehn, Felix 187, 198n. 5
Kuhn, Thomas S. 2, 23n. 5, 76, 100n. 14, 101n. 23, 132

Ladkin, Donna 83, 86–9, 102n. 31
Lai, David 79
Lakoff, George 27, 47, 66, 73, 78
Lang, Kurt 169n. 3
Lasswell, Harold 110
Lawrence Paradox 137
Lawson, Bryan 3
Layden, Joe 48
leadership moment 87
Lerer, Zeev xxin. 2
lessons learned (best practices) xiv, 4, 14, 23n. 4, 42, 46, 93, 101n. 30, 130, 132, 136, 156–8, 160
levels of war 65, 77–8, 117, 120, 152
Levi, Edward H. 202
Lévi-Strauss, Claude 135
Lewin, Kurt 101n. 30
Lewis, Adrian R. 202
Lewis, Marianne W. 24n. 14, 105
liberty 8, 110, 112–13, 139, 159
Lincoln, Yvonna S. 143n. 16
Lindblom, Charles E. 20, 26n. 31, 95, 133
line(s) of operation (line(s) of effort, logical line(s) of operation) 156, 187
logic x, xvi, xx, xxin. 3, 18, 25n. 24, 29, 31, 35, 38, 40, 45, 49, 57, 60–3, 75, 77, 79, 84, 90–1, 96, 100n. 19, 101n. 25, 103n. 39, 106–7, 115, 117, 120, 127, 132, 144n. 23, 146n. 44, 149, 151, 163–4, 171nn. 12, 14, 180, 182–3, 187, 191, 201
logical positivism 68n. 9, 176
logicoscientific 80
Luckmann, Thomas 4, 12, 71–2, 141n. 4, 144n. 27, 145n. 32, 147–8
Lutz, Bob 3
Lyotard, Jean-François 21, 82, 106, 140n. 3, 144n. 25, 158, 163, 172nn. 17, 19

Matta, Michael S. ix
McCabe, Judith A. 40
MacIntyre, Alasdair 41
McMaster, Herbert R. 107
McNamara, Robert S. 13, 96, 177
Mannheim, Karl ix, xxin. 1, 4, 7, 9, 16, 19–20, 22, 23nn. 3, 7, 24nn. 8, 12, 69n. 15, 70n. 26, 147, 201, 203
Marcella, Gabriel 100n. 13
March, James G. xxiiin. 11, 10, 12, 14, 23n. 6, 71, 76, 98n. 1, 145n. 35, 160, 167, 171n. 15, 192
Marion, Russ 38
Marshall, Monty G. 110, 154
Marshall, S. L. A. 141n. 7
Martin, Grant xx, 97
Martindale, Don 68n. 8
Martineau, Harriet 76, 143n. 20
Maruyama, Magoroh 138
Maslow, Abraham H. 111, 189, 199n. 8
Mastroianni, George R. xiii
Maton, Karl xxiin. 6

May, Ernest R. 43, 134
Mayer, Richard T. 126, 133, 143nn. 14, 19, 145n. 37
Meacham, John A. 6
meanings for action 23n. 5, 33, 57, 87, 107, 110, 113, 120, 124, 127, 130–1, 148, 170n. 7, 177, 186, 188, 194, 203
Medhurst, Martin J. 73
Mehra, Ajay 16, 76
Merkle, Judith A. xv, 3, 11, 103n. 39
Merton, Robert K. 153, 170n. 6, 171n. 15
metanarrative (grand narrative) 54, 82, 119–20, 122–3, 126, 140n. 3, 144n. 25, 156, 162–3, 167, 169, 172nn. 17, 23, 178, 186, 196
metaphoric reasoning 29, 33, 66, 141n. 3, 202–3
methodology (methods, methodological) viii–ix, xiii, xv, xxin. 4, xxiinn. 8–9, 22, 33, 35, 57–8, 68n. 8, 97, 102n. 30, 105, 114, 116, 143n. 19, 163, 187, 197, 203
Meyer, John W. 98n. 3
Miklaucic, Michael 157
Milbank, Dana 41
Millen, Raymond A. 141n. 7
Miller, Danny 110, 142n. 12
Miller, Peter 198n. 1
mindful (mindfulness) xix, xx, 6, 23n. 5, 31–2, 42, 49, 66, 69n. 18, 72, 78, 83, 101n. 29, 113, 136–7, 160, 163
mindless (mindlessness) 42, 77, 81, 120–2, 136, 141n. 4, 171n. 15
Mintzberg, Henry 8, 73, 99n. 6, 100n. 13, 153
Miser, Hugh J. 13
Mitchell, John G. 99n. 11, 102n. 31
Mitroff, Ian 130
modernism (modernist, modernistic) xix, xxii, 2, 14–17, 25n. 22, 66, 76, 84, 100n. 18, 114, 140n. 3, 143n. 13, 175–7
Mogahed, Dalia 202
Morgan, Gareth xx, 23n. 5, 24n. 12, 30, 33, 35, 67n. 6, 68n. 9, 71, 77, 84, 114, 138, 143n. 17, 146n. 43
morphology (morphological) 28–30, 33, 72–3, 75–6
Morris, Van Cleve xx
Moskos, Charles C. 3
Moyers, Bill 51, 109
muddling through (successive limited comparisons) 20, 26n. 31, 95, 133, 202
multi-frame approach 7, 10
multi-paradigmatic 183
Mumford, Lewis 128
Murphy, James R. 98n. 3
Murray, Williamson 25nn. 21, 26, 127
Mutch, Alistair 73

narratology 80
Nash, Ronald H. 143n. 16
Neustadt, Richard E. 43, 134
Newton, Sir Isaac 18, 36, 129
Nisbett, Richard E. 79
nomothetic taxonomies 33, 67n. 7

Oakley, Judith 81, 84, 122
Officer Professional Military Education Policy (OPMEP) 152–5, 171n. 14, 197, 199n. 11
oligarchy (oligarchic, oligarchical) 5, 17, 87, 120, 175, 192, 198
Olsen, Johan P. xxiiin. 11, 10, 12, 14, 71, 76, 98n. 1, 160, 171n. 15, 192
ontology (ontological) viii–x, xv, xxi–xxii, 3–4, 7, 17, 22, 33–6, 38, 71, 79, 105, 114, 120, 127, 132, 135, 160, 164, 187, 203
operationalism xxin. 9, 68n. 9, 107
operations research and systems analysis (ORSA) xii, xix, 5, 12–15, 22, 34, 93–5, 107, 141n. 8, 188, 190–2

Ortony, Andrew 28
Osinga, F. P. B. 101n. 24
Ostrom, Elinor 112

Pace, Peter 37
Paparone, Christopher R. 142n. 12, 146n. 39, 149, 166
paradigm xx, xxiinn. 7–8, 4, 10, 33, 38, 67n. 6, 68n. 9, 70n. 24, 71, 77–8, 81, 84, 95, 98, 100n. 14, 101nn. 22–3, 114–15, 118–20, 122, 126–7, 132, 134–40, 141n. 4, 144n. 23, 145n. 32, 146n. 44, 154, 156–7, 161, 164, 171n. 14, 172n. 23, 179, 183–4, 187, 195
paradigm shift 16, 23n. 5, 38, 78, 84, 101n. 22, 132, 183
paradox (paradoxical) 4, 8, 17, 21, 28, 41, 51, 56, 67n. 4, 69n. 15, 109–14, 116, 118–19, 137–8, 142nn. 10, 12, 161, 172n. 21
paralogy (paralogical, paralogically) 106, 110, 140, 140n. 3, 142n. 11, 143n. 13, 163–4, 166, 169
Paret, Peter 100n. 14
Parsons, Talcott 140n. 2, 143n. 18, 148, 159
Pasadena Sun xiv
Paul, Richard W. 67n. 5, 165, 173n. 25
Peirce, Charles S. 164
Pepper, Stephen C. 7
Perala, Chuck H. 173
performativity 158, 172n. 19
Perrow, Charles 93, 95
petit récit 168
Petraeus, David 103n. 43
Pfeffer, Jeffrey 84
Phillips, Denis C. xxiiin. 14, 16, 24n. 9, 105
Phillips, Nelson 77
Piaget, Jean 100n. 17
Pierce, James G. 103
pluralistic ethics 4, 126
Polyani, Michael 157
polysemic (polysemic language, polysemic meaning) 17, 28
Pondy, Louis R. 84
Popper, Karl 29
positivism 35, 113, 143n. 20, 201
positivism, logical 2, 68n. 9, 176
positivist ix, xviii, 3, 38, 68n. 9, 106, 109, 143n. 16, 172n. 17, 186
postinstitutional (postinstitutionalization) viii, xix–xxi, 3–4, 6, 10, xxiiin. 14, 16–17, 20–2, 23nn. 2, 5, 25n. 22, 28, 33–4, 64, 66–7, 68n. 10, 69n. 18, 76–7, 80, 82–90, 97, 98n. 1, 101n. 29, 113, 129, 134, 146n. 44, 160–1, 164, 166, 169, 175, 185, 203
postinstitutional reflexivity 23n. 5
postmodernism (postmodern, postmodernist) 3, 8, 16–18, 21–2, 24n. 12, 90, 140n. 3, 144n. 25, 195
Potter, Terrence M. 141n. 7
Powell, Walter W. xxiin. 5, 24n. 17, 190
PowerPoint xi, 37, 63, 180
practical drift 137
pretense of knowledge xx, xxiiin. 16, 65
problematization 10, 58, 61, 141n. 9, 187
professional doubt 152
professional military education (PME) 150, 152, 160, 170n. 10, 176, 183, 199n. 12
progressivism (progressive) + A138 ix, 15–16, 18, 22, 43, 76, 100n. 18, 117, 153, 158, 176–7, 195, 201–3
psychic prison(s) 6, 9, 23n. 5, 24n. 12, 64, 152
punctuated equilibrium 25n. 26, 127

quadigenous xx, 106, 112, 114, 203
quadrilectical reasoning 138
Quinn, Robert E. 8, 138, 142n. 10, 173n. 28

Rancière, Jacques 62
RAND (RAND Corporation) xii, xviii, 13, 69n. 16, 173
Rapoport, Anatol 197
rationalism (rationalize, rationalization, rationality, rationalist) 11, 14, 27, 42–3, 79, 88, 90, 93, 101n. 27, 104n. 44, 106–10, 113, 125–7, 134–6, 139, 141n. 9, 142nn. 9, 11, 143n. 14, 149–50, 154–5, 160–1, 167, 170n. 8, 172nn. 18, 20, 176, 189, 192–3
recapitulation theory 77, 100n. 18
Record, Jeffrey 170n. 6
reductionism 2, 60, 78, 97, 176
Reed, George 146n. 39, 149
reflecting-in-action 56, 85
reflection-in-action 20, 85
reflexive viii, xxiin. 5, 24n. 17, 33, 77–9, 82, 152, 154, 158–9, 183–4, 194, 196
reflexivity viii, x, xix–xx, xxinn. 2, 5, xxiin. 6, 23n. 5, 24n. 17, 26n. 28, 32–3, 66, 71–2, 76–80, 83, 98n. 1, 100n. 21, 113, 148, 173n. 29, 183, 192, 198, 203
reframing xx, 16, 23n. 3, 29, 33, 76, 78–80, 84, 86–7, 89, 101n. 22, 134, 139, 160, 177, 186, 188, 191
Rein, Martin 18, 72, 78, 101n. 22
Rescher, Nicholas 9, 26n. 30, 43, 69n. 16, 105–8, 201–2
retrodictability 46
retrogressivism 202
revolving door effect 190
rhetoric xx–xxi, xxiii, 18, 29, 38, 44, 64, 72–3, 79, 90, 115, 117, 120, 123, 127, 138, 144n. 23, 146n. 44, 171n. 14, 201
Ricœur, Paul 27, 74, 78, 99n. 8, 133
Rittel, Horst 102n. 33, 130–1, 134
Ritzer, George 170n. 8
Roberts, Andrew 25n. 23
Roberts, Karlene H. 136
Roberts, Nancy 144n. 21
Romjue, John L. 202
Ronfeldt, David 198n. 1
Root, Elihu 10–11, 24n. 18,
Rothenberg, Albert 142n. 12
Rouleau, Linda 144n. 23, 172n. 23
Rousseau, Jean-Jacques xix, xxiiin. 15
routine tasks (routinization) 93, 96
Rowan, Brian 98n. 3
Rutgers, Mark R. 125

Sabatier, Paul 9
Sandberg, Jorgen 187, 199n. 7
Sanders, Irene T. 40
Santayana, George 157, 172n. 18
Sarr, Robert A. 84
Sassaman, Nathan 48
Scales, Robert H. 48, 129
Schön, Donald A. 18, 20, 23n. 3, 26n. 28, 27, 29–32, 44, 69nn. 18–19, 72–3, 76–8, 81, 85, 101n. 22, 27, 32, 133, 155, 157–60, 167, 172n. 20, 193
Schütz, Alfred 69n. 19, 71, 161
Schlesinger, James R. 13
Schneider, Ann 3
Schoomaker, Peter J. 48
Scott, Wiber J. xiii, 73
Searle, John R. 4, 143n. 16
security xvi, 8, 12, 39, 84, 99n. 12, 110–13, 116–17, 122–3, 139, 144n. 22, 154, 184–8, 192–6
Segal, David R. 3
self-fulfilling prophecy 104n. 44, 153
Senge, Peter M. 23n. 2
sensemaking (collapse of sensemaking, "make" sense of + A28) ix, 4, 6, 16–17, 24nn. 9, 15, 33–4, 56, 64, 66, 73, 77, 79, 86, 105, 133–4, 136–7, 141n. 3, 146n. 38, 151, 160, 177–8
Shaw, George B. 120
Shrader, Charles R. 12–14, 94
Simons, Anna xxiiin. 16, 137–8, 173n. 27

Singer, Peter W. 129
single-loop learning 77, 104n. 44, 153, 155–6, 163, 186
Sjoberg, Gideon xxiin. 9
Smircich, Linda 84
Snider, Don M. 148, 150, 169n. 4
Snook, Scott A. 137
social constructionism 76, 152, 159
social construction of reality (cultural constructions of reality) 4, 71, 133, 147
social construction theory 147–8
Sookermany, Anders McD 3
Spanish-American War 10, 128, 198
special operations 157, 175–8, 183, 191, 194
Spengler, Oswald 77, 100n. 15
stabilitarianism 202
Staley, Dennis D. ix
Starkey, Ken 28, 41, 49
Sterling, Bruce S. 173
Stickle, Douglas R. 73
Stone, Deborah 8, 21, 51, 72, 110, 112–13, 125, 139, 165
storytelling (narratology) 53–4, 80, 101n. 21, 166, 191
Stowe, Christopher S. xvi
Strange, Joseph L. 67n. 3
stratégos (strategemata, strategema) 74, 99n. 10, 101n. 25
stratification (strata) 77, 115–16, 152, 170n. 10
sui generis 2, 4, 89
Summers, Harry G. 107
Sun, Kangyong 146n. 43
Sutcliffe, Kathleen M. 38, 136
Svechin, Alexandr A. 36
swarm theory (swarming, self-organizing) 31, 62, 79, 182, 198n. 1
synoptic (synoptic planning) 115–16, 144n. 21, 146n. 39, 152–3, 163–4
system of systems 34, 163

tacit knowledge 3, 28, 86, 134, 157–8, 162
taktikós A187 75, 101n. 25
Talbot, Philip A. 73
tame problems 88
tautology (tautological) 15, 26n. 27, 150, 161, 169n. 5
Taylor, Frederick W. xv, 11, 103n. 39
technical rationality 88, 101n. 27, 135, 155, 172n. 20, 193
technology of foolishness 167
Tempest, Sue 28, 41, 49
Thayer, Frederick C. xv
Thompson, William I. 98n. 5
thought trials 160
Thruelsen, Peter D. 199n. 6
Thucydides 25n. 25, 73
Toffler, Alvin 145n. 36
Toffler, Heidi 145n. 36
Tolbert, Pamela S. 10–12
True, James L. 127
Tsoukas, Haridimos 80
Turner, Mark 133
Tushman, Michael L. 127, 129

unconventional War (unconventional warfare) 45, 59, 176–7, 186
Universal Joint Task List (UJTL) 91, 94, 103n. 38

van Creveld, Martin 131
Van de Ven, Andrew H. 146n. 43
van Linschoten, Alex S. 187, 198n. 5
Vickers, Geoffrey 21, 88, 102n. 34
Vico, Giambattista 1, 28
Vietnam (Vietnam War, Military Assistance Command, Vietnam/MACV) xix, xxiin. 7, 13, 15–16, 44–5, 50, 53, 65, 96, 98n. 3, 103n. 41, 107–8, 111–12, 114, 135, 141n. 8, 142n. 10, 143n. 16, 154, 177, 183, 187, 194–5, 198

Wakefield, Wanda E. 47
Waldrop, Mitchell M. 79, 101n. 25
Walsh, James P. Gerardo Rivera Ungson 136
Walsh, W. H. 103n. 42

Wander, Philip 73
Waterman, Edward L. ix
Webber, Melvin 102n. 33, 130–1, 134
Weber, Max 149
Wedgwood, D. V. 41
Weick, Karl E. 6, 38, 55, 77, 105, 133–4, 136, 146n. 38, 160, 164
Westmoreland, William C. 15, 154
White, Hayden 8, 27, 42, 78, 141n. 4
Whitehead, Alfred N. 1, 102n. 31
wicked problems (wicked situations, wickedness) 102n. 33, 130, 134, 160, 165
Wiebe, Robert 97, 104n. 43
Wilbraham, Antony C. ix
Wildavsky, Aaron 90, 99n. 12
Wilkof, Marcia V. 124
Williams, John Allen 3
Williams, Blair 133
Winsor, Robert D.
Wolff, Kurt H. 106, 147
Wong, Leonard 141n. 7
Woolgar, Steve 2, 80, 100n. 21
World War II (WW II) 12–13, 25n. 23, 50, 88, 171n. 13, 186, 193, 197
World War I (WW I) xvii, 12, 127, 144n. 28, 170n. 9, 171n. 15, 197

Yanow, Dvora 57
Yarger, Harry R. 170n. 6
Yingling, Paul 45–6
ying::yang (ying and yang) 79, 106

Zelikow, Philip 9
zone of analogy 31, 36–8, 47, 69n. 18, 90
zone of indeterminate practice 165
Zucker, Lynne G. 10–12
Zweckrationalität 149–50, 154, 160
Zweibelson, Ben xx, 58, 64